Compensation for Dismissal

In memory of my father

EMPLOYMENT LAW LIBRARY

Compensation for Dismissal

Second Edition

Anthony Korn BA (Oxon), Barrister

Series editor: Simon Auerbach, Partner, Pattinson & Brewer

BLACKSTONE PRESS LIMITED

First published in Great Britain 1993 by Blackstone Press Limited,
9-15 Aldine Street, London W12 8AW. Telephone: 0181-740 2277

© Anthony Korn, 1993

First edition, 1993
Second edition, 1997

ISBN: 1 85431 636 2

British Library Cataloguing in Publication Data.
A CIP catalogue record for this book is available from the British Library

Typeset by Montage Studios Limited, Tonbridge, Kent
Printed by Livesey Ltd, Shrewsbury, Shropshire

All rights reserved. No part of this book may be reproduced or transmitted in any form or by any means, electronic or mechanical, including photocopying, recording, or any information storage or retrieval system without prior permission from the publisher.

Contents

Preface	ix
Table of Cases	xi
Table of Statutes	xxiii
Table of Statutory Instruments	xxvii

Part I Wrongful Dismissal	1
Introduction	1
1 Compensation for Wrongful Dismissal	2

1.1 What is wrongful dismissal? — 1.2 Lawful termination of contract — 1.3 Frustration — 1.4 Assessing compensation for wrongful dismissal — 1.5 Calculating the statutory notice entitlement — 1.6 Pay in lieu of notice — 1.7 Reduction of damages

2   Tax and Miscellaneous Matters 28

2.1 Tax — 2.2 Miscellaneous matters — 2.3 Calculating damages for wrongful dismissal

3   Other Remedies for Wrongful Dismissal 33

3.1 Equitable remedies (general principles) — 3.2 Equitable remedies and wrongful dismissal — 3.3 Other remedies

Part II Unfair Dismissal	38
Introduction	38
4 Re-employment Orders and the Additional Award	41

4.1 Introduction — 4.2 Orders for re-employment — 4.3 Terms of re-employment — 4.4 Enforcing a re-employment order — 4.5 Interim re-employment

5 Unfair Dismissal: the Basic Award 54

5.1 Introduction — 5.2 Calculating the basic award — 5.3 Minimum basic award — 5.4 Reducing the basic award — 5.5 Deductions from the basic award

6 Unfair Dismissal: the Special Award 61

6.1 Introduction — 6.2 Calculating the special award — 6.3 Reducing the special award

7 A Week's Pay 66

7.1 Problems of definition — 7.2 Normal working hours — 7.3 Remuneration — 7.4 The calculation date — 7.5 Methods of calculating a week's pay — 7.6 Statutory maximum

8 The Compensatory Award: General Principles 84

8.1 Introduction — 8.2 Compensation, not punishment — 8.3 Remoteness — 8.4 Heads of compensation — 8.5 Statutory maximum

9 Calculating the Compensatory Award: Loss of Earnings 93

9.1 Introduction — 9.2 What losses count — 9.3 Credits for payments received — 9.4 Assessing loss of earnings — 9.5 Loss of future earnings

10 Calculating the Compensatory Award: Fringe Benefits and Expenses 109

10.1 Introduction — 10.2 General principles — 10.3 Multiplier — 10.4 Valuing fringe benefits — 10.5 Company cars — 10.6 Accommodation — 10.7 Company loans — 10.8 Other benefits — 10.9 Expenses

11 Calculating the Compensatory Award: Pensions 118

11.1 Introduction and general principles — 11.2 Types of pensions — 11.3 Types of loss — 11.4 Methods of calculating loss — 11.5 Other principles — 11.6 The guidelines

12 Calculating the Compensatory Award: Manner of Dismissal 135

12.1 Introduction — 12.2 No compensation for injured feelings — 12.3 Disadvantage in the labour market — 12.4 Discrimination cases

13	**Calculating the Compensatory Award: Loss of Statutory Rights**	137

13.1 Introduction — 13.2 Redundancy and unfair dismissal — 13.3 Other statutory rights — 13.4 No award — 13.5 Reduced award

14	**Reducing Unfair Dismissal Compensation: Justice and Equity**	140

14.1 Limiting the compensatory award — 14.2 General principles — 14.3 Illustrations of the principles — 14.4 Other reasons for limiting compensation

15	**Mitigation of Loss**	151

15.1 Introduction — 15.2 Defining the duty to mitigate in unfair dismissal cases — 15.3 Re-employment orders — 15.4 Offers of re-employment — 15.5 Duty to find employment — 15.6 Limits to the duty to mitigate — 15.7 Onus of proof — 15.8 Assessing the deduction — 15.9 Mitigation in fact

16	**Contributory Fault**	163

16.1 Introduction — 16.2 General principles — 16.3 Amount of reduction — 16.4 Consistent reductions of awards — 16.5 New evidence after the hearing

17	**Ex Gratia Payments and Other Deductions**	175

17.1 Deducting redundancy payments from unfair dismissal compensation — 17.2 Ex gratia payments — 17.3 Ex gratia payment as a defence

18	**Recoupment Regulations, Tax and Miscellaneous Matters**	183

18.1 Recoupment of benefits from tribunal awards — 18.2 The monetary award — 18.3 Recoupment procedure — 18.4 Effect of regulations — 18.5 Tax — 18.6 Interest

	Part III Compensation for Redundancy	187
19	**Compensation for Redundancy**	187

19.1 Introduction — 19.2 Pre-conditions for payment — 19.3 Calculating a redundancy payment — 19.4 Reducing redundancy payments — 19.5 Strike dismissals generally — 19.6 Tax liability — 19.7 Ready reckoner for calculating the number of weeks' pay due

Part IV Compensation in Discrimination Cases 196

Introduction 196

20 Compensation in Discrimination Cases 197

20.1 Remedies in discrimination dismissals — 20.2 Relationship with unfair dismissal

Appendix Tribunal Form 209

Index 213

Preface

Since the advent of modern employment protection legislation many books have been written on employment law, but few of the established textbooks give a detailed account of the statutory and common law remedies available to employees who are dismissed. In practice, the remedies are almost as important as the rights themselves as most employees will want to know what they will get if they win and most employers will want to know the extent of their potential liability if they lose. It is a statistical fact that most cases are settled and the likely remedy, and in particular the level of any award of compensation, is obviously a critical factor in reaching a negotiated settlement. This book therefore aims to give a detailed, practical and balanced account of the statutory and common law remedies available on dismissal. It is written for all those involved in this area of law from the specialist lawyer to the non-lawyer.

The book is divided into four sections. The first section deals with wrongful dismissal and covers the remedies for dismissal at common law — in particular damages for wrongful dismissal. The second section, which is the longest, examines the statutory remedies for unfair dismissal. It analyses how an award of unfair dismissal compensation is calculated and the grounds on which an award may be reduced. The third section is devoted to the computation of redundancy payments and the grounds on which such payments may be reduced. The final section of the book considers the particular remedies available in cases of unlawful sex or race discrimination. Detailed consideration is given to the power of tribunals to award compensation for injured feelings and aggravated and exemplary damages in such cases. It should be noted that some common law concepts have been incorporated into the statutory provisions and for this reason wrongful dismissal cases are sometimes referred to in the context of unfair dismissal and unfair dismissal cases are sometimes referred to in the context of wrongful dismissal. With regard to the problem of gender, I would like to make it clear that, although it has been necessary on occasions to use 'he' rather than 'he or she', where the context so admits, the masculine includes the feminine and I apologise to anyone who may feel offended by the use of the masculine form.

Much of the original research for this book was carried out while I was a researcher at Industrial Relations Services and, in this context, I would like to acknowledge the respective contributions of Joe O'Hara and Edward Benson to the original manuscript. I would also like to acknowledge the contribution of Venessa

Robinson, who was Tolley's legal editor at the time when the book was first published and I would like to thank Tolley Publishing for releasing the copyright, thereby paving the way for the 'second' edition. In the same vein, I would like to thank those who contributed to the preparation of the first and second editions of this book for Blackstone Press: in particular David Cohen of Paisner & Co. who contributed the sections on profit-sharing and share options; Raymond Jeffers of Linklaters & Paines who rewrote and updated the material on pension loss; John Bowers who, as series editor at the time of the first edition, made a number of valuable comments on the manuscript; Stephen Levinson and Alexandra Davidson also at Paisner & Co., Gary Bowker and Richard Lister (both of IRS), Paul Jordan, who assisted me in updating the statutory references and Blackstone's editorial team. Last but not least, thanks go to my parents and friends for their continued encouragement and support.

The material in the new edition has been fully updated to take account of the changes in the law since October 1992. In particular, the chapter on compensation in discrimination cases (chapter 20) has been substantially rewritten because of removal of the statutory cap on compensation in discrimination after the ECJ decision in *Marshall (No. 2)*, which was anticipated at the time of the first edition, and the MOD cases. The text also incorporates the relevant provisions of the Employment Rights Act 1996 and the Industrial Tribunals Act 1996 as well as the consequential regulations made under those statutory provisions.

Inevitably there are a number of areas where conflicting EAT decisions mean that the law is somewhat unclear. It is possible that, after its ruling in *Digital Equipment Co. Ltd* v *Clements (No. 2)*, the EAT itself will take the initiative to resolve some of these issues but it should be noted that at the time of writing there are a number of cases pending before the Court of Appeal which may impact on the accuracy of some parts of the text.

One of the difficulties in updating a book of this kind is to ensure that the additions to the text do not result in the book becoming too long. With this in mind, I have not included some of the material from the first edition: for example, I have deleted the tables for valuing a company car. The relevant information is available from the Inland Revenue, AA and RAC but has a relatively short 'shelf life' because it is updated each year.

As to the future, it is unclear what impact the outcome of the 1997 General Election will have on the subject matter of this book. I have referred to the relevant provisions of the Employment Rights (Dispute Resolution) Bill in the text but it is unclear whether this bill would be introduced by an incoming Labour Government. It is also unclear whether a Labour Government would increase, or remove altogether, the present statutory cap on unfair dismissal compensation. This, of itself, would be unlikely to affect the principles described in this book.

The book therefore represents my understanding of the law as it existed on 1 April 1997.

Anthony Korn
Barnards Inn Chambers

Table of Cases

A and B v R1 and R2, reported in EOR 67	203
A v Solitaire Ltd case no: 16862/95	204
AB v South West Water Services [1993] 1 All ER 609	204
Abbotts v Wesson Glynwed- Steels Ltd [1982] IRLR 51	144
Abrahams v Performing Rights Society [1995] IRLR 486	19, 23, 25
Acorn Shipyard Ltd v Warren EAT 20/81	173
Adams v John Wright & Sons (Blackwall) Ltd [1972] ICR 463	73
Adams v Union Cinemas Ltd [1939] 3 All ER 136	2
Adapters and Eliminators v Paterson EAT 801/82	166
Adda International Ltd v Curcio [1976] IRLR 425	91, 98
Addis v Gramophone Co Ltd [1909] AC 488	10, 15
Addison v Babcock FATA Ltd [1986] IRLR 388	57, 97, 99, 101, 176, 178
Airscrew Howden Ltd v Jacobs EAT 773/82	144, 145
Akram v Lothian Community Council IRLIB 371	44
Alexander & Others v Standard Telephone & Cables Ltd (No. 2) [1991] IRLR 286	8, 9, 70
Alexander v The Home Office [1988] IRLR 190	200, 204
Allders International Ltd v Parkins [1981] IRLR 68	168
Allen v Hammett [1982] IRLR 89	168
Allen v Key Markets Ltd COIT 1425/41	98
Allen v N E Lancashire Dairies Ltd EAT 230/83	165, 172
American Cyanamid Co v Ethicon Ltd [1975] 1 All ER 504	34
Archbold Freightage Ltd v Wilson [1974] IRLR 10	151, 156
Armitage, Marsden and HM Prison Service v Johnson [1997] IRLR 162	201, 203, 204
Armstrong Whitworth Rolls Ltd v Mustard [1971] 1 All ER 598	71
Arthur Guinness & Son Co (GB) Ltd v Green [1989] IRLR 288	138, 139
Artisan Press Ltd v Srawley and Parker [1986] IRLR 126	49, 58, 62, 153, 169, 171
Aspden v Webbs Poultry & Meat Group (Holdings) Ltd [1996] IRLR 521	4, 26
Automatic Cooling Engineering Ltd v Scott EAT 545/81	45
Ayub v Vauxhall Motors Ltd [1978] IRLR 428	44, 50
Babcock FATA Ltd v Addison [1987] IRLR 173	85, 99, 100, 103, 177
Bailey, N G, & Co Ltd v Preddy [1971] 3 All ER 225	75
Baillie Brothers v Pritchard EAT 59/89	154
Bakr v Sade Bros Ltd EAT 470/83	149
Baldwin v British Coal Corporation [1995] IRLR 139	3, 26
Barber v Royal Guardian Exchange Assurance Group [1990] IRLR 240	76, 133

Barley v Amey Roadstone Corporation Ltd [1977] IRLR 299	91
Barnes v Gee Hogan (Convertors) Ltd EAT 198/77	138, 139
Barrell Plating and Phosphating Co Ltd v Danks [1976] IRLR 262	105
Barrett v National Coal Board [1978] ICR 1101	71
Basnett v J & A Jackson Ltd [1976] IRLR 154	15
Bateman v British Leyland UK Ltd [1974] IRLR 101	44, 108
Baxter v Wreyfield EAT 9/82	165, 172
Bell v Service Engines (Newcastle) Ltd IDS 309	169
Bennett v Tippins EAT 361/89	156
Benson v Dairy Crest Ltd EAT 192/89	91, 118, 129
Bessenden Properties Ltd v J K Corness [1974] IRLR 338	152, 160
Bickley, J & S, Ltd v Washer [1977] ICR 425	80
Bigham v Hobourn Engineering Ltd [1992] IRLR 298	91, 118, 133
Blackstone Franks Investment Management Ltd v Robertson EAT/434/96	10
Blick Vessels & Pipework Ltd v Sharpe IRLIB 274, February 1985	157, 160
Bliss v South East Thames Regional Health Authority [1985] IRLR 308	5, 15, 16
Bold v Brough, Nicholson and Hall Ltd [1963] 3 All ER 849	14
Bonner v H Gilbert & Co [1989] IRLR 475	191
Boorman v Allmakes Ltd [1995] IRLR 553	57, 175, 177
Boots Company Ltd, The v Lees-Collier [1986] ICR 728	44
Boston Deep Sea Fishing and Ice Co v Ansell [1888] 39 ChD 339	7, 191
Boulton & Paul Ltd v Arnold [1994] IRLR 532	143, 144, 146, 150
Bowker v Rose (1978) 122 SJ 147	24
Bowness v Concentric Pumps Ltd 1974 COIT 318/217	111
Boyo v London Borough of Lambeth [1995] IRLR 50	4, 6, 9
Brace v Calder [1895] 2 QB 253	22
Bracey, A G, Ltd v Iles [1973] IRLR 210	156
Braund, Walter, (London) Ltd v Murray [1991] IRLR 100	174, 181
British Coal Corporation v Cheeseborough [1989] IRLR 148	81
British Garages Ltd v Lowen [1979] IRLR 86	155
British Gas plc v Sharma [1991] IRLR 101	197
British Guiana Credit Corporation v Da Silva [1965] 1 WLR 248	21
British Steel Corporation v Williams EAT 776/82	165
British Telecommunications plc v Burwell IRLIB 293, November 1985	190
British Transport Commission v Gourley [1955] 3 All ER 796	28
Brittains Aborfield Ltd v Van Uden [1977] ICR 211	105, 135
Brownson v Hire Services Shops Ltd [1978] IRLR 73	93, 94, 188
Burdett-Coutts and others v Hertfordshire County Council [1984] IRLR 91	5
Burns v Boyd Engineering Ltd EAT 458/84	155
Butler v British Railways Board EAT 510/89	177
Butler v J Wendon & Son [1972] IRLR 15	114
Cadbury Ltd v Doddington [1977] ICR 982	60, 140
Callisher v Bischoffshein [1870] 5 QB 449	19
Carmichael, A M, Ltd v Laing (1972) 7 ITR 1	76
Cartiers Superfoods Ltd v Laws [1978] IRLR 315	106
Castleman & Patterson v A & P Appledore (Aberdeen) Ltd and Hall Russell Ltd EAT 478/90	144
Central Nottinghamshire Health Authority v Shine EAT 562/82	172
Chan v London Borough of Hackney (COIT 400002/92)	201
Chapell v The Times Newspapers Ltd [1975] 2 All ER 233	34

Table of Cases   xiii

Chaplin v Rawlinson [1991] ICR 553	172
Chapman v Aberdeen Construction Group plc [1992] IRLR 505	12
Chelsea Football Club and Athletic Co Ltd v Heath [1981] IRLR 73	60, 177, 178
Cichetti v K Speck & Son COIT 2041/209	108
City & Hackney Health Authority v Crisp [1990] IRLR 47	46, 48, 163
Clark v BET plc and another (unreported, 16 October 1996)	10
Clement-Clarke International Ltd v Manley [1979] ICR 74	179, 180
Co-operative Wholesale Society v Squirrell (1974) ITR 191	116
Coalter v Walter Craven Ltd [1980] IRLR 262	165
Cold Drawn Tubes Ltd v Middleton [1992] IRLR 160	45, 51
Coleman and Stephenson v Magnet Joinery Ltd [1974] IRLR 343	43, 44
Collen v Lewis IDS 390	156
Colwyn Borough Council v Dutton [1980] IRLR 420	173
Connor v Comet Radiovision Services Ltd EAT 650/81	165
Cook, James W, & Co (Wivenhoe) Ltd v Tipper and others [1990] IRLR 386	90
Cooner v P S Doal & Sons [1988] IRLR 338	73, 94
Cooper v Secretary of State for Employment COIT 1717/223	68, 69
Copson v Eversure Accessories Ltd [1974] IRLR 247	118, 120, 127, 128
Cort, Robert, & Son Ltd v Charman [1981] IRLR 437	15, 20
Courtaulds Northern Spinning Ltd v Moosa [1984] IRLR 43	87, 88, 89, 100, 154, 166
Cowley v Manson Timber Ltd [1995] IRLR 153	43
Cox v London Borough of Camden [1996] IRLR 389	16, 144
Cox v Philips Industries Ltd [1976] 3 All ER 161	15
Crossville Wales Ltd v Tracey and Ors [1996] IRLR 91	165
Crowther and Nicholson Ltd, Re (1981) 125 SJ 529	10
Crowther, John, & Sons (Milnsbridge) Ltd v Livesey EAT 272/84	153
Cruz, Dr v Airways Aero Association Ltd COIT 6066/72	115
Cullen v Kwik Fit Euro Ltd EAT 483/83	149
Daley v A E Dorsett (Almar Dolls) Ltd [1981] IRLR 385	138, 156, 160
Dandy v Lacy EAT 450/77	114
Darlington Forge Ltd, The v Sutton (1968) 3 ITR 196	70
Darr v LRC Products [1993] IRLR 257	178
Daykin v IHW Engineering Ltd COIT 1440/117	116
Deane v London Borough of Ealing [1993] IRLR 209	204
Delaney v Staples [1992] IRLR 191	18, 20
Department of Health v Bruce and the Department of Social Security EAT 14/92	42
Derwent Coachworks v Kirby [1994] IRLR 639	179, 180
Devine v Designer Flowers Wholesale Florist Sundries Ltd [1993] IRLR 517	136
Devis, W, & Sons Ltd v Atkins [1977] 3 All ER 40; [1977] IRLR 314	7, 141, 148, 163, 172, 174
Dews v National Coal Board [1987] IRLR 330	10
Dick v University of Dundee 1982 SCOIT 3814/81	208
Dicker v Seceurop Ltd EAT 554/84	107
Dietman v London Borough of Brent [1987] IRLR 146	6, 9
Digital Equipment Co. Ltd v Clements (No. 2) [1997] IRLR 140	144, 176, 179, 180, 211
Dixon v Stenor Ltd [1973] ICR 157	20
Dobson, Bryant, Heather v K P Morritt Ltd [1979] IRLR 101	154
Duffy v Eastern Health & Social Services Board [1992] IRLR 251	201, 203
Dundee Plant Co Ltd v Riddler EAT 377/88	88, 115, 157

Dundon v GPT Ltd [1995] IRLR 403	165, 174
Dunk v George Waller & Son Ltd [1970] 2 QB 163	16
East Lindsey District Council v Daubney [1977] IRLR 181	147
Eastern Counties Timber Co Ltd v Hunt EAT 483/76	106
Electronic Data Processing Ltd v Wright EAT 292/83	44, 47, 48
Enessy Co SA t/a The Tulchan Estate v Minoprio [1978] IRLR 489	44
Evans v Crown Eye Glass plc case no: 47660/92	204
Ever Ready Co (GB) Ltd v Foster EAT 310/81	159, 169
Farrell v Exports International Ltd EAT 569/89	154
Fentiman v Fluid Engineering Products Ltd [1991] IRLR 150	86, 88, 99, 100
Field v Leslie & Godwin Ltd [1972] IRLR 12	155
Finnie v Top Hat Frozen Foods Ltd [1985] IRLR 365	99, 167
Fisher v California Cake & Cookie Ltd [1997] IRLR 212	144
FMC (Meat) Supply Ltd v Wadsworth, Dey and Scrimshaw EAT 20/83	71
Ford v Milthorn Toleman Ltd [1980] IRLR 30	149
Fosca Services (UK) Ltd v Birkett [1996] IRLR 325	4, 9
Foster Wheeler (UK) Ltd v Chiarella EAT 111/82	47
Fougère v Phoenix Motor Co Ltd [1976] IRLR 259	84, 105, 106
Fowler v Westcliffe COIT 1001/164	115
Fox v C Wright Farmers Ltd [1978] ICR 98	68, 70, 167
Fraser v Tullos Business Services EAT 655/87	165
Freemans Plc v Flynn [1984] IRLR 486	44, 51, 122
Friend v PMA Holdings Ltd [1976] ICR 330	71
Fyfe v Scientific Furnishings Ltd [1989] IRLR 331	23, 151, 152, 154, 155, 160, 161
Gallear v J F Watson and Son Ltd [1979] IRLR 306	154
Gardiner-Hill v Roland Berger Technics Ltd [1982] IRLR 498	116, 157
Garner v Grange Furnishing Ltd [1977] IRLR 206	169
Gascol Conversions Ltd v Mercer [1974] IRLR 155	69
Gaskill v Preston [1981] 3 All ER 427	24
Gaskin v MSW Business Systems Ltd IDS 309	165
GEC Energy Systems Ltd v Gufferty EAT 590/87	145
Gee Walker & Sons Ltd v Churchill EAT 11/84	102
George v Beecham Group [1977] IRLR 43	44
Gibson and Others v British Transport Docks Board [1982] IRLR 228	171, 172
Gilham v Kent County Council [1986] IRLR 56	86, 90, 146, 159
Gill and Others v Cape Contracts Ltd [1985] IRLR 499	8
Ging v Ellward Lancs Ltd (1978) 13 IRT 265	85, 86, 88
Glen Henderson Ltd v Nisbet EAT 34/90	89, 94, 157, 158
Gothard v Mirror Group Newspapers [1988] IRLR 396	21
Gotts v Hoffman Balancing Techniques Ltd 1979 COIT 951/115	111
Gourley v Kerr EAT 692/81	28, 29, 138, 147
Gowland v BAT (Export) Ltd IRLIB 269	147
Greene v Church Commissioners for England [1974] ChD 467	19
Guest v A & P Appledore (Aberdeen) Ltd and Hall Russell Ltd SEAT 503/90	144
Gunton v London Borough of Richmond upon Thames [1980] 3 All ER 577	4, 5, 8, 9
Hadley v Baxendale (1854) 9 Exch 341	15
Halcyon Skies, The [1976] 1 All ER 856	14, 76

Table of Cases

Hall v Vincemark Ltd COIT 2029/54	165
Hammington v Berker Sportcraft Ltd EAT 344/79	106
Hardwick v Leeds Area Health Authority [1975] IRLR 319	157
Harrison v Norwest Holst Group Administration Ltd [1985] IRLR 240	5
Harvey v The Institute of the Motor Industry (No. 2) [1995] IRLR 416	137, 206
Hepworth Refractories Ltd v Lingard EAT 555/90	144
Highfield Gears Ltd v James EAT 702/93	143
Hill v C A Parsons Co Ltd [1971] 3 All ER 1345	2, 34, 35
Hilti (GB) Ltd v Windridge [1974] IRLR 53	100, 101, 127, 138
Hilton International Hotels v Faraji [1994] IRLR 267	102
Hollier v Plysu Ltd [1983] IRLR 260	58, 64, 164, 171
Holroyd v Gravure Cylinders Ltd [1984] IRLR 259	89, 158, 170
Hoover Ltd v Forde [1980] ICR 239	159, 160, 169
Hopkins v Norcros plc [1992] IRLR 304	26
Horizon Holidays Ltd v Grassi [1987] IRLR 371	177, 178
Hough v Leyland DAF Ltd [1991] IRLR 194	145
How v Tesco Ltd [1974] IRLR 194	154
Howman v A1 Bacon Ltd [1996] ICR 721	183
Hurley v Mustoe [1981] IRLR 208	202
Hurley v Mustoe (No. 2) [1983] ICR 422	198
Hutchinson v Enfield Rolling Mills [1981] IRLR 318	168
Igbo v Johnson Matthey Chemicals Ltd [1986] IRLR 215	6
Iggesund Converters Ltd v Lewis [1984] IRLR 431	85
ILEA v Gravett [1988] IRLR 497	44
Initial Textile Services v Rendell EAT 383/91	53
Initial Textile Services v Ritchie EAT 358/89	50, 51
Irani v Southampton & South-West Hampshire Area Health Authority [1985] IRLR 203	5, 35, 303
Isle of Wight Tourist Board v Coombes [1976] IRLR 413	105
Isleworth Studios Ltd v Rickard [1988] IRLR 137	4, 85, 101
Ivory v Palmer [1975] ICR 340	13
Jackson v Foster Wheeler (London) Ltd [1989] IRLR 283	21
Johnson v (1) Armitage (2) Marsden and (3) HM Prison Service [1997] IRLR 162	201, 204
Johnson v The Hobart Manufacturing Co Ltd EAT 210/90	152, 153
Johnston t/a Richard Andrews Ladies Hairdressers v Baxter EAT 492/82	136
Jones v International Press Institute EAT 571/81	121
Joseph v National Magazine Co Ltd [1958] 3 All ER 52	16
Josling v Plessey Telecommunications Ltd IRLIB 243, August 1982	76
Justfern Ltd v D'Inglethorpe and Ors [1994] IRLR 164	99, 102
Kennedy v Bryan (1984) The Times, 3 May 1984	111, 112
Kent Management Services Ltd v Butterfield [1992] IRLR 394	10
Kinzley v Minories Finance Ltd [1987] IRLR 490	94
Kraft Foods Ltd v Fox [1977] IRLR 43	166
Ladbroke Racing Ltd v Connolly EAT 160/83	162
Ladbroke Racing Ltd v Mason [1978] ICR 49	167
Ladbroke Racing Ltd v Mesher EAT 375/83	178
Ladup Ltd v Barnes [1982] IRLR 8	174

Lavarack v Woods of Colchester Ltd [1967] 1 QB 278; [1966] 3 All ER 683	10, 24, 26
Laws v Chronicle (Indicator Newspapers) Ltd [1959] 2 All ER 285	7
Lee v IPC Business Press Ltd [1984] ICR 306	96, 97
Leech v Berger, Jensen & Nicholson Ltd [1972] IRLR 58	116
Leech v Preston Borough Council [1985] IRLR 337	19, 20
Leonard, Cyril, & Co v Simo Securities Trust Ltd [1971] 3 All ER 1313	7
Les Ambassadeurs Club v Bainda [1982] IRLR 5	173
Leske v Rogers of Saltcoats (ES) Ltd EAT 520/82	95
Lewicki v Brown & Root Wimpey Highland Fabricators Ltd [1996] IRLR 565	26
Leyland Vehicles Ltd v Reston [1981] IRLR 19	10, 79, 95
Lifeguard Assurance Ltd v Zadrozny [1977] IRLR 56	85
Lignacite Products Ltd v Krollman [1979] IRLR 22	192
Lilley Construction Ltd v Dunn [1984] IRLR 483	48
Lincoln v Hayman [1982] 1 WLR 488	24
Links, A, Ltd v Rose [1991] IRLR 353	167
Linvar Ltd v Hammersley EAT 226/83	123
Lloyd v Scottish Co-operative Wholesale Society Ltd [1973] IRLR 93	114, 116
Lloyd v The Standard Pulverised Fuel Co Ltd [1976] IRLR 115	156
Lock v Connell Estate Agents Ltd [1994] IRLR 444	60, 90, 159
London Borough of Greenwich v Dell EAT 166/94	44
London Borough of Southwark v O'Brien [1996] IRLR 420	76
London Brick Company Ltd v Bishop EAT 624/78	75
London Underground v Edwards [1995] IRLR 355	205
Longmore v Dr Bernard Kei Kam Lee (Case No. 021743/88)	202
Lotus Cars Ltd v Sutcliffe [1982] IRLR 381	70
Lucas v Laurence Scott Electromotors Ltd [1983] IRLR 61	98
Lyford v Turquand (1966) 1 ITR 554	76
Lytlarch Ltd t/a The Viceroy Restaurant v Reid [1991] ICR 216; EAT 296/90	86, 99
Mabey Hire Co Ltd v Richens IDS Brief 468, May 1992, EAT 207/90 & 54/91	88
Mabrizi v National Hospital for Nervous Diseases [1990] IRLR 133	50
Mairs (HM Inspector of Taxes) v Haughey [1993] IRLR 551	194
Malik and another v Bank of Credit and Commerce International [1995] IRLR 375	16
Manning v R & H Wale (Export) Ltd [1979] ICR 433	121
Manpower Ltd v Hearne [1983] IRLR 281	122, 123, 124, 128
Mansfield Hosiery Mills Ltd v Bromley [1977] IRLR 301	147
Marbe v George Edwardes (Daly's Theatre) Ltd [1928] 1 KB 269	16
Marcusfield, A & B, Ltd v Melhuish [1977] IRLR 484	73, 74, 188
Maris v Rotherham Borough Council [1974] IRLR 147	172, 173
Marshall, Thomas, (Exports) Ltd v Guinle [1978] IRLR 174	5
Martin v British Railways Board [1989] ICR 198	142
Martin v Yeoman Aggregates Ltd [1983] IRLR 49	152, 153
Mason v (1) Wimpey Waste Management Ltd and (2) Secretary of State for Employment [1982] IRLR 54	184
MBS Ltd v Calo [1983] IRLR 189	98
McAndrew v Prestwick Circuits Ltd [1988] IRLR 514	159
McCarthy v British Insulated Callenders Cables plc [1985] IRLR 94	181, 182
McClaren v Home Office [1990] IRLR 338	36
McClelland v Northern Ireland General Health Services Board [1957] 2 All ER 129	4, 35, 36

Table of Cases xvii

Case	Page
McDonald v Capital Coaches Ltd EAT 140/94	58, 90
McFall, G M, & Co Ltd v Curran [1981] IRLR 455	173
McNee v Charles Tenant & Co Ltd EAT 338/90	148
McNicholas v AR Engineering IDS 309	165, 169
McQueen v Motherwell Railway Club EAT 652/88	50, 51
Meek v City of Birmingham [1987] IRLR 250	137
Meridian Ltd v Gomersall and another [1977] IRLR 425	43, 44
Micklefield v SAC Technology Ltd [1991] 1 All ER 275	12, 116
Millar, John, & Sons v Quinn [1974] IRLR 107	126, 135
Milnbank Housing Association v Murphy EAT 281/85	181
Mining Supplies (Longwall) Ltd v Baker [1988] IRLR 417	144
Minister of Labour v County Bake Ltd [1968] ITR 379	68
Ministry of Defence v Bristow	199
Ministry of Defence v Cannock [1994] ICR 918	198, 199, 200, 202, 204, 205, 207
Ministry of Defence v Hunt [1996] IRLR 139	198, 199, 200, 201
Ministry of Defence v Meredith [1995] IRLR 539	204
Ministry of Defence v Mutton [1996] ICR 590	119, 131
Ministry of Defence v Sullivan [1994] ICR 193	158, 199, 201, 202
Moeliker v A Reyrolle & Co Ltd [1976] ICR 253	198
Mole Mining Ltd v Jenkins [1972] ICR 282	73
Moncur v International Paint Co Ltd [1978] IRLR 223	166, 167
Moran v A D Hamilton EAT 509/89	145
Morgan Edwards Wholesale Ltd/Gee Bee Discount Ltd v Hough EAT 398/78	87
Morgan Edwards Wholesale Ltd v Francis EAT 205/78	110
Morganite Electrical Carbon Ltd v Donne [1987] IRLR 363	50, 107, 152
Morrish v Henlys (Folkestone) Ltd [1973] IRLR 6	165
Morrison v Amalgamated Transport and General Workers' Union [1989] IRLR 361	164, 170
Muffett, S H, Ltd v Head [1986] IRLR 488	137, 138
Muir, William, (Bond 9) Ltd v Lamb [1985] IRLR 95	159
Muirhead & Maxwell Ltd v Chambers EAT 516/82	59
Mulholland v Bexwell Estates Co Ltd [1950] TLR (Pt 2) 764	2
Mullett v Brush Electrical Machines Ltd [1977] ICR 829	109
Murray v Powertech (Scotland) Ltd [1992] IRLR 254	202
Mutual Life Assurance Society Ltd v Clinch [1981] ICR 752	161
Nairne v Highlands & Islands Fire Brigade [1989] IRLR 366	45
Napier v National Business Agency Ltd [1951] 2 All ER 264	15
Nelson v BBC (No. 2) [1979] IRLR 346	58, 64, 164, 165, 169
Nerva and Ors v RL & G Ltd [1996] IRLR 461	74
Nohar v Granitstone (Galloway) Ltd [1974] ICR 273	112, 114
Noone v North West Thames Regional Health Authority [1988] IRLR 530	200, 201
Norton Tool Co Ltd v Tewson [1973] 1 All ER 183	84, 85, 90, 93, 100, 101, 103, 135, 137
Notcutt v Universal Equipment Co (London) Ltd [1986] IRLR 218	7
Nothman v London Borough of Barnet No. 2 [1980] IRLR 65	44
O'Dea v ISC Chemicals Ltd [1995] IRLR 599	143, 145
O'Laoire v Jackel International Limited [1991] IRLR 170	11, 15, 25, 48, 115
O'Reilly v Welwyn and Hatfield District Council [1975] IRLR 334	156
Ogden v Ardphalt Asphalt Ltd [1977] 1 All ER 267	73
Onions v Apollo Design and Construction (Scotland) Ltd EAT 156/88	149

Orlando v Didcot Power Station Sports & Social Club [1996] IRLR 262	201, 202
Ouseburn Transport Co. Ltd, The v Mundell EAT 371/80	69
Pagano v HGS [1976] IRLR 9	88, 138
Page v Sheerness Steel plc [1996] PIQR Q26	125
Palmanor Ltd t/a Chaplins Night Club v Cedron [1978] IRLR 303	74, 94
Parker & Farr Ltd v Shelvey [1979] IRLR 434	179, 180
Parker Foundry Ltd v Slack [1992] IRLR 11	58, 164, 168
Parker v D & J Tullis Ltd EAT 306/91	142
Parry v Cleaver [1970] AC 1	26
Parsons v B N M Laboratories Ltd [1963] 2 All ER 658	24, 28, 29
Patterson v Bracketts EAT 486/76	165
Peara v Enderlin Ltd [1979] ICR 804	162
Pearson v Leeds Polytechnic Students' Union EAT 182/84	154
Penprase v Mander Bros Ltd [1973] IRLR 167	105
Perks v Geest Industries Ltd [1974] IRLR 228	105
Pirelli General Cable Works Ltd v Murray [1979] IRLR 190	43, 48
Plessey Military Communications Ltd v Bough IDS 310	155
Plewinski v McDermott Engineering London EAT 465/88	154
Plumley v A D International Ltd EAT 591/82	147
Polentarutti v Autokraft Ltd [1991] IRLR 457	164, 170
Polkey v A E Dayton Services Ltd [1987] IRLR 503	39, 44, 141, 143, 144, 176, 211
Port of London Authority v Payne & Others [1994] IRLR 9, reversing [1992] IRLR 447, 155560/89/LN/C	42, 43, 46, 51, 63, 77, 79
Post Office, The v Strange [1981] IRLR 515	4
Powell v London Borough of Brent [1987] IRLR 466	35
Powermatic Ltd v Bull [1977] IRLR 144	124, 126
Pratt v Pickford Removals EAT/43/86	43
Pringle v Lucas Industrial Equipment Ltd [1975] IRLR 266	124, 127
Property Guards Ltd v Taylor [1982] IRLR 175	165
Puglia v C James & Sons Ltd [1996] IRLR 70	102, 138
Qualcast (Wolverhampton) Ltd v Ross [1979] IRLR 98	44, 86
Quiring v Hill House International School EAT 500/88	178
R v British Broadcasting Corporation, ex parte Lavelle [1982] IRLR 404	36
R v East Berkshire Area Health Authority, ex parte Walsh [1984] IRLR 278	5, 36
R v Lord Chancellor's Department, ex parte Nangle [1991] IRLR 343	36
R v South Glamorgan Area Health Authority, ex parte Phillips IRLIB 223, February 1987	36
Ramsay v W B Anderson & Sons Ltd [1974] IRLR 164	157
Randell v Vosper Shiprepairers Ltd COIT 1723/13 (IDS 323)	75
Rank Xerox (UK) Ltd v Stryczek [1995] IRLR 568	47
Rao v Civil Aviation Authority [1992] IRLR 203	145, 147, 170, 173
Raynor v Remploy Ltd [1973] IRLR 3	117
Red Bank Manufacturing v Meadows [1992] IRLR 209	145
Richardson v Walker EAT 312/79	43
Ridgway v The Hungerford Market Co [1835] 3 Ad & El 171	7
Rippa v Devere Hotels COIT 144/83	115
Roadchef Ltd v Hastings [1988] IRLR 142	178
Robb v London Borough of Hammersmith [1991] IRLR 72	35

Table of Cases xix

Case	Page
Robertson, Charles, (Developments) Ltd v White and another [1995] ICR 349	173
Robinson v Harman (1848) 1 Exch 850	8
Rookes v Barnard [1964] AC 1129	204
Rose v RNIB COIT 26830/91	44
Ross v Yewlands Engineering Co Ltd COIT 17321/83/LN	115
Royal Court Hotel Ltd v Cowan EAT 48/84	89, 90
Royal Ordnance plc v Pilkington [1989] IRLR 489	190
RSPCA v Cruden [1986] IRLR 83	173
Rubenstein v McGloughlin [1996] IRLR 557	102
Rushton v Harcross Timber & Building Supplies Ltd [1993] IRLR 254	177, 178
S & U Stores Ltd v Lee [1969] 2 All ER 417	77
S & U Stores Ltd v Wilkes [1974] 3 All ER 401	72, 73, 76, 78
S & U Stores v Wormleighton EAT 477/77	113
Sahil v Kores Nordic (GB) Ltd EAT 379/90	60
Sainsbury, J, Ltd v Savage [1981] ICR 1	159
Samuels v Clifford Chance EAT 559/90	121
Sandown Pier Ltd v Moonan EAT 399/93	105
Saxton v National Coal Board [1970] 5 ITR 196	71
Scottish & Newcastle Breweries plc v Halliday [1986] IRLR 29	155
Scottish Co-operative Wholesale Society Ltd v Lloyd [1973] ICR 137	125
Sealy v Avon Aluminium [1978] IRLR 285; EAT 516/78	89, 158
Secretary of State for Employment v Haynes [1980] IRLR 270	75
Secretary of State for Employment v Wilson [1977] IRLR 483	24
Secretary of State for Employment v John Woodrow & Sons (Builders) Ltd [1983] IRLR 11; [1983] ICR 582	63, 73
Seligman & Latz Ltd v McHugh [1979] IRLR 130	159
Senlle v G Desai t/a Pizza Express COIT 29552/85 LN	94
Sharifi v Strathclyde Regional Council [1992] IRLR 259	201
Shepherd, F C, & Co Ltd v Jerrom [1986] IRLR 358	7
Shindler v Northern Raincoat Co Ltd [1960] 2 WLR 1038	22
Shove v Downs Surgical plc [1984] 1 All ER 7	5, 13, 23, 27, 29, 112
Sillifant v Powell Duffryn Timber Ltd [1983] IRLR 91	141
Simmonds v Merton, Sutton and Wandsworth Area Health Authority EAT 789/77	154
Simmons v Hoover Ltd [1976] IRLR 266	192, 193
Simpson v British Steel Corporation EAT 594/83	165
Simrad Ltd v Scott [1997] IRLR 147	87, 88, 89, 102
Skillen v Eastwoods Froy Ltd (1966) 2 ITR 112	76
Skyrail Oceanic Ltd v Coleman [1981] ICR 864	198, 203
Slaughter v C Brewer & Sons Ltd [1990] IRLR 426	147, 165, 167
Smith, H W, (Cabinets) Ltd v Brindle [1973] ICR 12	2
Smith & Smith v McPhee and Stewart EAT 338/339/89	168
Smith, Kline & French Laboratories Ltd v Coates [1977] IRLR 220	123, 124, 162
Smith v N E Transport & Plant Hire (Broughty Ferry) Ltd EAT 402/83	153
Smoker v London Fire and Civil Defence Authority [1991] IRLR 271	22
SMT Sales & Services Ltd v Irwin EAT 485/79	44
Snowball v Gardner Merchant Ltd [1987] IRLR 397	203
Soros and Soros v Davison and Davison [1994] IRLR 264	90, 149, 150
Southampton and South West Hampshire AHA v Marshall (No. 2) [1993] IRLR 445	206
Sparkes v E T Barwick Mills Ltd 1977 COIT 611/68	95, 117

Steel Stockholders (Birmingham) Ltd v Kirkwood [1993] IRLR 515	142, 143, 146
Steer v Messrs Primlock Ltd EAT 687/85	168
Stena Houlder Ltd v Keenan EAT(s) 543/93	48
Stewart v Glentaggart Ltd [1963] SLT 119	29
Stones v Hills of London EAT 12/83	198
Stowe-Woodward BTR Ltd v Beynon [1978] ICR 609	190
Sturdy Finance Ltd v Bardsley [1979] IRLR 65	123, 124
Sutton & Gates (Luton) Ltd v Boxall [1978] IRLR 486	167
Sweetlove v Redbridge and Waltham Forest Area Health Authority [1979] IRLR 195	152
Systems Floors (UK) v Daniel [1981] IRLR 475	70
Tarmac Roadstone Holdings Ltd v Peacock [1973] IRLR 157	69
TBA Industrial Products Ltd v Locke [1984] IRLR 48	85, 95, 100
Tele-Trading Ltd v Jenkins [1990] IRLR 430	141, 142, 165
Textet v Greenhough Ltd EAT 410/82	110, 112
Thomas v Gauges North West (Scientific Instruments) IRLIB 277, March 1985	172
Thompson v Imperial College of Science and Technology IDS 309	171
Thompson v Smiths (Harlow) Ltd EAT 952/83	93
Thompson v Woodland Designs Ltd [1980] IRLR 423	173
Tidman v Aveling Marshall Ltd [1977] IRLR 218	90, 107, 127
Timex Corporation Ltd v Thomson [1981] IRLR 522	44
Tipton v West Midlands Co-operative Society (No. 2) EAT 859/86	184
Tomlinson v Dick Evans 'U' Drive Ltd [1978] IRLR 77	76, 98
Townson v The Northgate Group Ltd [1981] IRLR 382	143
Tradewinds Airways Ltd v Fletcher [1981] IRLR 272	95, 97, 99, 100, 128, 167
Transport & General Workers' Union v Howard [1992] IRLR 170	64, 65
Trend v Chiltern Hunt Ltd [1977] IRLR 66	172
Trico-Folberth Ltd v Devonshire [1989] IRLR 396	148
Trimble v Supertravel Ltd [1982] IRLR 451	159
Trotter v Forth Ports Authority [1991] IRLR 419	20
Tsoukka v Ptoomac Restaurants Ltd (1968) 3 ITR 259	74
Tunnel Holdings Ltd v Woolf [1976] ICR 387	193
UBAF Bank Ltd v Davis [1978] IRLR 442	91, 110, 114, 148, 179, 180
United Freight Distribution Ltd v McDougall (S) EAT 218/94	117
Valentine v Great Lever Spinning Co Ltd (1966) 1 ITR 71	80
Vaughan v Weighpack Ltd [1974] IRLR 105	101, 135, 136
Vibert v Eastern Telegraph Co [1883] 1 Cab & El 17	2
Wadcock v London Borough of Brent [1990] IRLR 223	35
Wagstaff v Elida Gibbs Ltd and another (1991) 141 NLJ 1514	197, 201, 202
Walls v Brookside Metal Co Ltd EAT 579/89	165
Walker, J H, Ltd v Hussain [1996] IRLR 11	205
Washbrook v Podger EAT 123/85	167
Webb v EMO Cargo (UK) Ltd [1994] IRLR 482	198
Weevsmay Ltd v Kings [1977] ICR 244	73
Weston v Metzler (UK) Ltd EAT 303 and 304/91	145
Westwood v Secretary of State for Employment [1984] 1 All ER 874	18, 23, 24, 25
Whiting, Robert, Designs Ltd v Lamb [1978] ICR 89	168
Whittington v P Morris and Greenwich Health Authority (Case No. 17846/89)	197

Table of Cases

Wibberley v Staveley Iron and Chemical Company Ltd (1966) 1 ITR 558	77
Williams v Lloyds Retailers Ltd [1973] IRLR 262	160
Williams v Simmonds [1981] STC 715	20
Willment Bros v Oliver [1979] IRLR 393	123, 127
Wilson v Gleneagles Bakery Ltd EAT 40/88	157
Wilson v (1) Glenrose (Fishmerchants) Ltd and (2) Chapman and others (EAT/444/91)	158
Wilson v National Coal Board (1980) 130 NLJ 1146	25, 26
Wilson v Tote Bookmakers Ltd COIT 15570/81	95
Winterhalter Gastronom Ltd v Webb [1973] IRLR 120	147
Wolesley Centres Ltd v Simmons [1994] ICR 503	144
Yeats v Fairey Winches Ltd [1974] IRLR 362	122, 125
Yetton v Eastwoods Froy Ltd [1966] 3 All ER 353	22, 152, 154
York Trailer Co Ltd v Sparkes [1973] IRLR 348	95
York v Brown EAT 262/84	171
Yorkshire Engineering Co Ltd v Burnham [1974] ICR 77	107
Youngs of Gosport Ltd v Kendell [1977] IRLR 433	146

Table of Statutes

Act of Sederant (Interest in Sheriff Court Decrees or Extracts) 1975   207
Administration of Justice Act 1956
  s. 1(1)(o)   77
Administration of Justice Act 1982
  s. 15(1)   30

Companies Act 1985
  s. 316   29
  s. 316(3)   30
County Courts Act 1984
  s. 69   30

Disability Discrimination Act 1995   196
  s. 5(1)   205
  s. 8   197, 206
  s. 8(3)   197
  s. 8(4)   200
  s. 8(5)   206

Employment Act 1980   55
  s. 9(2)   169
  s. 9(5)   56
Employment Act 1982   61, 63
  s. 20   3
  Sch. 2   55
    para. 3   3
Employment Protection Act 1975   41, 54
Employment Protection (Consolidation) Act 1978
  s. 49   138
  s. 51   23
  s. 68(1)   43
  s. 69(2)   49
  s. 69(2)(a)   49
  s. 71(2)   49
  s. 74(1)   149
  s. 74(7)   177, 178

Employment Rights Act 1996   25, 66, 191, 207
  Part II   10
  s. 1(2)   3
  s. 1(4)(c)   70
  s. 86   16, 95, 138
  s. 86(1)   3, 18, 189
  s. 86(4)   191
  s. 86(6)   6
  s. 87   17, 18
  s. 87(4)   18
  s. 88   17, 18
  s. 88(1)–(3)   17
  s. 89   17, 18
  s. 89(1)–(2)   17
  s. 90   17, 18
  s. 91   17, 18
  s. 91(1)–(3)   18
  s. 91(5)   23
  s. 92   7
  s. 97   55
  s. 97(1)   38
  s. 97(2)   38, 55
  s. 97(4)   55
  s. 98(1)–(2)   38
  s. 98(4)   38
  s. 99   39
  s. 100   39
  s. 100(1)(a)–(b)   52, 56, 57, 61
  s. 104   39
  s. 107   172
  ss. 108–109   39
  s. 111   39
  s. 112   39
  s. 112(2)–(3)   42, 43
  s. 113   39
  s. 114   39, 42, 49, 52, 62
  s. 114(1)   41, 58

Employment Rights Act 1996 — *continued*
s. 114(2) 46, 49
s. 114(3)–(4) 46
s. 115 39, 42, 52, 62
s. 115(1) 42
s. 115(2) 47
s. 115(3) 48
s. 116 39
s. 116(1) 42, 46, 48, 51
s. 116(2) 46, 48, 51
s. 116(3) 42, 46, 48, 51
s. 116(4) 46, 48, 51
s. 116(5)–(6) 45
s. 117 39, 48
s. 117(1)–(2) 49
s. 117(3) 49, 62
s. 117(3)(b) 208
s. 117(4) 208
s. 117(4)(a) 50, 51
s. 117(5)(a) 210
s. 117(5)(b) 208, 210
s. 117(6) 208
s. 117(8) 52, 152
s. 118 39, 49
s. 119 39, 49, 209
s. 119(1)–(2) 54
s. 120 39, 49
s. 120(1) 56, 210, 211
s. 120(2) 56
s. 121 39, 49
s. 122 39, 49
s. 122(1) 58, 140, 169, 209
s. 122(2) 58, 140, 209
s. 122(3) 209
s. 122(4) 57, 140, 175, 176, 209
s. 123 39, 49, 88, 94, 109, 209
s. 123(1) 84, 88, 89, 96, 118, 140, 141, 149, 150, 163, 169, 173, 177, 179, 209, 210, 211
s. 123(2) 109, 118
s. 123(2)(a) 116
s. 123(2)(b) 94, 95
s. 123(3) 96, 140, 176, 210
s. 123(4) 52, 140, 151, 152
s. 123(5) 91, 172
s. 123(6) 44, 58, 128, 140, 163, 164, 169, 170, 209, 210
s. 123(7) 176, 178, 210
s. 124 39, 49
s. 124(1) 49
s. 124(2) 92

Employment Rights Act 1996 — *continued*
s. 124(3) 47, 48
s. 124(5) 180, 181
s. 125 39, 49
s. 125(1) 62, 210
s. 125(2) 211
s. 125(2)(b) 62
s. 125(3) 56, 64, 211
s. 125(4)–(5) 64, 140, 211
s. 125(6)–(7) 63
s. 126 39, 49
s. 126(2) 207
s. 127 49
ss. 128–132 52
s. 136(3) 193
s. 138(1) 61
s. 140(1) 191, 192, 193
s. 140(2) 193
s. 140(3) 191, 192
s. 141(1)–(2) 57
s. 141(4)(d) 57
s. 142 192
s. 142(2)–(3) 193
s. 143 193
s. 145(1) 188
s. 145(2)(a) 188
s. 145(2)(c) 188
s. 156(1) 188
s. 158 190
s. 162(1)–(2) 187
s. 162(3)–(4) 188
s. 177(5)(a)–(b) 50
s. 199 3
s. 203 3, 6, 116
s. 220 56, 66, 67
s. 221 56, 66, 67, 94
s. 221(2) 77
s. 221(3) 67, 80
s. 222 56, 66, 67, 94
s. 222(1) 74
s. 223 56, 66, 67, 94
s. 223(1) 77, 81, 82
s. 223(2) 81, 82
s. 223(3) 81
s. 224 56, 66, 67, 72, 74, 94
s. 225 56, 66, 67, 78, 94
s. 226 56, 66, 67, 94
s. 226(2)(a)–(b) 78
s. 226(3) 78
s. 226(5) 79, 189
s. 226(6) 78, 79, 189

Table of Statutes

Employment Rights Act 1996 — *continued*
   s. 227   56, 66, 67, 94
   s. 227(1)   189
   s. 228(1)   83
   s. 229(1)   83
   s. 229(2)   80
   s. 234   69
   s. 234(1)   67, 69
   s. 234(2)   67
   s. 234(3)   67, 69
   s. 235(1)   81

Fair Employment (Northern Ireland) Act 1989   196
Finance Act 1988
   s. 74(1)   20, 28, 185

Income and Corporation Taxes Act 1988
   s. 131   20
   s. 148   20, 29, 194
   s. 148(2)   185
   ss. 185–186   11
   s. 188   28, 29, 185
   s. 188(4)   20
   ss. 192–193   28
   s. 579(1)   194
   s. 580(3)   194
   s. 612(1)   29
   Schs. 8-10   11
   Sch. E   20, 194
Industrial Relations Act 1971
   38, 41
Industrial Tribunals Act 1996   183
   s. 14   186
   ss. 16–17   183

Judgments Act 1838
   s. 17   186

Law Reform (Miscellaneous Provisions) Act 1934
   s. 3   30
Limitation Act 1980
   s. 2   30
   s. 28   30

Race Relations Act 1976
   196, 204, 207
   s. 56(1)(a)   197
   s. 56(1)(c)   206

Race Relations Act 1976 — *continued*
   s. 56(4)   206
   s. 57(1)   197
   s. 57(3)   205
   s. 57(4)   200
Race Relations (Remedies) Act 1994
   206
Redundancy Payments Act 1965
   78
Rehabilitation of Offenders Act 1974
   165

Sex Discrimination Act 1975
   196, 198, 203, 207
   s. 65   197
   s. 65(1)(c)   206
   s. 65(3)   206
   s. 66(1)   197
   s. 66(2)   197
   s. 66(4)   200
Sex Discrimination Act 1986
   56
   s. 3   56
Supreme Court Act 1981
   s. 30   35
   s. 35A   30

Trade Union and Labour Relations (Consolidation) Act 1992
   s. 152   39, 56, 59, 61, 65
   s. 153   56, 57, 59, 61
   s. 155   59
   s. 155(2)   64
   s. 156(1)   56
   s. 157   39, 61
   s. 158(1)–(2)   62, 63
   s. 158(3)   63
   s. 158(4)–(5)   64
   s. 158(6)   63
   s. 159   56, 57, 63
   s. 160(1)   65
   s. 160(3)   65
   s. 161(1)–(4)   52
   s. 163   52, 53
   s. 163(4)–(6)   53
   s. 164   53
   s. 164(2)   53
   s. 164(5)–(6)   53
   ss. 165–166   53
   s. 236   34
   s. 238   166

Trade Union Reform and Employment Rights
    Act 1993
    s. 28   61
    Sch. 5   56, 61

Unfair Contract Terms Act 1977   12
    Sch. 1
        para. 1(a)   12
        para. 1(e)   12

Wages Act 1986   10

Table of Statutory Instruments

County Court Rules 1981
  ord. 6
    r. 1A 30
Court Funds Rules 1987
  r. 27(1) 207

Employment Protection (Recoupment of Jobseeker's Allowance and Income Support) Regulations 1996 183, 186
  reg. 2 184
  reg. 3 183
  reg. 4(1) 183
  reg. 4(3) 184
  reg. 4(8) 183
  reg. 7 184
  reg. 7(2)–(3) 184
  reg. 8 184
  reg. 8(2)–(3) 185
  reg. 8(4) 184
  reg. 8(6)(a)–(b) 184
  reg. 8(10) 184
  reg. 10 185
  Sch.
    para. 7 183

Fair Employment (Amendment) (Northern Ireland) Order 1995 (SI 1995/758(NI4)) 206

High Court and County Courts Jurisdiction Order 1991 (SI 1991/724) 30
  reg. 7(5)(a)–(d) 30

Income Tax (Employment) Regulations 1973 (SI 1973/334)
  reg. 13 28
  reg. 16(1) 28

Industrial Tribunals (Constitution and Rules of Procedure) Regulations 1993 (SI 1993/2687)
  reg. 8(1) 128
  r. 11(1)(e) 174
  Sch. 1
    para. 4 128
Industrial Tribunals Extension of Jurisdiction (England and Wales) Order 1994 (SI 1994/1623) 30
Industrial Tribunals Extension of Jurisdiction (Scotland) Order 1994 (SI 1994/1624) 30
Industrial Tribunals (Interest on Awards in Discrimination Cases) Regulations 1996 (SI 1996/2803) 206
  reg. 6(3) 207
  reg. 8 207
Industrial Tribunals (Interest) Order 1990 (SI 1990/479) 185
Industrial Tribunals (Rules of Procedure) Regulations 1985 (SI 1985/16)
  r. 4 160, 161
  r. 4(1)(b)(ii) 91
  r. 10(1) 107
  r. 10(1)(e) 174
  r. 11 117
  r. 12(2) 108

Occupational Pension Scheme (Disclosure of Information) Regulations 1986 (SI 1986/1046) 128
Occupational Pension Scheme (Transfer Values) Regulations 1985 (SI 1985/1931) 14, 122

Redundancy Payments Pensions Regulations 1965 (SI 1965/1932) 190

Rules of the Supreme Court
  Ord. 18
    r. 8 30
  ord. 53 35
    r. 9(3) 36

Sex Discrimination and Equal Pay Regulations 1993 (SI 1993/2798) 206
Sex Discrimination and Equal Pay (Miscellaneous Amendment) Regulations 1996 (SI 1996/438) 205
Social Security (Credits) Regulations 1975 (SI 1975/556)
  reg. 9(1) 98

Social Security (General Benefit) Amendment Regulations 1984 (SI 1984/1259) 25
Social Security (Unemployment, Sickness and Invalidity Benefit) Regulations 1983 (SI 1983/1598)
  reg. 7(1) 98

Transfer of Undertakings (Protection of Employment) Regulations 1981 (SI 1981/1794)
  reg. 8 39, 57

Unfair Terms in Consumer Contracts Regulations 1994 (SI 1994/3159) 12

PART I WRONGFUL DISMISSAL

Introduction

Two forms of financial compensation may be open to employees on dismissal — damages for wrongful dismissal (a common law remedy) or compensation for unfair dismissal (a remedy provided by statute). Wrongful dismissal claims are brought in the High Court and county courts whereas claims for unfair dismissal are made to industrial tribunals. The two kinds of claim are not mutually exclusive since the rules governing liability for each claim are distinct. A dismissal can therefore be wrongful, or unfair, both or neither.

A major drawback of the common law action for wrongful dismissal is that the courts cannot award compensation beyond the time when the contract could have been brought to an end in accordance with its terms. In most cases this means that compensation will not be awarded beyond the time when the notice period would have expired had notice been given. Such an action therefore offers limited financial compensation for most employees. However, it is still important for those employees who do not meet the statutory qualifications to bring an unfair dismissal claim and for highly paid directors or other senior executives, whose claims under their Service Agreements will often exceed the amount which tribunals are permitted to award by statute.

1 Compensation for Wrongful Dismissal

1.1 WHAT IS WRONGFUL DISMISSAL?

The law of wrongful dismissal is essentially an extension of the ordinary common law rules which govern the termination of a contract. A dismissal is therefore wrongful if the employer either terminates the contract in a manner which is contrary to its terms or does some other act which shows an intention not to be bound by it. Essentially, any termination by an employer which is not lawful will be wrongful. Apart from exceptional cases, where a contract of employment can be terminated on specified grounds, the law of wrongful dismissal is concerned with the mode of termination rather than the reasons for termination.

1.1.1 Dismissal without proper notice

The most common example of a wrongful dismissal is the failure of an employer to give an employee the correct period of notice which is required to terminate the employment contract lawfully. This period of notice may be expressly agreed between the parties or it may be implied. As regards the latter, there is a common law presumption that a contract for an indefinite period may be terminated by 'a reasonable period of notice'.

What is a reasonable period of notice depends on all the circumstances the employment. Particular importance is attached to such factors as the type of job, the employee's status and the period by which pay is calculated, e.g., weekly, monthly etc. The courts also take into account any custom or practice established in an industry or profession. It has been held that a clerk paid fortnightly was entitled to one month's notice (*Vibert* v *Eastern Telegraph Co* [1883] 1 Cab & El 17) whereas a 'superior' clerk was entitled to three months' notice (*Mulholland* v *Bexwell Estates Co Ltd* [1950] TLR (Pt 2) 764). A controller of cinemas was entitled to six months' notice (*Adams* v *Union Cinemas Ltd* [1939] 3 All ER 136) whereas a director and company secretary of a small firm was entitled to three months' notice (*H W Smith (Cabinets) Ltd* v *Brindle* [1973] ICR 12). In the rather special circumstances that existed in *Hill* v *C A Parsons Co Ltd* [1971] 3 All ER 1345, the court considered that a chartered engineer was entitled to at least six months' notice (see 3.2.1 below for the facts). However, it is always open to employees to waive their rights to notice, for example as part of a voluntary redundancy package, and in such circumstances it will not be open to them to seek damages for wrongful dismissal (*Baldwin* v *British Coal Corporation* [1995] IRLR 139).

Note: Employers are under a duty to specify the length of notice an employee is entitled to receive. They are obliged to give the employee this information in the written statement of particulars of employment which they must provide within two months from the commencement of employment (ERA 1996, s. 1(2)).

1.1.2 Failure to give statutory notice

Whatever period of notice is stated in the contract, whether express or implied, the notice actually given to the employee must not be less than the statutory minimum periods of notice laid down by the Employment Rights Act 1996.

The statutory periods are as follows (ERA 1996, s. 86(1)):

(a) not less than one week's notice for an employee who has been continuously employed for one month or more (before 2 January 1983, four weeks or more) but less than two years;
(b) not less than one week's notice for each year of continuous employment for an employee who has been continuously employed for two years or more but less than 12 years;
(c) not less than 12 weeks' notice for an employee who has been employed for 12 years or more.

Note: An agreement which purports to reduce the periods of notice guaranteed by the statutory provisions is void (ERA 1996, s. 203).

See 1.5 below for calculating the statutory notice entitlement.

1.1.2.1 Exceptions
The following employees do not have the right to be given the statutory minimum periods of notice:

(a) employees engaged in work wholly or mainly outside Great Britain unless they ordinarily work in Great Britain and the work outside Great Britain is for the same employer;
(b) employees who are employed under a contract made in contemplation of the performance of a specific task which was not expected to last longer than three months (before 2 January 1983, 12 weeks) unless they have been continuously employed for more than three months (ERA 1996, s. 86(1);
(c) merchant seamen and share fishermen (ERA 1996, s. 199).

1.1.3 Dismissal in breach of disciplinary procedures

Today, it is quite common for a disciplinary procedure to form part of the contract of employment and, in such circumstances, a failure to follow the disciplinary procedure may amount to a serious breach of contract (*The Post Office* v *Strange* [1981] IRLR 515). However, the precise effect of an employer's failure to follow a disciplinary procedure on termination is uncertain, although it has been held that the notice should be extended by the length of time it would have taken if the dismissal had been handled correctly (*Gunton* v *London Borough of Richmond upon Thames* [1980] 3 All ER 577 and *Boyo* v *London Borough of Lambeth* [1995] IRLR 50). But in *Fosca Services (UK) Ltd* v *Birkett* [1996] IRLR 325, the EAT ruled that this will be appropriate only where the evidence shows that the use of the disciplinary procedure would have extended the length of employment beyond the notice period. The EAT's reasoning is open to doubt on the ground an employee will not normally be given notice until the disciplinary process is completed.

1.1.4 Fixed term contract

Termination by an employer of a fixed term contract before the term has expired can also constitute wrongful dismissal. For example, if a scientist is employed on a project for a fixed term of four years, any unlawful termination by the employer before that time would amount to a breach of contract and give rise to an action for wrongful dismissal (*Isleworth Studios Ltd* v *Rickard* [1988] IRLR 137). Normally, the possibility of early termination will be taken into account by the inclusion of a provision that the contract may be terminated by either side giving a specified period of notice.

1.1.5 Restricted grounds of dismissal

Sometimes the parties may restrict the grounds on which the contract may be terminated to certain defined situations by providing for circumstances where notice will not be necessary, e.g., misconduct or incapacity. If an employee is dismissed where the grounds have been so restricted, such dismissal will be lawful only if the employer can justify it on one of the grounds specified in the contract. However, the precise effect of a failure to do this is uncertain.

In *McClelland* v *Northern Ireland General Health Services Board* [1957] 2 All ER 129, the House of Lords appear to have held that a dismissal for a reason other than one expressly permitted was of no legal effect. This decision involved the rather special rules of administrative law, and the more likely interpretation is that the employer's action would amount to a breach of contract with damages being quantified in the usual way (see, for example, *Aspden* v *Webbs Poultry & Meat Group (Holdings) Ltd* [1996] IRLR 521).

1.1.6 Contract for a specific task

An action for wrongful dismissal may lie if a contract for a specific task is terminated prematurely, i.e., before the task is complete. Here again, the employer will often take this into account by reserving the right to dismiss on certain grounds before the task is complete. A dismissal will not be wrongful if the employer is able to show that one or more of these grounds existed at the time of termination.

1.1.7 Repudiation and breach of fundamental term

An action for wrongful dismissal also arises where the employer is found to have 'repudiated' the contract or is in breach of one of the fundamental contractual obligations. The two concepts are often used by the courts interchangeably to describe the same kind of conduct. For example, a failure to give proper notice is both a breach of a fundamental term and a repudiation.

1.1.7.1 Repudiation
A repudiation occurs where the employer by his conduct displays an intention not to be bound by the contract. For example, in *Shove* v *Downs Surgical plc* [1984] 1 All ER 7, the defendant company admitted liability for repudiating its contract of employment with Mr Shove, its managing director, when it passed a motion of no confidence in him and suggested that he should make 'a dignified exit on grounds of ill health'.

Employers may also repudiate the contract if they act beyond the powers conferred on them by the contract itself. Thus in *Bliss* v *South East Thames Regional Health Authority* [1985] IRLR 308 the Court of Appeal ruled that the Authority had repudiated the contract by insisting that a consultant underwent a medical examination because the contract did not give it power to insist on a medical examinaton without just cause.

Employers may also repudiate the contract if they insist on imposing new terms and conditions of employment on their employees without their consent (see *Burdett-Coutts and others* v *Hertfordshire County Council* [1984] IRLR 91).

1.1.7.2 Breach of a fundamental term
A claim for wrongful dismissal will also arise where the employer is shown to be in breach of a fundamental term of the contract of employment such as pay, location, status etc. Thus, in some of the decisions cited above the employers were also found to be in breach of their essential contractual obligations. For example, in *Bliss* v *South East Thames Regional Health Authority* [1985] IRLR 308 the Authority was found to be in breach of the duty of mutual trust and confidence.

There is a difference of judicial opinion as to the effect of a breach of a fundamental term on the contract of employment. Some judges take the view that the wrongful dismissal ends the contract automatically (per Shaw LJ in *Gunton* v *London Borough of Richmond upon Thames* [1980] 3 All ER 577) whereas other judges are of the opinion that the dismissal will not terminate the contract of employment if the employee elects to affirm it (per Buckley LJ in *Gunton*). At the heart of the argument is the question whether the rules relating to contracts generally (which provide that a unilateral repudiation does not terminate a contract) can be applied to employment contracts in view of the special relationship which exist between employer and employee. The Court of Appeal appears to have affirmed that the 'elective' theory applies at least in cases of anticipatory breach, i.e., where one of the parties indicates an intention not to abide by the terms of the contract before the time fixed for performance (*Harrison* v *Norwest Holst Group Administration Ltd* [1985] IRLR 240). See also *Thomas Marshall (Exports) Ltd* v *Guinle* [1978] IRLR 174, *R* v *East Berkshire Health Authority ex parte Walsh* [1984] IRLR 278, *Irani* v *Southampton*

& *South-West Hampshire Area Health Authority* [1985] IRLR 203, *Dietman* v *London Borough of Brent* [1987] IRLR 146 and *Boyo* v *London Borough of Lambeth* [1995] IRLR 50.

In practical terms, if the courts decide that the 'elective' theory is correct, this may lengthen the period over which damages for wrongful dismissal are awarded. It may also encourage the development of other forms of legal redress for wrongful dismissal (see Chapter 3).

1.2 LAWFUL TERMINATION OF CONTRACT

An employment may be lawfully terminated by:

(a) *giving proper notice* (see 1.1.1 and 1.1.2 above);

(b) *expiry* — a contract for a fixed term, i.e., a specified period, will terminate automatically at the end of that period and a contract for a specified task will terminate automatically on the completion of that task;

(c) *agreement* — at common law, the employer and the employee may agree to terminate the employment contract and thereby release each other from their obligations thereunder. However, such agreements will be void under s. 203 of the Employment Rights Act 1996 if they purport to exclude the rights conferred on all employees by employment protection legislation (*Igbo* v *Johnson Matthey Chemicals Ltd* [1986] IRLR 215);

(d) *summary dismissal* — a dismissal without notice may be lawful if the employer can prove that the employee has committed a serious act of misconduct (see 1.2.1 below);

(e) *dismissal for cause* — some contracts confer power on the employer to terminate the contract lawfully in a specified set of circumstances (e.g., incapacity — see 1.1.5 above);

(f) *frustration* — where circumstances beyond the control of either party to the contract make it impossible to perform the contract in the manner originally contemplated by the parties (see 1.3 below).

1.2.1 Summary dismissal

At common law an employer may dismiss an employee summarily, i.e., without notice, in the event of a serious breach of contract on the part of the employee. This rule applies to all contracts of employment and is specifically preserved by s. 86(6) of the Employment Rights Act in relation to the statutory minimum notice requirements.

Whether the employee's conduct is sufficiently serious to justify summary dismissal depends on the particular circumstances and, to some extent, reflects changes in judicial attitudes to certain kinds of conduct as well as changes in the ordinary expectations of employers and employees. Typical examples of situations where summary dismissal would normally be justified include theft of the employer's property, disobedience to lawful orders, gross negligence, gross insubordination and other forms of gross misconduct.

An employee may be summarily dismissed for a single serious incident or a series of incidents. However, as a general rule, 'one act of disobedience or misconduct can justify dismissal only if it is of a nature which goes to show (in effect) that the servant is repudiating the contract, or one of its essential conditions' (per Lord Evershed in *Laws* v *Chronicle (Indicator Newspapers) Ltd* [1959] 2 All ER 285). He added that, in other words, there must be a 'deliberate flouting of the essential contractual conditions'.

1.2.2 Reasons for dismissal

The law of wrongful dismissal is primarily concerned with the form of dismissal rather than its substance. Employers may therefore exercise their right to dismiss without giving any reasons. As Lord Denman said in *Ridgway* v *The Hungerford Market Co* [1835] 3 Ad & El 171 'it is not necessary that a master, having a good ground of dismissal should either state it to the servant or act upon it. It is enough if it exist, and if there be improper conduct in fact'.

One consequence of this rule is that an employer who wrongly dismisses an employee for reason x may justify the dismissal by reason y even if the employer was unaware of reason y at the time of dismissal *Boston Deep Sea Fishing and Ice Co* v *Ansell* [1888] 39 ChD 339 confirmed by *Cyril Leonard & Co* v *Simo Securities Trust Ltd* [1971] 3 All ER 1313). This contrasts with the position in unfair dismissals where employers may rely only on the reason they put forward at the time of dismissal (see *W Devis & Sons Ltd* v *Atkins* [1977] 3 All ER 40). Employers are also under a statutory duty to give written reasons for dismissal to employees who have two years' continuous employment (ERA 1996, s. 92).

1.3 FRUSTRATION

There can be no claim for wrongful dismissal if the contract is terminated by frustration. This occurs when circumstances beyond the control of either party to the contract make it impossible to perform the contract in the manner originally contemplated by the parties. Thus it has been held that a contract of employment may be frustrated as a result of a sentence of imprisonment being imposed on an employee (see *F C Shepherd & Co Ltd* v *Jerrom* [1986] IRLR 358). A contract may also be frustrated as a result of the employee suffering from a serious illness which renders him incapable of performing the contract (*Notcutt* v *Universal Equipment Co (London) Ltd* [1986] IRLR 218).

A detailed consideration of the common law rules on frustration is beyond the scope of this book but it should be noted that where frustration is shown the contract terminates automatically and therefore there can be no claim for wrongful or unfair dismissal.

1.4 ASSESSING COMPENSATION FOR WRONGFUL DISMISSAL

The usual remedy for wrongful dismissal is an action for damages. The rules governing the assessment of compensation for wrongful dismissal are simply an extension of the ordinary rules which govern an award of damages for breach of contract. These differ in certain significant respects from the statutory rules which apply in assessing compensation for unfair dismissal.

Every breach of contract gives rise to a claim for damages. The basic object of damages for breach of contract is to put the plaintiff 'so far as money can do it ... in the same situation ... as if the contract had been performed' (*Robinson* v *Harman* (1848) 1 Exch 850 at p. 855). In the context of wrongful dismissal, this involves a consideration of two factors: first the period over which damages are awarded, 'the damages period', and secondly the items which can be included in such a claim.

In order to ensure that an employee is not better off than he would have been had the contract been performed and to prevent him from making a profit out of the employer's breach, an employee must give credit for payments received since dismissal such as earnings from a new job or social security benefits. These payments go towards reducing the employer's liability.

1.4.1 The damages period

The first stage in the calculation of damages for wrongful dismissal is to determine the 'damages period'. In determining this period the courts assume that the employer would have brought the contract to an end 'in the way most beneficial to himself, that is to say, that he would have determined the contract at the earliest date at which he could properly do so' (per Buckley LJ in *Gunton* v *London Borough of Richmond upon Thames* [1980] 3 All ER 577 at p. 589). This means that the period of loss ends at the time when the employer could have terminated the contract lawfully (*Alexander & Others* v *Standard Telephone & Cables Ltd (No. 2)* [1991] IRLR 286).

1.4.1.1 Damages for the notice period
Where the contract is terminable by notice, the damages period is fixed by reference to the period of notice. For example, where an employee receives insufficient notice, the damages period is the difference between the period of notice which the employee should have been given and the period he is actually given. If no notice is given, then the damages period is the full period of notice.

Example

An employee is entitled to receive four weeks' notice but is given two weeks' notice. The damages period is therefore two weeks.

See 1.1.1 for dismissal without proper notice.

1.4.1.2 Fixed term contracts
If the contract is for a fixed term without express provision for earlier termination by notice, the earliest date on which the employer could bring the contract to an end is the end of the term. Therefore, subject to the duty to mitigate, damages may be awarded for the remainder of the term. For example, in *Gill and Others* v *Cape Contracts Ltd* [1985] IRLR 499 the Northern Ireland High Court awarded Mr Gill and his colleagues six months' wages in compensation for breach of a collateral contract to work at Sullom Voe for six months (see also 1.1.4 above). However, if the

Compensation for Wrongful Dismissal 9

fixed term contract is terminable by notice, damages will be limited to the notice period.

Example

A scientist is employed on a research project under a contract for a fixed term of four years. If the contract was terminable on three months' notice, the damages period would be limited to three months.

1.4.1.3 Breach of contractual procedures

In *Gunton* v *London Borough of Richmond upon Thames* [1980] 3 All ER 577, the Court of Appeal ruled that, where the employers had failed to follow an established disciplinary procedure, the measure of damages should be based on the length of time it would have taken for the employment to have been terminated lawfully if the employers had followed the procedure correctly. The court therefore allowed 'a reasonable period' for carrying out those procedures plus the one month's notice provided for by the contract. (See also *Dietman* v *London Borough of Brent* [1987] IRLR 259 and *Boyo* v *London Borough of Lambeth* [1995] IRLR 50 where the Court of Appeal upheld the county court judge's ruling that five months was a reasonable period for carrying out the disciplinary procedure in the particular circumstances of the case; but contrast this decision with that of the EAT in *Fosca Services (UK) Ltd* v *Birkett* [1996] IRLR 325 where no damages were awarded.)

However, the court did not deal with situations where, had a disciplinary investigation been carried out, the employee would not have been dismissed.

This point arose in *Alexander & Others* v *Standard Telephones & Cables Ltd (No. 2)* [1991] IRLR 286, where it was argued that the employer's failure to follow a redundancy selection procedure whereby persons other than the plaintiffs would have been selected for redundancy meant that therefore damages should reflect the plaintiffs' loss of earnings for the remainder of their working lives, allowing for contingencies (see 9.4 below). By analogy, it could be argued, in disciplinary cases, that compensation should be awarded beyond the notice period if it can be shown that, had a proper procedure been followed, the employee would not have been dismissed. The argument was, however, rejected in *Alexander* by Hobhouse J who invoked the orthodox view that damages for breach of contract are assessed on the assumption that the contract breaker would have terminated the contract by giving the minimum period of notice necessary to terminate the contract lawfully. A similar argument was also rejected by the Court of Appeal in *Boyo* v *London Borough of Lambeth* [1995] IRLR 50 and *Fosca Services (UK) Ltd* v *Birkett* [1996] IRLR 325, where the EAT overturned a tribunal's decision to award damages by way of unfair dismissal compensation for the same reason.

1.4.2 Payments which count

Once the damages period has been calculated, the second stage in the calculation is to consider which items of loss may be included in a claim for damages. As a general rule, damages are awarded only for items to which the employee is contractually entitled. The result is that discretionary payments or other payments which the employee had a reasonable expectation of receiving are normally excluded (see

Lavarack v *Woods of Colchester Ltd* [1966] 3 All ER 683) but may be recoverable as unlawful deductions from wages under Part II of ERA (formerly the Wages Act) (see *Kent Management Services Ltd* v *Butterfield* [1992] IRLR 394 and *Blackstone Franks Investment Management Ltd* v *Robertson* EAT/434/96). Apart from this restriction, the award covers all foreseeable loss and includes such items as pay, commissions, bonuses, perks and pensions.

1.4.2.1 Pay
Normally, the largest item in a claim for damages is the amount in respect of the pay which the employee would have earned during the damages period. This should be relatively easy to calculate, but special rules apply in a claim for statutory notice pay (see 1.5 below). If, for some reason, the contract does not specify a rate of pay, the court will imply a 'reasonable' rate for the job.

A further difficulty may arise where a pay increase takes effect during the damages period, i.e, where annual pay negotiations are concluded outside the damages period but the agreement is back-dated. This point arose indirectly in *Leyland Vehicles Ltd* v *Reston* [1981] 1 IRLR 19, where the EAT had to decide whether a back-dated pay increase counted for the purpose of calculating a week's pay. The EAT ruled that it did not (see 7.4.5 below) but Slynn J suggested that Mr Reston might have been able to sue for back-pay had his contract so provided. (On the facts there was some doubt as to whether the terms of the collective agreement had been incorporated into Mr Reston's contract.) Thus it would seem that an employee whose contract provides for a pay increase to be back-dated should receive damages which allow for the increase from the time the increase takes effect to the end of the damages period.

Similarly, effect will be given to an inflation-proofing clause in a service agreement (*Re Crowther and Nicholson Ltd* (1981) 125 SJ 529) or a clause which provides for an annual review and an increase in salary 'by such amount as the board shall in its absolute discretion determine' (*Clark* v *BET plc and another* (unreported) 16 October 1996, HC on the basis that the powers conferred on the board by such a clause must be exercised in good faith. This will normally entitle an employee to the same increase in salary as was awarded to employees in a comparable position over the notice period.

A separate claim may be brought in the same action to recover back-pay or holiday pay which was outstanding at the time of dismissal or, where appropriate, the amount may be recovered as a unlawful deduction from wages under the Wages Act 1986 now Part II of the ERA 1996 which an employee would have contributed to his employer's pension scheme should not be included in a claim for lost earnings (*Dews* v *National Coal Board* [1987] IRLR 330).

1.4.2.2 Commission and bonus
If the employee would have been entitled to a bonus or commission during the damages period, that sum should be included in the award of damages (*Addis* v *Gramophone Co Ltd* [1909] AC 488 and *Clark* v *BET plc and another* (unreported), 16 October 1996, HC). However, damages will not be awarded for the loss of a discretionary bonus or commission even if the employee has reasonable grounds for believing that he would have received such a payment during the damages period. This rule is illustrated by the Court of Appeal's decision in *Lavarack* v *Woods of Colchester Ltd* [1966] 3 All ER 683. Part of Mr Lavarack's pay included a

discretionary bonus. Shortly after he was wrongfully dismissed, the employers discontinued the bonus scheme. Nevertheless, Mr Lavarack included it in his damages claim. The Court of Appeal, by a majority, rejected his claim since the bonus was discretionary. Lord Denning dissented, saying that the bonus should have been included if Mr Lavarack would in fact have received it during the period covered by the award. This case is an interesting illustration of the way in which the assessment of damages for wrongful dismissal contrasts with the assessment of compensation for unfair dismissal (see 9.2.1 below).

1.4.2.3 Profit sharing schemes

In principle, there is no objection to an employee claiming damages for the amounts which would have become due to him under a company profit sharing scheme, provided that such payments are guaranteed by the contract.

A profit sharing scheme — in the statutory meaning of the term — is a scheme for the distribution of shares amongst employees by trustees who purchase the shares with contributions from the employing company. Where a scheme has Inland Revenue approval under the Income and Corporation Taxes Act 1988, s. 186 and schs 9 and 10, both the employing company and the employees gain significant tax advantages. The number of shares available for distribution each year will depend upon the size of the grant from the employer, and this will almost invariably be in the complete discretion of the directors. This element of discretion will almost certainly defeat any claim for loss of future allocations.

Termination of employment does not however prejudice an individual's rights in respect of shares already allocated to him under a profit sharing scheme.

1.4.2.4 Profit-related pay schemes

A profit-related pay scheme is an arrangement whereby an amount linked to a company's profitability is distributed among its employees. A profit-related pay scheme which complies with the conditions in the Income and Corporation Taxes Act 1988, sch. 8 and has been registered with the Inland Revenue confers significant tax benefits on participating employees. Such schemes will often be established to run for a number of years. In principle, there is no reason why an employee should not claim damages for payments which would have been due to him under such a scheme provided such payments are a contractual right.

1.4.2.5 Share option schemes

Share options are an increasingly frequent and important part of an employee's remuneration package. More than 5,000 share option schemes have been approved by the Inland Revenue (under the Income and Corporation Taxes Act 1988, s. 185 and sch. 9) and a large number of other companies have introduced non-approved arrangements.

In spite of this proliferation of schemes, the question of whether an employee can claim damages for lost share option rights is far from resolved. What does seem clear is that an employee who, at the date of termination, has no more than a promise from his employers that he will be considered for the grant of options will not be able to recover damages for loss of those options (*O'Laoire* v *Jackel International Limited* [1991] IRLR 170).

In contrast, if an employee actually holds an option which he is prevented from exercising as a result of being dismissed, then on general principles there should be an entitlement to be compensated for the loss of the option. However, the position is complicated by the fact that the rules of share option schemes almost invariably include a clause purporting to exclude any right to be compensated for lost rights under the scheme. The validity of such a provision was judicially considered for the first time by John Mowbray QC in *Micklefield* v *SAC Technology Limited* [1991] 1 All ER 275. Mr Micklefield held a share option which was exercisable from 19 February 1988. On 11 February 1988 he was summarily dismissed and received six months' salary in lieu of his contractual notice. The hearing concerned the preliminary issue of whether, if Mr Micklefield had been wrongfully dismissed, he was entitled to damages for loss of his share option. The judge upheld the validity of the exclusion clause in the share option scheme and therefore ruled in favour of the employers.

Nevertheless, a more recent case suggests that the reasoning in *Micklefield* may be open to challenge. The judge in *Micklefield* decided that the Unfair Contract Terms Act 1977 did not strike out the exclusion clause because the 1977 Act does not apply to any contract relating to 'the creation or transfer of securities' 1977 Act, sch. 1, para. 1(e)). In the Scottish case of *Chapman* v *Aberdeen Construction Group plc* [1992] IRLR 505 the Court of Session has now upheld a claim for a lost share option on the basis that the 1977 Act did nullify the exclusion clause. The decision is not necessarily inconsistent with *Micklefield* because sch. 1, para. 1(e) does not apply in Scotland. However, the Court of Session treated the share option contract as a secondary contract (the service contract being the primary contract) and, even in England, sch. 1, para. 1(e) applies only to primary contracts. This uncertainty is now compounded by the Unfair Terms in Consumer Contracts Regulations 1994 (SI 1994 No. 3159). Arguably, the provision that excludes any contract 'relating to employment' from the ambit of the Regulations covers share option schemes (sch. 1, para. 1(a)). Pending further decisions, the position with regard to lost option rights remains far from clear.

Assuming that an entitlement to damages for a lost option can be established, the question of how to value the option will then need to be considered. The straightforward approach, and the one which was apparently adopted by the plaintiff in *Micklefield* v *SAC Technology Ltd* [1991] 1 All ER 275 (see above), is simply to calculate the profit which the holder of the option would have realised had he exercised the option at the date of termination of employment and then immediately sold the shares for their market value. For example, if an executive has an option to acquire 10,000 shares at 50p per share and the share value on termination is 75p, the loss would be £2,500 (10,000 × 25p). However, this method disregards the 'time value' of an option which can often be quite considerable. To take account of that value a more sophisticated approach would be required. Various techniques have been evolved for use in the traded options market of the Stock Exchange (of which the most popular is the Black-Scholes formula) but these are not necessarily appropriate in an employee-incentive context. The simpler approach of calculating the current worth of the option and ignoring the time value may be more appealing to a court.

1.4.2.6 Perks

'Perks' are an increasingly important part of an employee's remuneration package and damages may be awarded to cover the loss of any 'perk' to which the employee is contractually entitled.

Company car Damages may be awarded for the loss of a company car. In making such an award the court will have to assess the value of the benefit which the use of the car gives to the employee. Thus there would be no claim if the car was used exclusively for business purposes. Very often however the use of a company car is not subject to any restriction and in such circumstances, the judge will have to assess the ratio of private use to business use. For example, in *Shove* v *Downs Surgical plc* [1984] 1 All ER 7, Mr Shove successfully recovered £10,000 for the loss of use of a Daimler over a period of 30 months, the notice period under Mr Shove's contract. The judge based his assessment on the AA's estimate of the weekly cost of running a car of this kind and also took into account the ratio of private use to business use. The judge also found that Mr Shove was entitled to free petrol and included this in his award (see also 10.5).

Other perks Damages may also be awarded for the loss of other perks such as free travel passes, rent-free accommodation (*Ivory* v *Palmer* [1975] ICR 340), free medical insurance (*Shove* v *Downs Surgical plc*) and subsidised loans or mortgages. The loss of such perks must be measured in monetary terms, i.e., the cost to the employee of making equivalent arrangements. It should always be remembered that damages for the loss of these perks is limited to the damages period.

The assessment of compensation for loss of fringe benefits is considered in greater detail in Chapter 10.

1.4.2.7 Pensions

Damages may be awarded for the loss of pension rights, if there is a contractual right to a pension. The award is based on the difference between the value of the pension at the date of leaving (i.e., the date on which the employee was wrongfully dismissed), and the value of the pension had the contract been terminated lawfully (i.e., by giving the appropriate period of notice). Unlike unfair dismissal, no award is made for past loss (see 11.3.2). In calculating the loss, it is necessary to distinguish between a *defined contribution scheme*, typically a money purchase scheme, and a *defined benefits scheme*, typically a final salary scheme.

In relation to a *defined contribution scheme*, the loss is calculated by adding the total lost contributions over the damages period making appropriate allowance for mitigation (see 1.7.2), the possibility of withdrawal (i.e., the fact that the employee might have left the job for some reason during the damages period), and accelerated payment (see 1.7.3).

In relation to a *defined benefits scheme*, it is necessary to calculate the difference between what the pension was worth at the time of dismissal and what it would have been worth at the end of the notice period, thereby reaching a capitalised value based on the difference between the two. This will usually be the difference between a deferred pension at the date of dismissal and what a deferred pension would have been at the end of the notice period/expiry of a fixed term contract. However, the position is complicated where the employee takes an early retirement pension at the date of dismissal. The Court of Appeal in *Johnson v Walter Runciman plc* held that the comparison should be between that early retirement pension and what the deferred pension would have been at the end of the notice period/expiry of a fixed term contract. Thus, the employer takes credit for a 'generous' early retirement pension. The difference in value is normally calculated on an actuarial basis. Sometimes the capital value will include an accelerated discount to allow for the accelerated nature of the payment (see 1.7.3). Otherwise allowance will have to be made for this as well as mitigation and the possibility of withdrawal.

As an alternative, the 'contributions' method (see 11.4.1), may be used to value the benefit where the damages period, i.e., the contractual notice period, is relatively short (see *The Halcyon Skies* [1976] 1 All ER 856 and *Bold v Brough, Nicholson and Hall Ltd* [1963] 3 All ER 849). But the contributions method is a very rough and ready method of valuing pension loss and becomes increasingly unreliable the longer the period of notice. It should also be noted that, in the case of a contributory scheme, the employee may have the right to a return of his contributions and, in any event, has a statutory right to the transfer value of the pension to another scheme.

Where pension loss is included as part of the terms of settlement, it may be possible to structure the terms of settlement in such a manner that the employee's pension will be increased in the same way as if he had remained in employment during the notice period. Moreover, under Inland Revenue regulations, it will often be possible for an employee to secure tax advantages by augmenting his pension up to the maximum permitted by the Inland Revenue.

Table: Calculating pension loss

(a) Ascertain the damages period (subject to the duty to mitigate) by reference to:

— the period of notice or
— the remainder of the term where there is a fixed term contract without express provision for early termination.

(b) Loss = either the lost contributions during the damages period or the value of an annuity which would yield the benefits which could be purchased with those contributions

less

(c) an allowance for the possibility of withdrawal from the scheme.

Note: Where a full transfer value is offered, there may be no loss at all (Occupational Pension Scheme (Transfer Values) Regulations (SI 1985 No. 1931)).

The issue of pension loss in unfair dismissal cases is considered in Chapter 11.

1.4.2.8 Expenses

Expenses cannot be recovered as damages for wrongful dismissal because such payments are mere reimbursement for expenditure incurred by the employee on the

Compensation for Wrongful Dismissal 15

employer's behalf. The payment of 'phoney' expenses may result in the contract being held illegal, thereby preventing the employee from recovering any damages at all (see *Napier* v *National Business Agency Ltd* [1951] 2 All ER 264).

1.4.3 Other items

Damages for wrongful dismissal may include compensation for the loss of other rights either arising out of or connected with the employment so long as the loss is forseeable within the rule in *Hadley* v *Baxendale* (1854) 9 Exch 341. These include the loss of the chance of receiving redundancy pay and the loss of the right to bring an unfair dismissal claim.

1.4.3.1 Loss of chance of redundancy pay
Damages may be awarded for loss of redundancy pay where it is shown that the employee would have been made redundant in the damages period. For example, in *Basnett* v *J & A Jackson Ltd* [1976] IRLR 154, Mr Basnett was made redundant three years before his fixed term contract was due to expire. He argued that if he had been kept on he would have been entitled to an enhanced payment at the end of that period due to his longer service. The judge, having heard evidence as to the fluctuating state of the building industry, concluded that there was 'half a chance' of this happening and awarded half the enhanced payment.

For a claim to succeed it must be shown that the risk of redundancy was a real one, i.e., that the employee was likely to be made redundant at the relevant time. The more remote the possibility, the lower the award.

1.4.3.2 Loss of right to bring an unfair dismissal claim
It has been suggested that where an employer dismisses an employee with no notice or less notice than that required and thereby prevents the employee from being able to bring an unfair dismissal claim successfully, damages may be recovered to compensate him for the loss of his statutory rights (per Browne-Wilkinson J in *Robert Cort & Son Ltd* v *Charman* [1981] IRLR 437). However, there are no reported cases in which the courts have tackled the rather speculative task of quantifying the loss in such circumstances. The court would be required to estimate both the chances of the claim succeeding and the kind of sum the employee would have recovered as compensation.

1.4.3.3 Damages for distress
As a general rule, no damages are awarded for the distress and vexation associated with a wrongful dismissal (*Addis* v *Gramophone Co Ltd* [1909] AC 488 confirmed in *Bliss* v *South East Thames Regional Health Authority* [1985] IRLR 308 and *O'Laoire* v *Jackel International Ltd* [1991] IRLR 70). Rather surprisingly, the same rule applies in unfair dismissals (see 12.2 below).

In certain exceptional circumstances it appears that damages for distress may be awarded where this is contemplated by the terms of the contract. This is suggested by the High Court's decision in *Cox* v *Philips Industries Ltd* [1976] 3 All ER 161.

Mr Cox commenced employment with Intertherm Ltd, a company owned partly by the defendants, in 1946. In July 1963, faced with the prospect of losing him to a rival company, Intertherm agreed to give him a better position within the company. In December 1964 he was dismissed and became ill as a result. Allowing the claim, the judge awarded him £500 for vexation and distress on the ground that it was in the contemplation of all the parties that a breach of the agreement made in July 1963 might cause Mr Cox the anxiety, frustration and sickness which he did in fact suffer.

However, in the light of the critical remarks made by the Court of Appeal in *Bliss v South East Thames Regional Health Authority* [1985] IRLR 308, a real question mark hangs over the correctness of the decision in *Cox*.

1.4.3.4 Damage to career prospects

As a general rule, damages will not be awarded to compensate an employee for damage to his or her career prospects or reputation caused by the dismissal, or for any 'stigma' caused by the employer's actions (*Malik and another v Bank of Credit and Commerce International* [1995] IRLR 375). However, this principle does not apply where the pecuniary loss suffered by the employee is a foreseeable consequence of the breach of contract in accordance with normal contractual principles. Such cases include those where the nature of the contract is to provide for status (for example, apprenticeships), or for the promotion or preservation of a reputation (for example, advertising) or for the opportunity to appear in a prestigious place or part. The successful cases are almost all concerned with actors or writers who have argued that their career prospects were damaged as a result of the dismissal. For example, in *Marbe v George Edwardes (Daly's Theatre) Ltd* [1928] 1 KB 269, an American actress, wishing to establish her reputation in London, sued her employers when, in breach of contract, they refused to give her a part in a play. The Court of Appeal awarded her damages for the duration of the contract plus an amount representing the loss to her reputation which had been caused by the defendant's action. (See also *Joseph v National Magazine Co Ltd* [1958] 3 All ER 52.) The same principle may apply to other employments where such an opportunity was an essential part of the consideration, or in the rather exceptional cases where the employer is under an obligation to provide the employee with work as well as wages.

As stated above, damage to career prospects is foreseeable in contracts of apprenticeship. For example, in *Dunk v George Waller & Son Ltd* [1970] 2 QB 163 it was held that an apprentice who was wrongfully dismissed was entitled to recover damages for the unexpired period of the apprenticeship and for a period of nearly two years thereafter as compensation for the damage to his future prospects caused by the loss of tuition and training. It is unclear whether the same principles would apply to young persons on a youth training scheme.

1.5 CALCULATING THE STATUTORY NOTICE ENTITLEMENT

1.5.1 Statutory notice periods

There are special statutory rules which apply to the calculation of the periods of notice guaranteed by s. 86 of the Employment Rights Act 1996.

The following table sets out the minimum periods of notice an employee, other than an excepted employee (see 1.1.2.1 above), is entitled to receive for each year of employment.

Period of continuous employment (years)	Minimum period (weeks)
Less than 2 (but one month or more)	1
At least 2 but less than 3	2
At least 3 but less than 4	3
At least 4 but less than 5	4
At least 5 but less than 6	5
At least 6 but less than 7	6
At least 7 but less than 8	7
At least 8 but less than 9	8
At least 9 but less than 10	9
At least 10 but less than 11	10
At least 11 but less than 12	11
12 or more	12

1.5.2 The statutory formula

Statutory minimum notice is calculated in accordance with the rules set out in the Employment Rights Act 1996, ss. 87–91, and depends on whether the employee has normal working hours or no normal working hours.

Where the employee has normal working hours, an employer has to pay him a week's pay, or an appropriate proportion thereof, for each week (or part week) of the statutory notice period during which the employee is (ERA 1996, s. 88(1)):

(a) ready and willing to work, but is not given work by his employer,
(b) incapable of work through sickness or injury, or
(c) absent from work wholly or partly because of pregnancy or childbirth, or
(d) absent from work in accordance with the terms of his employment relating to holidays.

Where there are normal working hours, a week's pay shall be 'not less than the amount of remuneration for that part of normal working hours calculated at the average hourly rate of remuneration produced by dividing a week's pay by the number of normal working hours' (s. 88(1), (2) and (3)). This formula takes account of the different patterns of employments with normal working hours.

Where the employee has no normal working hours he is entitled to 'a sum not less than a week's pay' for each week of the statutory notice period during which he is ready and willing to do work of a reasonable nature to earn a week's pay. This latter condition does not apply where the employee is incapable of work due to sickness, is absent because of pregnancy or childbirth, or is absent from work in accordance with the terms of his employment relating to holidays (s. 89(1) and (2)). Holiday pay and sick pay are set off against the employer's liability (see below).

See Chapter 7 for the meaning of 'normal working hours', 'a week's pay' and 'remuneration'.

Any sick pay, statutory sick pay, statutory maternity pay, maternity pay or holiday pay paid to the employee may go towards meeting the employer's statutory liability as may any payment for sickness or injury benefit (ss. 88(1), (2), 89 and 90).

Payments which the employer has already made in respect of the statutory liability may also be set-off. So, for example, if the employer wrongly terminates the contract halfway through the notice period, the employee is entitled to recover only those damages which relate to the outstanding period (s. 91(3))

The employer is not under an obligation to make payments in respect of periods when the employee has requested time off work for public duties, trade union duties or activities, or job seeking (s. 91(1)). Neither is the employee entitled to statutory notice pay if he takes part in a strike during the notice period (s. 91(2)).

The right to notice pay ceases if the employee breaches the contract and the employer rightfully treats the breach as terminating the contract. So, for example, the employer's obligation ceases if an employee commits an act of gross misconduct during the notice period (s. 91(3)).

Note: Damages may also be reduced if the employee has failed to mitigate his loss (*Westwood* v *Secretary of State for Employment* [1984] 1 All ER 874). See 1.7.2 below.

1.5.3 Calculating statutory notice pay

Damages period = statutory notice period (subject to duty to mitigate).

£

(a) Number of weeks of statutory notice period multiplied by amount of one week's pay =
  (b) *less*
     — sick pay
     — holiday pay
     — other payments made by the employer
     — social security benefits
  (c) Final award

1.5.4 Relationship with contractual notice

Sections 87–91 do not apply if the notice 'to be given' by the employer is 'at least one week more' than the notice required by s. 86(1) of the Employment Rights Act 1996, s. 87(4). Thus, if the contractual notice, express or implied, exceeds the employee's statutory entitlement, the statutory provisions do not apply. For example, if a clerk has been employed for six months and the contract states that the contract may be terminated by one month's notice, the employee's entitlement is based on the contractual one-month period, not the statutory period of one week.

1.6 PAY IN LIEU OF NOTICE

It is common practice for employers to make a 'payment in lieu of notice' but, as Lord Browne-Wilkinson has recently pointed out in *Delaney* v *Staples* [1992] IRLR 191, the expression 'payment in lieu' may be used 'to describe many types of payment the legal analysis of which differs'. His Lordship identified four principal categories:

(a) Where the employer gives proper notice of termination to the employee but does not require the employee to attend his/her place of working during the notice period. This is commonly referred to as 'garden leave'. The wages due to the employee during such a period of garden leave may be either paid as a 'lump sum', i.e., as a payment in lieu, or payments may continue to be made on a weekly or monthly basis.

(b) The contract of employment may itself provide for the employment to be terminated on notice or on payment in lieu of notice. Such a provision is common in service agreements of more senior executives as it enables the employer both to terminate lawfully by making such a payment and to continue to enforce any contractual provisions which take effect after the termination, such as restrictive covenants.

(c) The contract of employment may itself provide that an agreed sum is payable on termination, i.e., an agreed damages clause. Again there will be no breach of contract provided the employer pays the agreed sum.

(d) The employer may terminate the contract without notice, i.e., dismiss the employee summarily and at the same time tender a payment in lieu of proper notice. In *Delaney*, the House of Lords confirmed that such a payment is an advance payment of damages for wrongful dismissal and cannot be regarded as 'wages'.

(See also *Leech* v *Preston Borough Council* [1985] IRLR 337, where the EAT classified Lord Browne-Wilkinson's fourth category as the 'technical' meaning of a payment in lieu and the first as its 'colloquial' meaning, and *Abrahams* v *Performing Rights Society* [1995] IRLR 486, where the Court of Appeal appears to have treated a clause which gave the employer a right to terminate a contract by giving two years' notice or an equivalent payment in lieu as falling within Lord Browne-Wilkinson's second category.)

Below the phrase payment in lieu is used to cover both its technical and more colloquial usage but not cases where the payment is provided for by the contract itself.

1.6.1 What the payment should cover

Although it is customary for a payment in lieu to cover wages or salary only, the payment should in fact cover all those items which could have been included in a claim for damages. Thus the loss of fringe benefits, use of a company car, mortgage subsidy etc. should all be taken into account and an approximate value calculated and added to the payment. Any contractual bonuses, overtime or shift premia which would have been earned during the notice period should also be included. However, where an employee accepts a payment consisting of wages alone in *full and final settlement* of his contractual claims, the acceptance is likely to be seen as a binding agreement not to sue in respect of the outstanding common law claims, and therefore precludes a claim for any further sums due. Such acceptance may be express or implied. (*Greene* v *Church Commissioners for England* [1974] ChD 467; *Callisher* v *Bischoffshein* [1870] 5 QB 449.) On the other hand, *mere* acceptance of a termination payment of itself will not necessarily prevent an employee from claiming damages for other losses consequent upon dismissal.

For example, in *Robert Cort & Son* v *Charman* [1981] IRLR 437, the EAT suggested that acceptance of payment in lieu would not prevent an employee from claiming damages for the loss of his statutory right to bring an unfair dismissal claim. Nor does the acceptance of a redundancy payment under a Government Compensation Scheme necessarily preclude a dockworker from suing for his statutory notice pay (*Trotter* v *Forth Ports Authority* [1991] IRLR 419). In *Trotter*, the Court of Session rejected the employer's argument that acceptance of a redundancy payment itself meant that the employee had waived his rights to his statutory notice pay.

1.6.2 Taxation of pay in lieu

If the expression 'payment in lieu' is used in the colloquial sense (see 1.6 above), it has the status of an ordinary payment and therefore tax under Schedule E (Income and Corporation Taxes Act 1988, s. 131) and national insurance should be deducted. However, if it is used in the technical sense, as compensation for breach of contract, the position is less straightforward.

Where the contract itself gives an employee a right to receive a payment in lieu or contains an agreed damages claim, i.e., a set payment which is due on breach, then the resultant payment is taxable because it constitutes an emolument of the employment. For example in *Williams* v *Simmonds* [1981] STC 715, Mr Simmonds received an agreed sum determined in accordance with his service agreement as compensation for 'loss of office'. It was held that the sum was subject to income tax in the ordinary way as an emolument of Mr Simmonds' employment (Income and Corporation Taxes Act 1988, s. 131). It is probable that national insurance should also be deducted from such payments in the normal way.

Service contracts apart, it is relatively uncommon for a contract to confer such rights expressly. The more common situation is for the payment to be made outside the contract. The status of such payments for tax purposes has led to a difference of opinion among tax inspectors. Some local inspectors consider that a payment received in such circumstances is taxable under ordinary Schedule E rules because the employee may be said to have a 'reasonable expectation' of receiving such a payment on dismissal. However, the better view is that since non-contractual pay in lieu is compensation for the employer's breach of contract in not giving notice, it is not taxable as an 'emolument', although it will usually be caught by the special provisions which apply to 'golden handshakes' and other lump sum termination payments. This view is supported by the Inland Revenue's own booklet, *'The employer's guide to PAYE'*, although it should be remembered that statements in IR Handbooks are not legally binding. It is also consistent with the judiciary's view of the legal nature of the payment (see *Dixon* v *Stenor Ltd* [1973] ICR 157, *Leech* v *Preston Borough Council* [1985] IRLR 337 and *Delaney* v *Staples* [1992] IRLR 191).

However it should be noted that any payment made in connection with the termination of employment (or loss of office) which is not a taxable emolument under the Income and Corporation Taxes Act 1988, s. 131 is taxable under s. 148 of the Act, unless it falls within the exemption covering so called 'golden handshakes' (see Income and Corporation Taxes Act 1988, s. 188(4) and Finance Act 1988 s. 74(1)). Thus a payment in lieu which is in excess of the current £30,000 limit is liable to higher rate income tax, currently 40%.

1.6.3 Payment gross or net

It is common practice for employers to make a payment in lieu on the basis of an employee's gross wage or salary. However, the employer's strict legal obligation is simply to pay the sum which would have been awarded as damages by a court, i.e., the net amount which the employee would have received after deduction of tax and national insurance (*Jackson* v *Foster Wheeler (London) Ltd* [1989] IRLR 283). In exceptional cases however it may be established that the employer is under an obligation to pay gross rather than net. For example, in *Gothard* v *Mirror Group Newspapers* [1988] IRLR 396, it was shown that a lump sum payment in lieu of notice was made as part of an early retirement scheme which was expressed to be 'tax free', and was accepted by Mr Gothard on that basis. The court held that there was a clear intention, and consequently a contractual obligation, to make the payment gross rather than net.

In any event, there is nothing to prevent an employer from paying the gross amount, and there may be sound reasons for doing so, e.g., to maintain good industrial relations and/or as a financial inducement not to bring a claim for wrongful dismissal. Indeed it could be argued that the employer must make the payment on this basis if it has become customary to do so.

1.7 REDUCTION OF DAMAGES

1.7.1 General principles

The object of contractual damages is to compensate employees for the loss caused by the employer's breach of contract, but the award should not result in the employee making a profit (*British Guiana Credit Corporation* v *Da Silva* [1965] 1 WLR 248). Thus the third stage in the calculation of damages for wrongful dismissal is to take account of the different factors which might lead to an award being limited to a certain period of time. These include the duty to mitigate, contingencies such as the possibility that the employee would have left the job anyway, and the fact that payments due under the contract are being received earlier than would otherwise have been the case. Allowance must also be made for tax liabilities.

Some of these factors, such as the duty to mitigate, apply even where the contract is terminable by a relatively short period of notice, but in general, the factors considered in this section are more important where the 'damages period' is substantial.

1.7.2 Mitigation

The common law requires a dismissed employee to take all reasonable steps to reduce the loss caused by the wrongful dismissal.

There are two elements to the duty to mitigate:

(a) Employees are not entitled to sit back and wait until the time when the contract could have been lawfully terminated and then sue for the loss which accrues during that period. They must take positive steps to find alternative employment. If they fail to do this, the award will be limited to the time when the court believes that they should have found a new job.

(b) Employees must give credit for any benefits which accrue as a result of dismissal. For example, credit must be given for any income received from a new job during the notice period or for any social security benefits received during that time. It is possible that credit should also be given for payments received under an early retirement scheme (*Smoker* v *London Fire and Civil Defence Authority* [1991] IRLR 271).

Lawyers often refer to the first element as the duty to mitigate in law and the second element as the duty to mitigate in fact, but it should be stressed that both are aspects of what is essentially the same general duty. The distinction is used below purely as a matter of convenience.

Note: The duty to mitigate also applies to the assessment of unfair dismissal compensation (see Chapter 15 where the case law is considered in greater detail).

1.7.2.1 Mitigation in law

The duty to mitigate means that the employee must take reasonable steps to minimise the loss caused by the dismissal by seeking other employment. If he fails to do this, he will be penalised. What is reasonable is essentially a question of fact for the court to determine. On the one hand, the employee is not bound to accept the first offer that comes along, particularly if it involves a change of work, reduction in status or a reduction in pay or other terms and conditions. On the other hand, the employee may in some circumstances be required to accept an offer of re-employment from the old employer or even less favourable employment elsewhere if there is no prospect of obtaining a similar position. The following case decisions illustrate the above principles.

(a) The plaintiff was dismissed as a result of a change in the partnership. The new partners offered him his old job back but he declined their offer. *Held:* he was unreasonable in turning down their offer and was therefore awarded only nominal damages (*Brace* v *Calder* [1895] 2 QB 253).

(b) The plaintiff was dismissed from his position as managing director of the defendant company. The company offered to re-employ him as assistant managing director in the same company at the same salary but he refused because acceptance would have meant 'a significant step down'. The judge was satisfied that the plaintiff had acted reasonably in turning down the offer and found that he had also taken other reasonable steps to look for work. *Held:* full damages would be awarded up to the trial, but would be limited thereafter because the plaintiff had agreed to look for a new job at a lower salary which he was likely to find soon after the trial (*Yetton* v *Eastwoods Froy Ltd* [1966] 3 All ER 353).

(c) The plaintiff was dismissed from his job as managing director of the defendant company. The parent company offered to re-employ him at the same salary. He turned down its offer because he would have had to work with people with whom he had had major disagreements and it was a condition of the offer that he drop his wrongful dismissal claim. *Held:* it was reasonable for him to reject the company's offer on these grounds (*Shindler* v *Northern Raincoat Co Ltd* [1960] 2 WLR 1038).

On the positive side, employees may be held to have satisfied their duty to mitigate their loss by setting up a business or becoming self-employed. For example, in *Shove v Downs Surgical plc* [1984] 1 All ER 7, the judge held that Mr Shove had taken reasonable steps to mitigate his loss by setting himself up as a consultant even though the consultancy was not expected to make a profit until its third year.

The duty to mitigate and statutory notice   In *Westwood v Secretary of State for Employment* [1984] 1 All ER 874, the House of Lords ruled that the duty to mitigate applies to statutory notice. Their Lordships said that the reference to the employer's 'liability for breach of contract' in s. 51 of the Employment Protection (Consolidation) Act (now s. 91(5) of the Employment Rights Act 1996) showed that the ordinary common law rules for assessing damages for breach of contract also applied to an employer's liability under the statutory provisions.

Assessing the deduction   The effect of a failure to mitigate is that the award of damages will be reduced. The reduction may be made in one of the following ways:

(a) it may be taken into account in determining the appropriate multiplier (see 1.7.3 below);

(b) damages may be awarded only in respect of the period up to the time when the court considers that the employee should have found a new job on equivalent terms.

It is also open to the court to reduce damages on the grounds that the employee should have found a new job even if it meant a drop in salary. In these circumstances the recoverable loss will be the difference between the old salary and the new one.

The duty to mitigate and payments in lieu of notice   The duty to mitigate does not apply where an employee sues for the recovery of a payment in lieu of notice. This was the rather surprising conclusion of the Court of Appeal in *Abrahams v Performing Rights Society* [1995] IRLR 487, where the court classified such a payment as a 'sum due under a contract' (i.e., a contractual debt) rather than damages for wrongful dismissal. Furthermore, Hutchinson LJ stated that the duty to mitigate did not apply even if (as the employers had contended) the sum should be regarded as liquidated damages.

Onus of proof   The burden of showing that the employee has failed to mitigate his loss is on the employer (*Fyfe v Scientific Furnishings Ltd* [1989] IRLR 331). As a result, the employer is entitled to particulars of any attempts, (successful or otherwise) that the employee has made to find other employment since dismissal.

1.7.2.2 Mitigation in fact

The second element to the duty to mitigate is that the employee must give credit for any benefits received as a result of the dismissal.

Earnings from a new job   The main effect of this rule is that the employee must give credit for any earnings received during the damages period. This may include giving credit for other benefits received from the new employment. For example, in *Lavarack* v *Woods of Colchester Ltd* [1967] 1 QB 278, the court held that it was entitled to take into account the income Mr Lavarack had received as a result of acquiring shares in his new employer's company. It is also open to the court to take into account the value of other benefits received by the employee in making its overall assessment. Credit must also be given for earnings received in the period of statutory notice (*The Secretary of State for Employment* v *Wilson* [1977] IRLR 483).

However, in working out what proportion of the earnings should be taken into account, allowance will be made for any reasonable expenses incurred by the employee in looking for work or setting up in business on his own account. This may even include expenditure incurred outside the damages period (see *Westwood* v *Secretary of State for Employment* [1984] 1 All ER 874).

Example: Mitigation of loss — earnings from new job.

Ms Firth was engaged to work as a designer in London for a fixed term of one year. She is dismissed after 6 months. She finds a new job in Cheltenham three months after her dismissal. She used to take home £400 net a week and now takes home £300 net a week. She claims £200 as expenses in looking for a new job. Her damages claim is calculated as follows:

		£
Loss of earnings	26 weeks @ £400 a week	10,400
Less earnings from new job	13 weeks @ £300 a week	3,900
		6,500
Add expenses		200
Total claim (subject to further reduction in respect of such items as state benefits (see below))		£ 6,700

Social security benefits   Credit must be given for jobseeker's allowance and other social security benefits received during the damages period.

It has been held therefore that jobseeker's allowance must be deducted from the award (*Parsons* v *B N M Laboratories Ltd* [1963] 2 All ER 658). The same rule applies to supplementary benefit (now income support) (*Lincoln* v *Hayman* [1982] 1 WLR 488). However, some state benefits are excluded. For example, mobility and attendance allowances have been held to be non-deductible (*Bowker* v *Rose* (1978) 122 SJ 147). In relation to family income supplement, it has been held that FIS which has been received is deductible, but FIS which is to be received in respect of loss of future earnings is ignored because of the difficulty in valuing the future benefits (*Gaskill* v *Preston* [1981] 3 All ER 427). Other statutory payments such as redundancy pay have been held to be too remote to be deductible (see 1.7.2.3 below).

State benefits and statutory notice pay   Credit must be given for state benefits received during the statutory notice period (*Westwood* v *Secretary of State for Employment* [1984] 1 All ER 874).

This ruling led to a particular problem in relation to the long-term unemployed. It was argued that in deducting the full benefit received during the statutory notice period no account was taken of the fact that employees would exhaust their entitlement to state benefits sooner than they would have done had employers fulfilled their statutory or contractual obligations. This problem was considered by the House of Lords in *Westwood*, where the employee was dismissed without the statutory notice or pay in lieu, owing to the insolvency of his employers. Their Lordships held that although the duty to mitigate applied to the provisions guaranteeing minimum periods of notice, and hence the benefits fell to be deducted from the entitlement, the employee need give credit only for the net gain received during the notice period. In the particular circumstances, the net gain was not the sum of the actual benefits received in the notice period of 12 weeks, but the difference between the sum and the lesser amount of supplementary benefits received as a result of his entitlement to unemployment benefit being prematurely curtailed.

Following the House of Lords' decision in *Westwood*, the Department of Health and Social Security issued new regulations which deal specifically with employees who claim benefit at a time when they have a valid legal claim against their employers for lost notice pay. The Social Security (General Benefit) Amendment Regulations 1984 (SI 1984 No. 1259) provide that days covered by payments under the insolvency provisions of the Employment Rights Act 1996 do not count in determining eligibility for jobseeker's allowance.

Payments in lieu of notice Despite the decision in *Abrahams v Performing Rights Society* [1995] IRLR 487, a payment in lieu of notice is deductible if it is made by an employer in discharge of the employer's liability to an employee under the employment contract.

Ex gratia payments If these are intended to discharge the employer's liability for wrongful dismissal they should be deducted from the assessment of damages.

Unfair dismissal compensation The compensatory element in an award for unfair dismissal is deducted in computing a wrongful dismissal award if it covers the same loss, namely notice pay and other benefits (*O'Laoire v Jackel International Ltd* [1991] IRLR 70). On the other hand, it will not be deducted if it can be shown that the compensatory award relates to loss suffered outside the notice period since there would be no 'double' recovery in such circumstances (*O'Laoire*). It may be open to an applicant who is bringing both unfair and wrongful dismissal proceedings to ask the industrial tribunal not to make an award in respect of notice pay so as to retain the right to claim these sums in wrongful dismissal proceedings and preserve the right to recover maximum compensation within the statutory limits. It is doubtful whether the basic award is deductible because it represents compensation for loss of job security and not damages for dismissal (see *Wilson v National Coal Board* (1980) 130 NLJ 1146).

1.7.2.3 Remoteness

Credit need not be given for benefits which are too remote or which accrue to the employee independently of the employer's breach. These are known as 'collateral benefits'. Often the dividing line between these non-deductible benefits and those discussed above is a narrow one.

Collateral employment benefits   In *Lavarack* v *Woods of Colchester Ltd* [1967] 1 QB 278, the Court of Appeal rejected the company's argument that, as Mr Lavarack had been released from a restriction that prohibited him from making investments in other companies quoted on the stock exchange whilst in its employment, he should give credit for the profits he had made on all his investments in other companies. The court said that these benefits did not arise as a 'direct result of the dismissal' but were 'collateral' to it and so non deductible.

Disability insurance and other private pensions   Payments received from a private pension scheme or disability insurance (*Lewicki* v *Brown & Root Wimpey Highland Fabricators Ltd* [1996] IRLR 565) are considered to be collateral benefits and are not therefore deductible from damages for wrongful dismissal. In *Parry* v *Cleaver* [1970] AC 1, the House of Lords held that a policeman's compensation for personal injuries should not be reduced by the amount he received as a disablement pension from the police pension fund. Their Lordships did not think that it made any difference whether the pension was payable as of right or discretionary. The same rule applies to damages for wrongful dismissal, even where the pension is a contractual benefit (*Hopkins* v *Norcros plc* [1992] IRLR 304, upheld by the Court of Appeal [1994] IRLR 18).

Redundancy payments   It has been held by the House of Lords that it is not normally reasonable to deduct a redundancy payment in the assessment of damages for wrongful dismissal since it represents compensation for the loss of an established job and not compensation for loss of earnings (*Wilson* v *National Coal Board* (1980) 130 NLJ 1146). It is uncertain whether the same is true where the redundancy package includes an enhanced notice entitlement, although it is likely that credit should be given for the additional payment in such circumstances (see *Aspden* v *Webbs Poultry and Meat Group (Holdings) Ltd* [1996] IRLR 521). Similarly, in *Baldwin* v *British Coal Corporation Ltd* [1995] IRLR 95, the High Court held that credit should be given for a 'special' incentive redundancy payment where the employee would not have received that payment but for the failure to receive proper notice. In such circumstances the payment received was a direct consequence of the employer's breach and therefore was not too remote.

1.7.3   Contingencies and accelerated receipt of payments

Some reduction is made for contingencies such as the possibility that the employee might have died or resigned before the date on which the contract could have been lawfully terminated. This is likely to arise only where the period of notice, or the unexpired period of the contract, is substantial. A further reduction is made to take into account the accelerated receipt of the payment. This acknowledges the fact that the employee receives the payments due under the contract sooner than would otherwise have been the case.

Two methods are commonly used to make the reduction:

(a) *Annuity method.* This involves finding out the current value of an annuity that would yield the same income annually as that which the employee would have received during the damages period. The effect of the duty to mitigate may be taken into account by reducing the period covered by the annuity.

(b) *Multiplier.* This method takes account of all the relevant contingencies by discounting them from the maximum period of the employee's contractual entitlement. For example, if the damages period was five years, the multiplier may be limited to three years on account of the contingencies outlined above and the accelerated receipt of the payments. Accordingly, the award would be three times the employee's annual salary.

The need to use one of the above methods is only likely to arise if the damages period is considerable. In other cases, allowance for the accelerated receipt of the payment is based on a simple percentage reduction, e.g., in *Shove* v *Downs Surgical plc* [1984] 1 All ER 7 the award was reduced by 7% for this reason.

1.7.4 Contributory fault

In assessing the employer's liability, no reduction will be made for contributory fault since liability for breach of contract is strict. Thus the courts are not interested in whether the employee was partly to blame for the dismissal. See Chapter 16 for the position in unfair dismissal cases.

1.7.5 Deducting tax from damages

Tax liability is taken into account both in the assessment of damages and in the final award of damages. See 2.1 below.

2 Tax and Miscellaneous Matters

2.1 TAX

2.1.1 Deducting tax from damages

The principle that employees should be placed in no better position than they would have been in if the contract had been performed means that damages for wrongful dismissal are awarded net of tax and national insurance contributions. This is known as 'the Gourley principle' (see *British Transport Commission* v *Gourley* [1955] 3 All ER 796, a personal injuries case, which was applied to wrongful dismissal by the Court of Appeal in *Parsons* v *B N M Laboratories Ltd* [1963] 2 All ER 658).

2.1.2 Deducting tax from the final award

At the time of the decision in *Gourley*, post-cessation receipts such as damages for wrongful dismissal, were not taxable in the hands of the employee. The law was subsequently changed and the present position is that payments on the termination of an office or employment (including damages for wrongful dismissal) are taxed on a sliding scale (Income and Corporation Taxes Act 1988, s. 188; Finance Act 1988, s. 74(1)). This general statutory liability is however subject to a number of exemptions and reliefs. Furthermore special provisions apply to employees who work overseas (ICTA 1988, ss. 192 and 193). The position is as follows:

(a) The first £30,000 is tax free.
(b) The balance is taxed at the higher rate of tax, currently 40%.

These provisions also apply to payment in lieu of notice (see 1.6.3 above) if they are not regarded as ordinary emoluments. Where such payments are taxable, i.e., exceed £30,000, and are made prior to termination taking effect, tax should be deducted in the ordinary way under normal PAYE arrangements (Income Tax (Employment) Regulations 1973 (SI 1973 No. 334), reg. 13). On the other hand, where the payment is made after termination, the employer should deduct basic rate tax (currently 25%) and leave the employee to account to the tax authorities for the balance. This means that the employee is entitled to the benefit of the use of the money in the meantime (Income Tax (Employment) Regulations 1973, reg. 16(1)). Special rules apply to the

Tax and Miscellaneous Matters

taxation of payments made on death or retirement (ICTA 1988, ss. 148, 188 and 612(1)).

2.1.3 The 'Gourley' principle and payments above £30,000

A problem arises where the lump sum payment or an award of damages exceeds the tax free exemption. The excess is taxable even though, in line with the *Gourley* principle, tax liability has already been included in the assessment of damages. In theory, this means that an employee could be placed in the unfortunate position of being taxed twice. However the court said, *per curiam*, in *Parsons* v *B N M Laboratories Ltd* [1963] 2 All ER 658 that where this situation arises the two amounts of tax should be left by way of set-off against each other.

The simplest way of achieving this effect is as follows:

(1) deduct the full tax which would have been payable on the earnings an employee would have received during the damages period, and

(2) add back a sum which is equivalent to the tax payable under s. 188 of the Income and Corporation Taxes Act 1988 so that this additional sum cancels out the amount of that tax.

This involves a kind of grossing-up of the tax liabilities. The employee is therefore left with the net amount after the tax has been deducted from the damages. This approach was applied by the courts in *Shove* v *Downs Surgical plc* [1984] 1 All ER 7 and *Stewart* v *Glentaggart Ltd* [1963] SLT 119.

However, in assessing the employer's tax liability under (1) above, it is important to take into account the following factors:

(a) future changes in rates of tax — movements in the rates of tax in the period covered by the award are unknown at the time the damages are assessed and it may therefore be difficult to work out the employee's net liability over the period;

(b) personal allowances — the employee's own personal allowances may change in future years and this may affect his tax liability over the period;

(c) other income — the employee may have other income which affects tax liability; and

(d) employment overseas — there are special rules which govern the taxation of employees who spend a considerable amount of time overseas.

The task of adding back the tax which is going to be paid on the award (see (2) above) is not quite as difficult because the tax falls due in the tax year when the dismissal took place and therefore the employee's other income and the other variable factors will generally be known at the time of the assessment.

2.2 MISCELLANEOUS MATTERS

2.2.1 Payments to directors

Payments made to a director by way of compensation for loss of office are unlawful unless they are first disclosed to and approved by the company (Companies Act 1985,

s. 316). However, this provision does not apply to 'any bona fide payment by way of damages for breach of contract or by way of pension in respect of past services' (Companies Act 1985, s. 316(3)).

2.2.2 Interest

The High Court and county court may award interest on damages for wrongful dismissal from the date when the cause of action arose to the date of judgment, or in the case of a payment made before that date, the date of the payment. (Supreme Court Act 1981, s. 35A; County Courts Act 1984, s. 69; Administration of Justice Act 1982, s. 15(1).) The statutory rate of interest is currently 15% but this is subject to variation by statutory instrument. All claims for interest must be pleaded (RSC Order 18, Rule 8; County Court Rules 1981, Order 6, Rule 1A). A higher rate of interest may be awarded if the contract so provides.

The Court of Appeal (civil division) also has the power to award interest on damages for wrongful dismissal (Law Reform (Miscellaneous Provisions) Act 1934, s. 3).

2.2.3 Court proceedings

An action for wrongful dismissal may be brought in the High Court or county court. The upper limit on the county courts' jurisdiction has now been abolished. All claims below £25,000 must now be commenced in the county court (High Court and County Courts Jurisdiction Order 1991 (SI 1991 No. 724)). Such claims may be transferred to the High Court if one or more of the grounds for transfer specified in reg. 7(5)(a)–(d) of the High Court and County Courts Jurisdiction Order 1991 apply, e.g., if it can be shown that complex points of law or fact are involved.

2.2.4 Time limits

The time limit for bringing a claim for wrongful dismissal is six years from the time the cause of action accrues (normally the date of the employer's breach of contract) though special provision is made for certain persons under disability (Limitation Act 1980, ss. 2 and 28).

2.2.5 Tribunal proceedings

Pursuant to the Industrial Tribunals Extension of Jurisdiction (England and Wales) Order 1994 (SI 1994 No. 1623) and the Industrial Tribunals Extension of Jurisdiction (Scotland) Order 1994 (SI 1994 No. 1624), industrial tribunals have the power to hear claims for damages for breach of contract (or any other claims connected with employment), or for a sum due under such a contract or recovery of a sum in pursuance of any enactment relating to the terms or performance of such a contract. The value of the total claim cannot exceed £25,000. The tribunal's jurisdiction is concurrent with that of the county court and High Court.

Such a claim must be brought within the period of three months beginning with the effective date of termination of the contract giving rise to the claim, or, where the termination is brought about by operation of law, within three months of the last day on which the employee worked in the employment. The time limits may be extended if the tribunal accepts that it was not reasonably practicable to bring the claim within the three-month time limit if proceedings were commenced within a reasonable time period thereafter.

2.3 CALCULATING DAMAGES FOR WRONGFUL DISMISSAL

The table below sets out the way in which an award for wrongful dismissal is assessed.

(1) Damages for loss of earnings

    (a) Work out the damages period by reference to

        — contractual period of notice, or
        — statutory period of notice, or
        — unexpired period of fixed term.

            £

    (b) *Calculate* net pay in accordance with (a) above.
        Add overtime, bonuses, commission.

(2) *Add* damages for loss of benefits by reference to   £
    same damages period as before in respect of loss of

        — company car
        — loans
        — subsidised mortgage
        — pension
        — profit sharing scheme
        — medical insurance
        — other contractual benefits.

Total additions
    (3) *Deduct*

        — earnings from new job
        — social security payments received
            in the damages period
        — payment in lieu
        — ex gratia payments
        — award of unfair dismissal compensation
            (but not basic award or redundancy
            payments).

Total deductions
Add
Total additions
Balance

Add   £
  (4)   Further additions for loss of statutory rights and
        distress

        — loss of the chance of redundancy payment
        — loss of reputation
        — loss of chance to bring an unfair dismissal
          claim.

Total of (4) plus balance
Add/deduct tax adjustment
Add interest

Final award

3 Other Remedies for Wrongful Dismissal

In the vast majority of cases, financial compensation is the only remedy available to an employee who claims that his dismissal is wrongful. However, in exceptional circumstances, it may be open to the employee to seek reinstatement under the ordinary law or to challenge the legality of the dismissal in public law (see 3.3.1 below).

3.1 EQUITABLE REMEDIES (GENERAL PRINCIPLES)

The only common law remedy for breach of contract is damages, but during their existence the courts of equity developed other 'equitable' remedies. Thus in certain types of cases equity would grant an order for specific performance or an injunction to compel the party in breach to perform its obligations under the contract. When the courts of common law and equity became fused these 'equitable remedies' continued to be available.

Unlike the common law remedy of damages, equitable remedies are discretionary and are subject to a number of technical restrictions, such as the rule on mutuality, which lie outside the scope of this book. For present purposes, the most important of these principles is that equitable remedies are granted only where an award of damages would be an inadequate remedy.

3.1.1 Injunctions

An injunction is an order of the court directing a party to do or refrain from doing a particular act. Such injunctions may be interlocutory or perpetual.

An interlocutory or 'interim' injunction is an injunction which is granted before the trial of an action with the object of maintaining the status quo until the full trial. Success at the interim stage does not necessarily mean that the plaintiff will succeed in getting a perpetual injunction at the trial because the criteria which determine whether an injunction will be granted are different at each stage of the proceedings.

To obtain an interim injunction the court must first be satisfied that the plaintiff's claim is not 'frivolous' or 'vexatious' and that there is a 'serious issue to be tried'. Unless the plaintiff has no real prospect of getting a perpetual or 'permanent' injunction at the full trial of the action, the court will normally go on to consider whether the balance of convenience lies in favour of granting or refusing an injunction. In weighing the balance of convenience, the court will have regard to such factors as the nature of the damage the plaintiff is likely to suffer if the injunction is refused and whether damages are an adequate remedy. The court will also take into account the effect the injunction will have on the defendant and will consider whether the defendant would be adequately compensated by the plaintiff's 'undertaking in damages'. This is an undertaking to compensate the defendant for any loss suffered as a result of the injunction being granted if the plaintiff's claim is not upheld at the full trial. In cases where both parties are likely to suffer 'uncompensatable disadvantage' the court may investigate the relative strength of each party's case. There may also be other special factors which are relevant in particular circumstances. See *American Cyanamid Co* v *Ethicon Ltd* [1975] 1 All ER 504 where the House of Lords explained the criteria which determine whether an interim injunction will be granted.

A perpetual injunction may be granted once the plaintiff has established liability at the trial.

3.1.2 Specific performance

An order for specific performance compels the party in breach to perform the terms of the contract.

3.2 EQUITABLE REMEDIES AND WRONGFUL DISMISSAL

3.2.1 Rule against specific enforcement

An employer cannot obtain an injunction or an order for specific performance against an employee (Trade Union and Labour Relations (Consolidation) Act 1992, s. 236). Nor can an employee usually obtain an injunction against his employer restraining dismissal, because the courts are reluctant to make an order which has the effect of compulsorily reinstating an employee.

Three reasons have been given in support of this rule. The first and main reason is that it is considered wrong to force one party to serve or to employ another 'if one party has no faith in the honesty, integrity or loyalty of the other' (per Lane LJ in *Chapell* v *The Times Newspapers Ltd* [1975] 2 All ER 233). Secondly, it is said that such an order would require the court's constant supervision and could not therefore be effectively enforced by the court. The third reason is that, until recently, it was thought that the employer's breach automatically terminated the contract with the result that there was no contract to enforce. However, this 'unilateralist' view of the termination of employment contracts is no longer generally accepted as many judges now favour the alternative 'acceptance' view which, in the event of a serious breach by an employer, gives the employee the choice of either affirming the contract or bringing it to an end (see 1.1.7.2 above).

There are now some signs of a relaxation in the courts' traditional stance. Thus, in *Hill* v *C A Parsons Ltd* [1971] 3 All ER 1345, the Court of Appeal said that the rule against the enforcement of employment contracts is not a fixed rule of law and recognised that there may be 'exceptions' where the usual reasons against enforcement do not apply. For example, the 'rule' may not apply where there is no

Other Remedies for Wrongful Dismissal 35

loss of trust and confidence between the parties (see *Powell* v *London Borough of Brent* [1987] IRLR 466).

Perhaps a more significant illustration of the new, less restrictive attitude, is to be found in the High Court's ruling in *Irani* v *Southampton and South West Hampshire Health Authority* [1985] IRLR 203. Mr Irani, a part-time ophthalmologist employed by the Authority was dismissed after he had a quarrel with the consultant who was in charge of the clinic. An ad-hoc panel of inquiry was set up by the Authority after the incident which concluded that the differences between the two men were irreconcilable. It therefore recommended that Mr Irani, the more junior of the two, should be dismissed. The Authority accepted this recommendation and gave Mr Irani six weeks' notice, even though it had no complaint about his conduct or professional competence. Mr Irani sought an interim injunction to prevent the dismissal from taking effect until the Authority had exhausted the elaborate grievance procedure which formed part of his contract of employment.

Granting the interim injunction, the judge said that the special features which existed in *Hill* also existed in *Irani*. First, there was still complete confidence between the employer and employee. Secondly, Mr Irani was seeking to protect his legal rights under the grievance procedures, of which he would be deprived were the injunction not granted. Thirdly, damages would not be an adequate remedy, because if Mr Irani lost his appointment with the Authority he could never again secure employment in the NHS.

Recent cases, such as *Wadcock* v *London Borough of Brent* [1990] IRLR 223 and, in particular, *Robb* v *London Borough of Hammersmith* [1991] IRLR 72, suggest that where an employer fails to follow an agreed recruitment procedure or disciplinary procedure, the court should determine whether an interim injunction is 'workable' and that the employer's loss of confidence in the employee is just one factor among many in determining the question of 'workability'. It remains to be seen whether this approach is endorsed by the Court of Appeal.

3.3 OTHER REMEDIES

3.3.1 Public law remedies

In certain restricted cases, the legality of a dismissal may be challenged in public law, that is the law regulating the exercise of statutory powers by public bodies. Here it may be argued that the dismissal is invalid either because it was handled in a manner which was contrary to the rules of natural justice or because the authority had no power to dismiss the employee in the particular circumstances, i.e., it was *ultra vires*. The legal result of a successful claim in this respect is that the dismissal is of no legal effect with the result that the parties remain bound by the terms of the contract. See *McClelland* v *Northern Ireland General Health Services Board* [1957] 2 All ER 129, where the House of Lords held that a dismissal for a reason other than that permitted in the particular contract of employment was *ultra vires*.

Such a claim must now be made under the Rules of the Supreme Court, ord. 53 (which gives effect to the Supreme Court Act 1981, s. 30). This provides for special administrative law remedies such as *certiorari* (an order quashing an illegal decision), *prohibition* (an order which prohibits a public body acting in a particular way) and *mandamus* (an order to compel an authority to act in a particular way). It also makes provision for a *declaration* (a court order which states whether or not the action complained of was lawful — see 3.3.2 below) and an injunction to restrain the illegal action.

These 'administrative law' remedies are available only where an issue of public law is involved and therefore are generally confined to holders of a public office. Furthermore, employment by a public authority does not of itself inject any element of public law. This point was stressed by the Court of Appeal in *R* v *East Berkshire Health Authority, ex parte Walsh* [1984] IRLR 278. In that case, Mr Walsh, a senior nursing officer, whose terms and conditions of employment were fixed by the Whitley Council, applied to have the Authority's decision to dismiss him quashed on the grounds that the decision was taken in breach of the rules of natural justice. Dismissing the claim, the Court of Appeal ruled that the contractual relationship between Mr Walsh and the Authority was one of pure master and servant, i.e., a matter of private law, not public law. The court ruled that public law remedies would only be available in those rare cases where parliament had underpinned the position of public servants by directly restricting the freedom of the authority to dismiss (e.g., in *McClelland* above). The recent case of *McClaren* v *Home Office* [1990] IRLR 338 and *R* v *Lord Chancellor's Department, ex parte Nangle* [1991] IRLR 343 further limit the scope of public law remedies in an employment context, with the result that such remedies are likely to be available to only a very limited number of employees in the public sector.

3.3.2 Declaration

Another remedy open to an employee is to seek a declaration from the court as to the lawfulness or otherwise of an employer's conduct. Such declarations are frequently sought where the legality of a public body's action is being challenged in public law. However, a number of cases suggest that the remedy may also be invoked to challenge the lawfulness of an employer's conduct under the contract of employment in private law.

For example, employees have sought declarations to the effect that their dismissal (or other disciplinary action taken against them) was unlawful due to a 'serious' procedural irregularity such as a denial of natural justice (*R* v *British Broadcasting Corporation, ex parte Lavelle* [1982] IRLR 404), or a failure to abide by the express terms of a disciplinary procedure (*R* v *South Glamorgan Area Health Authority, ex parte Phillips* IRLIB 223, February 1987). Furthermore, it should be noted that where an application for judicial review is unsuccessful, e.g., because the public law element is lacking, the court may still make a declaration or issue an injunction if these remedies are sought in the application for judicial review (Rules of the Supreme Court, Order 53, Rule 9(3), cf *R* v *East Berkshire Area Health Authority, ex parte Walsh* [1984] IRLR 278).

The power to grant a declaration is however discretionary. Furthermore, even if it is granted, it is of little use to most employees since it does no more than declare the rights of the parties under the contract. In most cases this will not give an employee a right to anything more than a normal award of damages for wrongful dismissal. However, a declaration may prove to be an important remedy in itself for public sector workers, since their employers may feel that they are under a moral and political duty to reconsider the case in accordance with the terms of their procedure. This possibly explains why the leading authorities so far have involved public sector workers.

PART II UNFAIR DISMISSAL

Introduction

The right to complain of unfair dismissal was established by the Industrial Relations Act 1971 and introduced in 1972. In substance, the law has remained relatively unchanged since its introduction.

In the year to March 1995, there were 40,039 complaints of unfair dismissal. However, not all employees qualify for protection against unfair dismissal: the right to complain is subject to a number of qualifying conditions and certain categories of workers are excluded altogether. The most important qualifying requirement is that the complainant, at the 'effective date of termination' (ERA 1996, s. 97(1) and (2)), must have worked for a period of two years or more.

In unfair dismissal cases, unlike a case of wrongful dismissal, it is necessary for employers to establish a *valid* reason for dismissal, i.e., a reason which falls within one of the five categories of valid reasons permitted by ERA 1996, s. 98(1) and (2), and to show that it was 'reasonable' to dismiss for that reason.

The following reasons for dismissal are permitted by statute:

(a) a reason relating to the capability or qualifications of the employee for performing the work he is employed to do;
(b) a reason relating to the conduct of the employee;
(c) redundancy;
(d) the fact that the employee cannot continue to do his job without contravening a statutory duty or requirement;
(e) some other substantial reason of a kind such as to justify the dismissal of an employee holding the position which that employee held.

Having established a valid reason for dismissal, ERA 1996, s. 98(4) provides that a tribunal must be satisfied that the employer acted 'reasonably or unreasonably in treating it [the reason for dismissal] as a sufficient reason for dismissing the employee' and that question 'shall be determined in accordance with equity and the substantial merits of the case'. In approaching the question of reasonableness, tribunals attach greater importance to the procedure by which employers reach their decision rather than to the merits of the decision itself. This trend has been

Unfair Dismissal

strengthened by a series of Court of Appeal and Employment Appeal Tribunal decisions which have stressed that a tribunal should not substitute its view for a decision which lies within the 'range of reasonable responses' of a reasonable employer. In the vast majority of cases, the critical question is whether the procedure followed by the employer is a reasonable one. In *Polkey v A E Dayton Services Ltd* [1987] IRLR 503, the House of Lords reasserted the importance of procedural fairness and stressed that a failure to follow a fair procedure will only be justified in the most exceptional of circumstances.

Certain reasons for dismissal are deemed to be automatically unfair, e.g., dismissals for pregnancy-related reasons (ERA 1996, s. 99) and dismissals for the assertion of statutory rights (ERA 1996, s. 104). A dismissal is also automatically unfair if it is for a reason connected to the transfer of an undertaking unless the employer can establish an 'economic, technical or organisational reason entailing changes in the workforce', in which case the dismissal must still be shown to be 'reasonable' in accordance with ordinary unfair dismissal principles (Transfer of Undertakings (Protection of Employment) Regulations 1981 (as amended), reg. 8).

Special provisions also apply where the dismissal is for union-related reasons, i.e., where the reasons for dismissal relates to union membership or non-membership, or relates to an employee's participation in the activities of an independent trade union, and where the dismissal is for health and safety reasons contrary to ERA 1996, s. 100. A dismissal for one or more of these reasons is automatically unfair and the usual qualifying requirements do not apply (TULR(C)A 1992, s. 152 and ERA 1996, ss. 108–109). The same protection has been extended to elected employee representatives who are performing (or proposing to perform) the functions and activities as such, or candidates for election as employee representatives (ERA 1996, s. 103). Special rules apply to the 'mass' dismissal of strikers and in certain circumstances the tribunal will have no jurisdiction to determine such claims.

As far as sex and race discrimination is concerned, although there is no specific statutory provision relating to dismissals for reasons connected with a person's race or sex, it is clear that such reasons are not 'valid' reasons for dismissal and therefore it is unfair to dismiss someone because of their sex or race. The same is likely to apply to the dismissal of disabled persons.

The rules governing the remedies for unfair dismissal are laid down in ss. 111 to 126 of the Employment Rights Act 1996. An award of unfair dismissal compensation is usually limited to a basic award (ERA 1996, ss. 119–122) and a compensatory award (ss. 123–124). However, where an industrial tribunal makes an order for reinstatement or re-engagement pursuant to s. 113 and an employer fails to comply with it, the tribunal has the power to make an additional award (s. 117) or, in union membership dismissals, a special award (TULR(C)A 1992, s. 157). A special award may also be made where re-employment is requested by the employee but not ordered by the tribunal.

Chapters 4 to 17 describe how each of these awards is calculated and the circumstances in which the statutory award may be reduced. Each of the statutory awards is subject to prescribed maxima. Readers will be aware that these maxima are reviewed annually by the Secretary of State for Employment. The review normally takes place in December and increases normally take effect from 1 April the following year.

A table setting out the factors which should be taken into account in quantifying an award of unfair dismissal compensation is to be found in the Appendix.

The current median award for unfair dismissal is £3,289 (*Labour Market Trends*, July 1996).

4 Re-employment Orders and the Additional Award

4.1 INTRODUCTION

A novel feature of the statutory provisions relating to unfair dismissal is the power of tribunals to order reinstatement or re-engagement. Specific performance of an employment contract is a legal remedy which is rarely available in other circumstances (see 3.2.1 above).

As a result of the recommendation of the Donovan Commission that tribunals be given the power to order re-employment, a power to recommend re-engagement was included in the Industrial Relations Act 1971. The statutory powers were strengthened by the Employment Protection Act 1975 and remain in the form laid down in that Act to the present day.

It was Parliament's intention that reinstatement or re-engagement should be the primary remedy for unfair dismissal but, in practice, there has been a noticeable reluctance on the part of employees to request re-employment and an even greater reluctance on the part of tribunals to make such orders when requested to do so. The result is that in 1994/95 re-employment orders were made in only 1.6% of cases in which the dismissal was held to be unfair (and accounted for a mere 0.2% of all applications (*Labour Market Trends, July 1996*). Thus, instead of being the primary remedy, such orders are a rarity. Nonetheless, the statutory powers are still important, since failure to comply with such orders gives rise to an enhanced right to compensation — the additional award.

This chapter looks at the circumstances in which reinstatement and re-engagement orders are made, the circumstances in which an additional award becomes payable and how it is calculated.

4.2 ORDERS FOR RE-EMPLOYMENT

Industrial tribunals can make two types of permanent re-employment order. These are an 'order for reinstatement' or an 'order for re-engagement'.

An order for reinstatement requires an employer to 'treat the complainant in all respects as if he had not been dismissed'. This means that the employee must be restored to his or her former position (ERA 1996, s. 114(1)).

An order for re-engagement is a more flexible remedy. The order, which can be made against either the employer, a successor of the employer or an associated employer, requires the ex-employee to be taken on 'in employment comparable to that from which he was dismissed or other suitable employment' (ERA 1996, s. 115(1)). Civil servants are regarded as being employed by the department in which they work rather than by the civil service as a whole. However, in exceptional circumstances where, for example, two departments are linked for historical reason, a re-engagement order may be made against a different government department (*Department of Health* v *Bruce and the Department of Social Security* EAT 14/92).

Industrial tribunals may also make an interim re-employment order in certain circumstances (see 4.5 below).

4.2.1 Statutory procedure

The statutory provisions lay down a detailed procedure which tribunals should normally follow in deciding which of the statutory remedies to award.

The first step is to explain to the complainant what orders for reinstatement and re-engagement can be made under ss. 114 and 115 of the ERA 1996. The tribunal must then ask the complainant whether he wishes to be reinstated or re-engaged (ERA 1996, s. 112(2) and (3)).

The second step is for the tribunal to decide whether to order *reinstatement*. The tribunal has a general discretion whether or not to order reinstatement (*Port of London Authority* v *Payne & Others* [1992] IRLR 447) but, in reaching its decision, the tribunal must take into account the following considerations (s. 116(1)):

(a) whether the complainant wishes to be reinstated;

(b) whether it is practicable for the employer to comply with an order for reinstatement;

(c) where the complainant has caused or contributed to some extent to the dismissal, whether it would be just to order his reinstatement.

The third and final step is for the tribunal to decide whether to order *re-engagement*. The tribunal has a general discretion whether or not to order re-engagement (*Port of London Authority* v *Payne & Others*) but, in reaching its decision the tribunal must take into account the following considerations (s. 116(3)):

(a) any wish expressed by the complainant as to the nature of the order to be made;

(b) whether it is practicable for the employer, or as the case may be, a successor or associated employer, to comply with an order for re-engagement;

(c) where the complainant has caused or contributed to some extent to the dismissal, whether it would be just to order re-engagement and, if so, on what terms.

Tribunals may take other factors into account. For example, in *Port of London Authority* v *Payne & Others* the EAT thought that the tribunal should have taken account of the applicants' ability to repay the £35,000 severance payments they had received from their employers. On the other hand, the EAT accepted that employer objections or one or more of the grounds referred to above are not necessarily conclusive at this stage.

4.2.2 Wishes of the complainant

No order can be made if the employee does not want to be reinstated or re-engaged (ERA 1996, s. 112(2) and (3)). For this reason, tribunals are under a statutory duty both to explain their powers to make such orders and to find out whether the employee wishes to be reinstated or re-engaged.

It has been held that the tribunal's duty in this respect is mandatory and applies even where the employee is represented (*Pirelli General Cable Works Ltd* v *Murray* [1979] IRLR 190). However, more recently, the EAT ruled that the terms of s. 68(1) of the Employment Protection (Consolidation) Act 1978 (now ERA 1996, s. 112(2) and (3)) were discretionary only and need not be followed where either the employee had found another job and was not seeking re-employment or the tribunal found the employee 100% to blame for the dismissal since it is 'pointless' to consider re-employment in these circumstances. (See *Richardson* v *Walker* EAT 312/79 and *Pratt* v *Pickford Removals* EAT/43/86). These unreported authorities do not appear to have been placed before the Court of Appeal in *Cowley* v *Manson Timber Ltd* [1995] IRLR 153. However, the Court appears to have taken the view that a tribunal's failure to comply with the statutory provisions may be challenged only where this failure causes unfairness or injustice to the complainant. Furthermore, the Court ruled that a failure to comply with the statutory procedure will not nullify its decision on compensation.

4.2.3 Practicability of compliance

Assuming that the employee wishes the tribunal to make an order of re-employment, the central issue is whether it is practicable for the employer to comply with the order. The requirement of practicability must be considered both in relation to reinstatement and re-engagement. Although 'impracticability' is also a defence where the employer fails to comply with such an order (see 4.4.6 below), a tribunal must consider the issue at each stage. It should not postpone its consideration of practicability until the enforcement hearing, but by necessity any determination at the first hearing will be provisional (*Port of London Authority* v *Payne & Others* [1992] IRLR 447 (EAT), [1994] IRLR 9 (CA)).

The issue of practicability is primarily a question of fact and the EAT has recommended that tribunals adopt a 'broad common sense view' of the question and avoid trying to analyse the word 'practicable' in too much detail (per Kilner Brown J in *Meridian Ltd* v *Gomersall and another* [1977] IRLR 425). In *Port of London Authority* v *Payne & Others*, the EAT suggested that the question of practicability must be judged by the standards of a 'reasonable employer' and tribunals must take care not to substitute their own judgment for that of a reasonable employer, but this approach does not appear to have been accepted by the Court of Appeal.

In deciding whether a re-employment order is practicable, the tribunal should consider whether, having regard to the industrial relations realities of the situation, it is capable of being put into effect with success (per Stephenson LJ in *Coleman and*

Stephenson v *Magnet Joinery Ltd* [1974] IRLR 343). Thus, what is practicable should not be equated with what is 'possible'. A tribunal may take into account the fact that its order may lead to serious industrial strife (see *Coleman* above and *Bateman* v *British Leyland UK Ltd* [1974] IRLR 101) or cause resentment amongst the workforce (*Meridian Ltd* v *Gomersall and another* [1977] IRLR 425). However, mere 'inexpediency' is no bar to re-employment (*Qualcast (Wolverhampton) Ltd* v *Ross* [1979] IRLR 98). Thus employers' fears that a re-employment order will undermine their authority or lead to embarrassment as a result of adverse publicity are irrelevant (*George* v *Beecham Group* [1977] IRLR 43 and *Ayub* v *Vauxhall Motors Ltd* [1978] IRLR 428).

It should also be remembered that the tribunal is only required to 'consider' the question of 'practicability' at this stage and may make an order to test whether employers claims of impracticablity are justified (*Timex Corporation Ltd* v *Thomson* [1981] IRLR 522 and *Freemans Plc* v *Flynn* [1984] IRLR 486). A tribunal may therefore order re-engagement even where the employer claims that there is no existing vacancy (*Electronic Data Processing Ltd* v *Wright* EAT 292/83) or where the employee was originally dismissed for redundancy (*Polkey* v *A E Dayton Services (formerly Edmund Walker (Holdings) Ltd*) [1987] IRLR 503), but such an order is unlikely if there is no prospect of a suitable vacancy arising in the near future. Such orders are also unlikely where the employer believes that the employee is incapable of doing the job (*SMT Sales & Services Ltd* v *Irwin* EAT 485/79) or is not qualified for the job (*Rose* v *RNIB* COIT 26830/91), or has a genuine fear that the employee will not be able to do the job without endangering those in his care (*ILEA* v *Gravett* [1988] IRLR 497). Similarly, in *London Borough of Greenwich* v *Dell* EAT 166/94, the EAT overturned an industrial tribunal's decision to order the re-engagement of a member of the National Front in a position which did not involve contact with ethnic minorities on the ground that such an order was impracticable and offensive to the Borough Council as an equal opportunities employer.

An order is also unlikely where there has been a fundamental loss of trust between the parties (e.g., *Nothman* v *London Borough of Barnet No. 2* [1980] IRLR 65, where the employee believed that there had been a conspiracy against her by her employers). However, in *The Boots Company Ltd* v *Lees-Collier* [1986] ICR 728 a tribunal ordered reinstatement despite the employer's lingering belief in the employee's dishonesty. Re-employment was considered impracticable where compliance with an order might result in a withdrawal of funding for the employer (*Akram* v *Lothian Community Council* IRLIB 371).

Tribunals will also take the size of the employer organisation into account, particularly where the employment involves a close working relationship between the dismissed employee and the employer (*Enessy Co SA t/a The Tulchan Estate* v *Minoprio* [1978] IRLR 489).

4.2.4 Contributory fault

Tribunals must also consider whether re-employment is appropriate in the light of the employee's contributory conduct. The EAT has said that the test to be applied is the same as that under what is now s. 123(6) of the Employment Rights Act 1996 (see *The Boots Company Ltd* v *Lees-Collier* [1986] ICR 728). Thus an employee will not be held to have caused or contributed to the dismissal unless he has been guilty of 'blameworthy' conduct (see Chapter 16).

A finding of contributory fault does not necessarily preclude a tribunal from making an order of reinstatement or re-engagement. Such orders are not uncommon where the employee is to blame only to a small extent. More exceptionally, in *Automatic Cooling Engineering Ltd* v *Scott* EAT 545/81, the EAT upheld an industrial tribunal's order of reinstatement despite a finding that the employee, an apprentice, had been 75% to blame for the dismissal. But, in *Nairne* v *Highlands & Islands Fire Brigade* [1989] IRLR 366, the EAT held that re-engagement was impracticable in a job which required a driving qualification where the employee had been disqualified from driving for three years as a result of a second offence of drink-driving within a two-year period. The EAT held the employee 75% to blame for his dismissal and overturned the tribunal's order of re-engagement. The EAT's decision was later confirmed by the Court of Session ([1989] IRLR 366).

The extent of the employee's contributory conduct may however be reflected in the terms of an order of re-engagement and in particular in a tribunal's refusal to award compensation for loss of back-pay (see 4.3.2 below).

4.2.5 Permanent replacements

Reinstatement or re-engagement is not considered impracticable simply because the employer has taken on a permanent replacement, though it may be held impracticable for this reason in the circumstances set out in s. 116(6) of the Employment Rights Act 1996:

> (5) Where ... an employer has engaged a permanent replacement for a dismissed employee, the tribunal shall not take that fact into account in determining ... whether it is practicable to comply with an order for reinstatement or re-engagement.
> (6) Subsection (5) does not apply where the employer shows—
> (a) that it was not practicable for him to arrange for the dismissed employee's work to be done without engaging a permanent replacement, or
> (b) that—
> (i) he engaged the replacement after the lapse of a reasonable period, without having heard from the dismissed employee that he wished to be reinstated or re-engaged, and
> (ii) when the employer engaged the replacement it was no longer reasonable for him to arrange for the dismissed employee's work to be done except by a permanent replacement.

The effect is that large employer organisations who cannot invoke s. 116(6) successfully will often be unable to resist a re-employment order and may have to consider the possibility of dismissing the permanent replacement in order to comply with it. The effect of this provision appears to have been overlooked by the EAT in *Cold Drawn Tubes Ltd* v *Middleton* [1992] IRLR 160.

4.2.6 Duty to give reasons

The tribunal must give reasons for exercising or declining to exercise its discretion under ERA 1996, s. 116(1), (2), (3), and (4). Thus it should say why it considers re-employment to be practicable or impracticable in the particular circumstances (*Port of London Authority* v *Payne & Others* [1992] IRLR 447).

4.3 TERMS OF RE-EMPLOYMENT

4.3.1 Terms of reinstatement

On making an order of reinstatement, the tribunal must specify (ERA 1996, s. 114(2)):

(a) any amount payable by the employer in respect of any benefit which the complainant might reasonably be expected to have had but for the dismissal, including arrears of pay, for the period between the date of termination of employment and the date of reinstatement;
(b) any rights and privileges, including seniority and pension rights, which must be restored to the employee;
(c) the date by which the order must be complied with.

The tribunal can therefore require the employer to award full back-pay, holiday pay etc. between the date of dismissal and the date of reinstatement. This may include any improvement in an employee's terms and conditions (for example a pay rise) which takes effect during the above period, since it is provided that the complainant is to be treated as if 'he had benefited from that improvement from the date on which he would have done so but for being dismissed' (s. 114(3)).

However, in calculating the amount payable by the employer, tribunals must deduct (s. 114(4)):

(a) wages in lieu of notice or any ex gratia payment received by the employee from the employer in respect of the period between the date of termination and the date of reinstatement;
(b) any payments received by the employee in respect of employment with another employer during the above period (i.e., wages etc.); and
(c) such other benefits as the tribunal thinks fit in the circumstances.

No deduction should be made for contributory fault or a failure to mitigate (*City & Hackney Health Authority* v *Crisp* [1990] IRLR 47).

Jobseeker's allowance and other social security benefits are recovered by the State through the operation of the regulations dealing with recoupment (see Chapter 18).

Example

An employee who was earning £150 a week is unfairly dismissed. The hearing takes place 3 months after the dismissal. At the time of the dismissal, the employee received one month's wages in lieu. He commenced a temporary job two weeks before the hearing from which he received wages of £100 a week. The tribunal ordered reinstatement.

The calculation of back-pay is as follows:

	£
Total arrears	1,800
Less	
—payment in lieu	600
—earnings from new job	200
Balance of arrears	£1,000

Note: There is no statutory limit to the amount a tribunal may award for loss of back-pay under these provisions (see *Foster Wheeler (UK) Ltd* v *Chiarella* EAT 111/82) and the statutory cap on compensation does not apply to this part of the tribunal's award (ERA 1996, s. 124(3)).

4.3.2 Terms of re-engagement

On making an order of re-engagement, the tribunal must specify (ERA 1996, s. 115(2)):

(a) the identity of the employer;
(b) the nature of the employment;
(c) the remuneration for the employment;
(d) any amount payable by the employer in respect of any benefit which the complainant might reasonably be expected to have had but for the dismissal, including arrears of pay, for the period between the date of termination of employment and the date of re-engagement;
(e) any rights and privileges, including seniority and pension rights, which must be restored to the employee;
(f) the date by which the order must be complied with.

There is no power to order re-engagement on significantly more favourable terms than the employee would have obtained if the employee had been reinstated (*Rank Xerox (UK) Ltd* v *Stryczek* [1995] IRLR 568, where the EAT held that an industrial tribunal had erred in law when it ordered an employer to re-engage the complainant in a position which carried a substantially higher salary and the added benefit of a company car). In addition, it has been held that the tribunal should specify the employee's place of work if this differs from the employee's original place of work (*Electronic Data Processing Ltd* v *Wright* [1986] IRLR 8). But in general it is undesirable for a tribunal to order re-engagement in a specific job as distinct from identifying the nature of the proposed employment (*Rank Xerox (UK) Ltd* v *Stryczek*).

The tribunal is again entitled to award the full amount of back-pay etc. which has accrued between the date of the dismissal and the date when the re-engagement will take effect. The arrears are normally calculated on the basis of the employee's pre-dismissal rate of pay, even where the employee is to be re-engaged at a lower rate of pay (*Electronic Data Processing Ltd* v *Wright*).

It is likely that the employee is entitled to the benefit of any pay rise or other improvement in terms and conditions which takes effect between the date of the dismissal and the date of re-engagement by virtue of the tribunal's duty under s. 116(2), (3) and (4) of the Employment Rights Act 1996 (see below). However, there is no authority on this point.

Credit must be given for payments that have been made to the employee since dismissal, such as wages in lieu, ex gratia payments and any payments made by a new employer (see 4.3.1 above) (ERA 1996, s. 115(3)), but no deduction should be made for a failure to mitigate (*City & Hackney Health Authority* v *Crisp* [1990] IRLR 47).

The tribunal's broad discretion in deciding the terms of re-engagement, is subject to the restriction that it is under a duty to ensure 'so far as is reasonably practicable' that the terms of re-engagement are 'as favourable as an order for reinstatement'. This does not, however, apply where the employee is found to have contributed to the dismissal. In such circumstances, it is open to tribunals to penalise an employee for contributory fault in the terms of the re-engagement order (ERA 1996, s. 116(1), (3) and (4)).

4.3.3 Tribunal's duty to state terms

The tribunal is under a duty to state the statutory terms of re-engagement. In effect, this means that it must write a new contract for the parties. It will not discharge its duty in this respect by leaving it to the parties to decide the terms of re-engagement (*Pirelli General Cable Works Ltd* v *Murray* [1979] IRLR 190), or by leaving the parties to agree the nature of the work and the rate of pay (*Stena Houlder Ltd* v *Keenan* EAT(s) 543/93). Similarly, it has been suggested that the practice adopted by some tribunals of making an 'offer direction', i.e., directing the employer to make an offer of re-engagement within a stated period on certain terms specified by the industrial tribunal, is invalid for the same reason. See *Lilley Construction Ltd* v *Dunn* [1984] IRLR 483, where the distinction between an offer direction and a full re-employment order is explained.

4.4 ENFORCING A RE-EMPLOYMENT ORDER

The penalty for non-compliance with an order for reinstatement or re-engagement is prescribed by s. 117 of the ERA 1996 and is purely financial. It is not open to the applicant to seek to enforce the industrial tribunal's orders for back-pay or any other ancillary matter in a High Court or county court action (*O'Laoire* v *Jackel International Ltd* [1990] IRLR 70) but the statutory cap on compensation does not apply in relation to arrears of pay (ERA 1996, s. 124(3)). The statutory remedy is in the nature of compensation and depends on whether the employer has failed to comply with the order or has partially complied with it. This distinction is considered below.

Re-employment Orders and the Additional Award

4.4.1 Partial compliance

Where a re-employment order is made and the complainant (the employee) is reinstated or re-engaged but the 'terms of the order are not fully complied with', then, subject to s. 124(1) of the Employment Rights Act 1996, which fixes the statutory limit on the compensatory award, the tribunal is empowered to award compensation of such amount as it thinks fit, having regard to the loss sustained by the complainant in consequence of the employer's failure to comply with the terms of the order (ERA 1996, s. 117(2)). Thus, in such circumstances, the tribunal's power is limited to making an award of compensation up to the statutory limit for the compensatory award of £11,300. There is no power to make an additional award.

4.4.2 Failure to reinstate or re-engage

Where an order for reinstatement or re-engagement is made 'but the complainant is not reinstated or re-engaged in accordance with the order' the tribunal is required, subject to the defence of impracticability (see 4.4.6 below) to make an additional award under s. 117(3) of the Employment Rights Act 1996 as well as the standard award of compensation for unfair dismissal under ss. 118 to 127.

4.4.3 Partial compliance and failure to comply distinguished

The precise distinction between a failure to comply with the tribunal's order and a failure to reinstate or re-engage in accordance with it is not entirely clear from the wording of s. 117(1) and (3) of the Employment Rights Act 1996, but the point was considered by the EAT in relation to an order for *reinstatement* in *Artisan Press Ltd v Srawley and Parker* [1986] IRLR 126.

In that case, the tribunal ordered two security officers, who were found to have been unfairly dismissed on union membership grounds, to be reinstated by their employers. The employers purported to comply with the tribunal's order by re-employing the two employees as cleaners with minor security functions (i.e., in a different job), but they argued that they had done enough to achieve partial compliance with the tribunal's order for reinstatement. The EAT, however, did not agree. It said that reinstatement on less favourable terms did not amount to reinstatement for the purpose of s. 69(2) of the Employment Protection (Consolidation) Act 1978 (now see ERA 1996, s. 114) and therefore held that the employers were in breach of s. 71(2) (now see ERA 1996, s. 117(3)). (In the particular circumstances the employees qualified for a special award since the dismissal was for a union-related reason.) By way of contrast, the EAT said that an employer would be treated as having failed to comply fully with the tribunal's order for reinstatement if the employer had failed to comply with the 'ancillary matters' in s. 69(2)(a) (now see ERA 1996, s. 114(2)) (see 4.3.1 above). For example, if the employers had merely failed to pay off arrears due to the employee.

4.4.4 Additional award

The additional award is calculated as follows:

(a) in unfair dismissals which are not union or discrimination-related, the additional award is between 13 and 26 weeks' pay (ERA 1996, s. 177(5)(b)); but

(b) if the dismissal is for an unlawful act of race or sex discrimination, the additional award is increased to between 26 and 52 weeks' pay (ERA 1996, s. 117(5)(a)). For compensation in discrimination cases, see 19.2 below.

The statutory rules governing the calculation of a week's pay are considered in detail in Chapter 7.

4.4.4.1 Fixing the penalty — the employer's conduct

The additional award is a financial penalty for non-compliance with the tribunal's order and in fixing its award tribunals are likely to adopt a 'tariff approach'. It follows that if the employer is guilty of a flagrant violation of the order, the award is likely to be at the higher end of the scale whereas if the employer fails to observe the order because of genuine re-employment difficulties which fall short of the impracticability defence the award will be at the lower end (*Morganite Electrical Carbon Ltd* v *Donne* [1987] IRLR 363). Considerations of public policy may also play a part in sex and race discrimination cases.

4.4.4.2 Fixing the penalty — other factors

Although it is clear that the employer's conduct is the most influential factor in determining the amount of an additional award, tribunals may also take account of other factors. One such factor is the extent to which the compensatory award fully compensates the applicant. For example, in *Initial Textile Services* v *Ritchie* EAT 358/89, the EAT reduced the additional award from 26 to 20 weeks' pay on account of the fact that the employee had already received full compensation for the loss she suffered as a result of her dismissal; on the other hand, a higher additional award may be justified where the loss exceeds the statutory limit (see also *Morganite Electrical Carbon Ltd* v *Donne*). Another factor is whether the employer has complied with the ancillary parts of the order; for example, whether the employer has paid any of the back-pay due to the employee under the order. These factors may be balanced against other general factors such as whether the employee has taken steps to mitigate his or her loss (*Mabrizi* v *National Hospital for Nervous Diseases* [1990] IRLR 133) and the extent to which the employee contributed to the dismissal (*Ayub* v *Vauxhall Motors Ltd* [1978] IRLR 428). However a failure to mitigate should not lead to a quantifiable reduction in the additional award (see *Mabirizi*). Another relevant factor is whether the employee would have been fit and able to return to work on the date specified in the order if the employer had complied with it (see *McQueen* v *Motherwell Railway Club* EAT 652/88).

4.4.5 Defence of impracticability

No additional award is payable if the employer can show that 'it was not practicable to comply with the order' (ERA 1996, s. 117(4)(a)). (See 4.2.3 on the meaning of 'practicability'.)

In determining whether the defence is made out, the tribunal is not restricted to considering the events which have taken place since the order was made. Thus the tribunal may take account of all the relevant facts both before and after the date of the order (*Freemans plc* v *Flynn* [1984] IRLR 486).

This provision gives the employer 'a second bite at the cherry' since the employer is entitled to raise the same arguments twice — both at the time the order is made and at the enforcement stage. However, it should be noted that 'practicablity' is only a 'consideration' under s. 116(1), (2), (3) and (4) of the Employment Rights Act 1996, whereas it is a complete defence under s. 117(4)(a).

It follows that where the original order is made to put pressure on the employer to reinstate or re-engage the employee, it will still be open to the employer to argue that it was not practicable to comply with the order in the light of what happened subsequent to the order being made. For example, if, at the time the order was made, there was no vacancy (see 4.2.3 above), and this is still the case when an application is made to enforce the order, it will still be open to the employer to argue that it was not practicable to comply with the order for this reason.

Employers are not under a duty to create a special job for the employee to do or to dismiss existing employees to enable them to re-employ the complainant (*Freemans plc* v *Flynn* [1984] IRLR 486). Neither will it be practicable to comply with the order if this would result in overmanning or a redundancy situation (*Cold Drawn Tubes Ltd* v *Middleton* [1992] IRLR 161, where the EAT rejected the argument that the applicant should have been reinstated and then, if necessary, the employers should have gone through a proper redundancy selection exercise). Furthermore, as the Court of Appeal pointed out in *Payne and Ors* v *Port of London Authority* [1994] IRLR 9, employers cannot be expected to explore every possible avenue which ingenuity might suggest. On the other hand, tribunals will scrutinise the genuineness of the employer's attempts to look for a vacancy and, in redundancy dismissals, may consider it appropriate for an employer to seek volunteers for redundancy if this is practicable. Some employer objections, e.g., that non-compliance is justified on the ground of inexpediency, are unlikely to meet with any greater success the second time round. Similarly, the fact that the employer has taken on a permanent replacement does not necessarily mean that it is impracticable to comply with the order (see 4.2.3 above).

An additional award will be made even though, unknown to the employer, the employee would not have been able to return to work had the employer complied with the order. Thus, in *McQueen* v *Motherwell Railway Club* EAT 652/88 the EAT upheld an additional award of 20 weeks' pay when, unknown to the employers, one of the applicants would not have been able to start work on the day specified in the order on health grounds. The EAT said this factor did not justify the employer's failure to comply with the order, although it did justify the award being limited to 20 weeks rather than the full 26 weeks.

Lodging an appeal against an industrial tribunal decision does not make it impracticable to comply with the order (*Initial Textile Service Ltd* v *Ritchie* EAT 358/89).

4.4.6 Union-related dismissals

Where the dismissal is for union membership, refusal to join a union or trade union activities, the tribunal must make a special award instead of an additional award. For the special award, see Chapter 6.

4.4.7 Non-compliance by employee

Where the tribunal finds that the complainant has unreasonably prevented an order under ss. 114 or 115 of the Employment Rights Act 1996 from being complied with, it must treat the employee's conduct in this respect as a failure to mitigate under s. 123(4) (ERA 1996, s. 117(8)).

This provision would seem to be aimed at the employee who changes his mind after an order for reinstatement or re-engagement has been made. Similar provisions apply where the employee unreasonably refuses an employer's offer of reinstatement or re-engagement (see 5.4.2 and 15.4 above).

4.5 INTERIM RE-EMPLOYMENT

At present, there is no general statutory right to interim re-employment in unfair dismissal cases, i.e., re-employment on an interim basis until the complaint is determined at the hearing. However, special provision is made for a form of interim re-employment in cases where the dismissal is for union-related reasons or, in the case of employees with designated health and safety responsibility, or health and safety representatives or committee members, for carrying out health and safety responsibilities. This is known as 'interim relief'.

4.5.1 Interim relief

An application for interim relief may be made by an employee who claims that he has been dismissed for reasons relating to union membership or in circumstances where he can invoke the statutory right to non-union membership (TULR(C)A 1992, s. 161(1)). The right has also been extended to those who have been dismissed for carrying out health and safety responsibilities pursuant to ERA 1996, s. 100(1)(a) and (b) and ERA 1996, ss. 128–132.

An application for interim relief must be made within seven days of the effective date of dismissal (s. 161(2)). In the case of dismissals for union membership, it must be supported by a certificate in writing, signed by an authorised official of the 'independent union of which the employee was or had proposed to become a member' stating that there are 'reasonable grounds for supposing that the reason or principal reason for his dismissal ... was the one alleged in the complaint' (s. 161(3)). On the receipt of such an application, the industrial tribunal is under a statutory duty to determine the matter 'as soon as practicable', though the employer must be given at least seven days' notice of the hearing (s. 161(2)). Furthermore, in cases where it is proposed to join the trade union as a party to the proceedings (see 6.3.4 below) the union must be given at least three days' notice of the hearing (s. 162(3)). The tribunal may postpone the hearing in special circumstances (s. 162(4)).

If, at the hearing of the application for interim relief, the tribunal is satisfied that it is likely that on determining the complaint to which the application relates, the tribunal will find that the complainant was unfairly dismissed, it must announce its findings and explain to both parties its powers under TULR(C)A 1992, s. 163. Broadly stated, these are:

(a) if the employer is willing to reinstate the employee, to order interim reinstatement until the case is heard or settled (s. 163(4));

(b) if the employer is willing to re-engage the employee, to order interim re-engagement until the case is heard or settled (s. 163(5));

(c) if the employer is unwilling to reinstate or re-engage the employee, to order that the contract of employment shall continue in force, irrespective of whether it has been terminated, until the case is heard or settled (ss. 163(6) and 164(2)). The tribunal is required to specify in its order 'the amount which is to be paid by the employer to the employee' (s. 164(2)), though in making the order it will take account of any payment made by the employer as damages for wrongful dismissal or as a payment in lieu of notice (s. 164(5) and (6)).

On the application of either party, the tribunal may, 'at any time between the making of an order' under ss. 163 and 164 and 'the determination or settlement of the complaint', revoke or vary its order on the ground of a relevant change in circumstances (s. 165).

The penalty for a failure to comply with the terms of a continuation order is set out in s. 166. This provides that if, on the application of the employee, the tribunal is satisfied that the employer has failed to comply with an order of continuation of the contract, for example by not paying the employee the amount stated under s. 164(2), the tribunal is required to determine the amount of pay owed by the employer and to order that the sum due is paid to the employee by way of additional compensation at the 'full' hearing. In cases where the employer has failed to comply with some other aspect of the tribunal's order, for example in relation to pension rights or similar matters, the tribunal may award such compensation as it considers just and equitable in the circumstances.

In effect, these provisions enable the tribunal to ensure that the employee is either reinstated or re-engaged on an interim basis or suspended on full pay until the case is resolved.

The sum paid to an employee under a continuation order is irrecoverable even if the employee subsequently loses his or her unfair dismissal application (*Initial Textile Services* v *Rendell* EAT 383/91).

5 Unfair Dismissal: the Basic Award

5.1 INTRODUCTION

The basic award was introduced by the Employment Protection Act 1975 with the aim of compensating employees for the loss of job security brought about by dismissal. In a sense, the policy behind the award is similar to that underlying the redundancy payments scheme and this is reflected in the way the award is calculated. The award is normally calculated by referencce to the employee's age and length of service at the effective date of termination, but in union-related dismissals there is a statutory obligation to award a fixed amount as a minimum basic award. This amount is unrelated to the employee's age or length of service.

5.2 CALCULATING THE BASIC AWARD

There are two main elements in the calculation of the basic award. These are the employee's length of service at the effective date of termination and the employee's age at the time of dismissal. The award is calculated by working out the number of reckonable years of continuous employment and then multiplying those years by the appropriate statutory factor. The employee is allowed (ERA 1996, s. 119(1) and (2)):

(a) one and a half weeks' pay for each year of employment in which he was not below the age of 41;
(b) one week's pay for each year of employment in which he was below the age of 41 but not below the age of 22;
(c) half a week's pay for each year of employment in which he was below the age of 22.

The method of calculation is illustrated below:

Example 1: Employee aged 30 has worked for the employer since the age of 20. Weeks' pay @ £150 at the calculation date.

Basic award:	one year × half a week's pay =	£75
	nine years × one week's pay =	£1,350
	Total award =	£1,425

Example 2: Employee aged 50 has worked for the employer for 20 years. Week's pay @ £180 at the calculation date.

Basic award:	10 years × one week's pay =	£1,800
	10 years × one and a half week's pay =	£2,700
	Total award =	£4,500

Note: In both these examples we have assumed that the years spanning the 22nd and 41st years count at the higher rate.

5.2.1 Effective date of termination

The effective date of termination as defined by s. 97 of the Employment Rights Act 1996 depends on whether or not the employee is dismissed with the requisite period of statutory notice (see 1.5.1 above).

Where an employer summarily dismisses an employee or gives him less than the period of notice guaranteed by the statutory provisions, the effective date of termination is the date on which the statutory notice would have expired had it been given (ERA 1996, s. 97(2)). Similarly, if an employee is constructively dismissed, the effective date of termination is extended by the minimum period of notice which the employer was required to give the employee by statute (ERA 1996, s. 97(4)). However, where the employer gives the employee notice which is equivalent to or greater than the statutory minimum, the effective date of termination is the date on which that notice expires (ERA 1996, s. 97(2)).

Note: Establishing the correct effective date of termination can be important because extra years of employment may fall to be included in the calculation.

5.2.2 Straddling years of employment

Prior to the Employment Act 1980 there was some doubt as to whether years of employment which spanned an employee's 22nd or 41st birthday counted. This was because years of service counted only if the employee was above the relevant age limit for the whole of the year. However, the new wording makes it clear that the years which span the 22nd or 41st birthday do count.

The problem now is whether the 'appropriate statutory factor' for such years is the higher rate (i.e., one week's pay for a year which spans an employee's 22nd birthday and one and a half weeks' pay for a year which spans an employee's 41st birthday) or the lower rate (i.e., half a week's pay and one week's pay respectively). Before the Employment Act 1980 was amended it was thought that the lower rate applied because continuity of employment was calculated in weeks. Thus the higher rate would have applied only if the employee was above 22 or 41 in each week of the relevant years, which plainly would not have been the case. However, sch. 2 to the Employment Act 1982 deleted the crucial words 'which consist wholly in weeks' and substituted a calculation based on years of employment with the result that it is now generally thought that such years now count at the higher rate.

5.2.3 Age

In contrast to a redundancy payment, the basic award is not subject to a lower age limit, so employees under the age of 18 are entitled to a payment. Thus, years of employment under the age of 18 count towards the aggregate award.

The basic award is scaled down as employees approach the statutory retirement age of 65. Thus the basic award of an employee who is dismissed after reaching the age of 64 (but before the age of 65) will be scaled down by one-twelfth for every month that the employee's age at the effective date of termination exceeds 64 (ERA 1996, s. 125(3)). For example, an employee who is dismissed one month before his or her 65th birthday would have his or her basic award reduced by eleven-twelfths. Originally the scaling down provisions applied to women in their fifty-ninth year but the Sex Discrimination Act 1986 introduced a unitary statutory retirement age of 65 for men and women and the relevant provisions of s. 73 was amended accordingly (SDA 1986, s. 3).

5.2.4 A week's pay

The rules governing the statutory calculation of a week's pay are set out in ss. 220–229 of the Employment Rights Act 1996 and are considered in Chapter 7.

5.3 MINIMUM BASIC AWARD

5.3.1 Union-related and health and safety dismissals

Generally, there is no statutory right to a minimum basic award, the previous provisions which guaranteed a minimum basic award having been repealed by s. 9(5) of the Employment Act 1980. However, in the case of union membership dismissals, i.e., dismissals which are to be regarded as unfair by virtue of ss. 152 and 153 of the Trade Union and Labour Relations (Consolidation) Act 1992 because they are for a 'union-related' reason, the minimum basic award has been retained and this has been extended by sch. 5 of TURERA 1993 to cases where a health and safety representative is dismissed for carrying out his duties under ERA 1996, s. 100(1)(a) and (b). The statutory minimum is currently £2,770 (TUL(C)RA 1992, s. 156(1) and ERA 1996, s. 120(1)).

The 'statutory minimum' is reviewed annually by the Secretary of State for Employment. Any increase may be made only with parliamentary approval (TULR(C)A 1992, s. 159; ERA 1996, s. 120(2)). The new limits normally take effect on 1 April.

The intention behind these provisions is to ensure that the victims of union-related dismissals receive a guaranteed minimum award. Thus employees will receive the guaranteed minimum if, having calculated the basic award in the ordinary way, the award would be less than the amount guaranteed by the statutory provisions. On the other hand, the statutory minimum is ignored if the award exceeds the minimum guaranteed by the statutory provisions.

Unfair Dismissal: the Basic Award

5.3.2 Redundancy dismissals

An employee is not entitled to receive both a basic award and a redundancy payment. In cases of redundancy, therefore, the redundancy payment is deducted from the basic award (ERA 1996, s. 122(4)). However, such a deduction will not be made if the tribunal finds that redundancy was not the real reason for dismissal (*Boorman* v *Allmakes Ltd* [1995] IRLR 553). For example, if an employer mistakenly makes a redundancy payment in circumstances where the dismissal is automatically unfair under the Transfer of Undertakings (Protection of Employment) Regulations 1981, reg. 8, then the employee will be entitled to recover a basic award despite receiving a redundancy payment.

5.3.2.1 Union dismissals
This general exclusion does not apply where an employee is selected for redundancy in breach of s. 153 of the Trade Union and Labour Relations (Consolidation) Act 1992, i.e., for a reason related to trade union membership, or where a workers' representative is selected for redundancy for carrying out health and safety duties pursuant to ERA 1996, s. 100(1)(a) and (b). In such circumstances, an employee is entitled to a minimum basic award as well as a redundancy payment (TULR(C)A 1992, s. 159). It also does not apply where the employee is dismissed for a reason other than redundancy but receives a redundancy payment as part of the compensatory award (see *Addison* v *Babcock FATA Ltd* [1986] IRLR 388).

5.3.2.2 The 'unreasonable' employee
Where the principal reason for dismissal is redundancy but the employee is not entitled to a redundancy payment because he has:

(a) unreasonably refused an offer of suitable employment (ERA 1996, s. 141(2));
or
(b) unreasonably terminated or given notice to terminate a trial period of employment (s. 141(4)(d)); or
(c) had his contract of employment renewed or is re-engaged under a new employment contract pursuant to s. 141(1) of the Employment Rights Act 1996, so that there is no dismissal,

the maximum basic award is limited to two weeks' pay. The purpose behind this is to prevent the 'unreasonable' employee from recovering the statutory equivalent to a redundancy payment in the form of a basic award.

5.3.3 Maximum basic award

The maximum basic award is fixed by reference to the maximum number of reckonable years of employment, the maximum multiplier provided for under the statutory provisions and the maximum amount of pay which qualifies as a week's pay.

There is a maximum of 20 years' service at a maximum of one and a half weeks' pay for each year of service, the limit of a week's pay being £210 where the effective date of termination is on or after 1 April 1992. Thus the maximum award is £6,300.

5.4 REDUCING THE BASIC AWARD

5.4.1 Contributory fault

The basic award may also be reduced or further reduced where any conduct of the employee (including conduct which did not contribute to the dismissal) was such that it would be 'just and equitable' to reduce or further reduce the award (ERA 1996, s. 122(2)).

This provision is wider than the similar provision in relation to the compensatory award under s. 123(6) of the Employment Rights Act 1996 (see Chapter 16), because it provides for any conduct to be taken into account if that would be just and equitable, whereas only conduct which contributes to the dismissal can be taken into account under s. 123(6). As a result, misconduct which was not known at the time of the dismissal may be taken into account even though it did not contribute to the dismissal (see *Parker Foundry Ltd* v *Slack* [1992] IRLR 11).

Example

An employee is dismissed for fighting. Three weeks after the dismissal, the employer discovers that the employee was working for a trade rival in his spare time. The dismissal is found to be unfair because the employers failed to investigate the question of provocation. In deciding whether to reduce the basic award for contributory fault, the tribunal may take into account both the conduct which led to the dismissal and the conduct which was not known at the time of dismissal.

Apart from this wider power, the general principles are the same as those examined in Chapter 16. Effectively, the award will not be reduced unless the employer is guilty of blameworthy conduct as explained by the Court of Appeal in *Nelson* v *BBC (No. 2)* [1979] IRLR 346. The amount of the reduction is a matter for the tribunal to decide and an appellate court is unlikely to interfere with the tribunal's decision on this point (*Hollier* v *Plysu Ltd* [1983] IRLR 260).

5.4.2 Unreasonable refusal of offer of reinstatement

The basic award may also be reduced by such extent as a tribunal considers just and equitable having regard to its finding that the employee 'has unreasonably refused an offer by the employer which (if accepted) would have the effect of reinstating the complainant in his employment in all respects as if he had not been dismissed' (ERA 1996, s. 122(1)). This provision will apply only where the employer makes an offer which complies with the statutory provisions. An invitation to 'discuss' the situation surrounding dismissal will not amount to such an offer (*McDonald* v *Capital Coaches Ltd* EAT 140/94. Furthermore, it would seem that the employer can rely on this provision only if the offer is one of reinstatement as defined by s. 114(1) of the Employment Rights Act 1996. Thus an offer of re-employment on less favourable terms will not amount to an offer of reinstatement. Neither will an offer of a different job on the same salary (*Artisan Press Ltd* v *Srawley and Parker* [1986] IRLR 126).

Unfair Dismissal: the Basic Award

See 15.4.1.2 below for factors which are taken into account in determining the reasonableness of the employee's refusal.

Although a reduction will normally be made where the employee is found to have acted unreasonably, the tribunal is not bound to make one if it feels that this would not be just and equitable. For example, in *Muirhead & Maxwell Ltd v Chambers* EAT 516/82 the EAT held that the tribunal was entitled to conclude that it was inequitable to reduce the award where the employee's reason for refusing the employer's offer of reinstatement was that he 'feared victimisation'.

5.4.3 Restrictions in union membership dismissals

The same general principles as in ordinary dismissals apply in determining whether the basic award should be reduced for contributory fault in 'union-related' cases. No reduction, therefore, should be made unless the complainant is guilty of 'blameworthy' conduct which contributed to the dismissal (see Chapter 16). However, certain special statutory rules apply to the calculation of the basic award in union membership cases.

5.4.3.1 Matters to be disregarded

No reduction or further reduction in the basic award should be made where the employee's conduct amounts to a breach of a requirement to be a union member or non-member or to take part in trade union activities (TULR(C)A 1992, s. 155). Tribunals should also ignore a refusal to comply with a requirement to make a payment in lieu of union subscriptions or an objection to deductions from pay for that purpose.

Thus an employee who previously agreed to such a payment may not be held to have contributed to the dismissal if that agreement is subsequently withdrawn. It is hard to imagine a case where the employee would be held to have contributed to the dismissal under ss. 152 and 153 of the Trade Union and Labour Relations (Consolidation) Act 1992.

5.4.3.2 Minimum award

As a general rule, there can be no reduction of the basic award for contributory fault where the reason or principal reason for dismissal is redundancy. This provision is intended to preserve an employee's full entitlement to a redundancy payment. However, the restriction does not apply where an employee would be entitled to receive a minimum basic award, e.g., where a dismissal is automatically unfair under s. 153 of the Trade Union and Labour Relations (Consolidation) Act 1992 due to selection on the grounds of trade union membership or non-membership (see 5.3.1 above). In such circumstances, the statutory minimum basic award may be reduced for contributory fault but the reduction may not exceed the minimum an employee is entitled to receive as a basic award. For example, where an employee with two years' service who is aged 25 and who earns £200 a week is selected for redundancy for union-related reasons, he would normally be entitled to a redundancy payment of £400 but is entitled to a minimum basic award of £2,700. In such circumstances, the award may be reduced for contributory fault by £2,300.

5.5 DEDUCTIONS FROM THE BASIC AWARD

The basic award is a statutory award and may be reduced only where this is authorised by the statutory provisions (*Cadbury Ltd* v *Doddington* [1977] ICR 982); it therefore cannot be reduced where, for example, the employee has failed to mitigate his loss (*Lock* v *Connell Estate Agents Ltd* [1994] IRLR 444) or where the tribunal considers this to be 'just and equitable' (*Sahil* v *Kores Nordic (GB) Ltd* EAT 379/90).

Deductions in respect of redundancy payments are dealt with at 5.3.2.1 above.

It has been held that where an ex gratia payment is specifically referable to the employee's statutory right to unfair dismissal compensation, the payment may be relied on as a defence to the employer's statutory liabilities (see *Chelsea Football Club and Athletic Co Ltd* v *Heath* [1981] IRLR 73). (See also Chapter 17 for the effect of an ex gratia payment on unfair dismissal compensation generally.)

6 Unfair Dismissal: the Special Award

6.1 INTRODUCTION

The Employment Act 1982 introduced provisions for a special award in substitution for an additional award to be made to employees whose dismissal is regarded as unfair by reason of what is now ss. 152 and 153 of the Trade Unions and Labour Relations (Consolidation) Act 1992, namely that the employee:

(a) was, or proposed to become, a member of an independent trade union; or
(b) had taken, or proposed to take part at an appropriate time in the activities of an independent trade union; or
(c) had refused, or proposed to refuse, to become or remain a member of a trade union which was not an independent trade union; or
(d) was selected for redundancy for a reason falling within (a)-(c) above.

This was extended by s. 28 and sch. 5 of TURERA 1993 to employees who are dismissed for carrying out health and safety responsibilities prusuant to ERA 1996, s. 100(1)(a) and (b). The special award is made in addition to the basic and compensatory awards.

6.1.1 Entitlement to special award

Entitlement to a special award is conditional on the complainant (i.e., the employee) making a request for re-employment.

Furthermore, a special award will not be made if the principal reason for dismissal is redundancy and the employee has:

(a) unreasonably refused an offer of suitable alternative employment; or
(b) unreasonably terminated a trial period of employment; or
(c) is not regarded as having been dismissed by virtue of s. 138(1) of the Employment Rights Act 1996, i.e., the contract has been renewed or the employee re-engaged consequent upon redundancy. (TULR(C)A 1992, s. 157.)

Subject to these two qualifications, entitlement to a special award is triggered automatically by a request for re-employment and does not depend on the industrial tribunal making such an order.

There is no lower age limit, but the award will be scaled down in the year immediately preceding the statutory retirement age (see 6.2.10 below). In practice the statutory retiring age acts as an upper age limit.

6.2 CALCULATING THE SPECIAL AWARD

Unlike the basic award, the special award is not dependent on an employee's age or length of service. Instead, the level of the award is fixed by statute and depends, in the first instance, on whether or not the tribunal makes an order for re-employment.

6.2.1 No order for re-employment

Where re-employment is requested by the employee but is not ordered by the tribunal, the amount of the special award is fixed at 104 weeks' pay or £13,775 (whichever is the greater) subject to a maximum of £27,500 (TULR(C)A 1992, s. 158(1); ERA 1996, s. 125(1)).

6.2.2 Re-employment order complied with

Where re-employment is ordered by the tribunal and the employer complies with the order, compensation is assessed in the same way as if an ordinary order of reinstatement or re-engagement was made under s. 114 or 115 of the Employment Rights Act 1996. Such an order may be conditional on the employer paying the arrears of pay between the date of dismissal and the date of re-employment. The amount of the award is limited to the current maximum for the compensatory award (see 8.4.3 below).

6.2.3 Re-employment order not complied with

Where an order for re-employment is not complied with, the special award will be either 156 weeks' pay or £20,000, whichever is the greater. However, if the employer satisfies the tribunal that it was not practicable to comply with the re-employment order, the special award will be assessed as if no order had been made (TULR(C)A 1992, s. 158(2); ERA 1996, s. 125(2)(b)).

6.2.3.1 Meaning of compliance
It has been held that an employer who offers an employee a different job does not 'comply' with an order for re-employment. The EAT has said that re-instatement means treating the employee as if he had not been dismissed. Thus re-employment on less favourable terms is insufficient for the purpose of s. 117(3) of the Employment Rights Act 1996 — see 4.4.4 above — and employees are therefore entitled to a full special award (*Artisan Press Ltd* v *Srawley and Parker* [1986] ICR 328).

6.2.3.2 Re-employment not practicable
In general, the same legal principles as in non-union dismissals probably apply in determining whether it was practicable for the employer to comply with an order for re-employment (see 4.2.3 above).

Unfair Dismissal: the Special Award

6.2.3.3 Permanent replacements

The fact that an employer takes on a permanent replacement will normally be disregarded by the tribunal in determining whether it was practicable to comply with an order for re-employment. However, this factor may be taken into account if the employer can show that it was not practicable for him to arrange for the employee's work to be done without engaging a permanent replacement (TULR(C)A 1992, s. 158(6) and ERA 1996, s. 125(6)).

It is possible that employers will be able to rely on this provision where the dismissed employee was a key worker and the dismissal necessitated the employment of a permanent replacement in a labour market where such skills were at a premium.

6.2.4 Review of statutory payments

The financial limits set by s. 159 of the Trade Union and Labour Relations (Consolidation) Act 1992 and the Employment Rights Act 1996, s. 125(7) are subject to periodic review and have been increased many times since they were introduced by the Employment Act 1982. The review normally takes place towards the end of the year (together with the review of other employment protection payments) and the new limits normally take effect on 1 April the following year.

6.2.5 A week's pay

The rules governing the statutory calculation of a week's pay are considered in detail in Chapter 7. The following points have particular relevance to the special award.

First, the statutory maximum which limits the reckonable amount of a week's pay does not apply to the special award. Thus, provided a particular payment counts towards a week's pay, the full amount will be recoverable. An employee's pay is the gross amount, not the net amount (*Secretary of State for Employment* v *John Woodrow & Sons (Builders) Ltd* [1983] ICR 582).

Secondly, the statutory provisions do not specify the calculation date for the special award (see 7.5.3 below). But, in *Payne* v *Port of London Authority* 15560/89/LN/C, the industrial tribunal rejected the argument that the failure to provide for a calculation date meant that a tribunal could award only the amounts specified under what is now s. 158(1) and (2) of the Trade Union and Labour Relations (Consolidation) Act 1992. The industrial tribunal considered that 'in default of a statutory method of calculating a week's pay, the matter is at large and we have to do the best we can in the circumstances applying our knowledge of industry and common sense to give effect to the statutory provisions for a remedy in the case of trade union dismissals'.

6.2.6 Scaling down

As with redundancy payments and the basic award, the special award is scaled down as employees approach the statutory retirement age of 65 (TULR(C)A 1992, s. 158(3)) (see 5.2.3 above). Thus the special award of an employee who is dismissed after the age of 64 but before the age of 65 will be scaled down by one-twelfth for every month that the employee's age at the date of termination exceeds 64 (ERA 1996, s. 125(3)).

6.3 REDUCING THE SPECIAL AWARD

Like other statutory awards for unfair dismissal, the special award may be reduced in certain circumstances. Some of the grounds for reduction, such as contributory fault, are similar to those to be found elsewhere in the statutory provisions. Other grounds of reduction are more specific to the special award and there are certain matters which tribunals should ignore.

6.3.1 General grounds for reduction

The special award may be reduced where the tribunal considers that any conduct by the complainant before the dismissal (or, where the dismissal was with notice, before the notice was given) was such that it would be just and equitable to reduce or further reduce it (TULR(C)A 1992, s. 158(4) and ERA 1996, s. 125(4)).

The same general principles as in other cases will apply in determining whether the special award should be reduced for contributory fault (see Chapter 16). Thus before the award is reduced, it will be necessary for the employer or the trade union (in cases where the trade union is a party to the proceedings) to show blameworthy conduct on the part of the employee (*Nelson* v *BBC (No. 2)* [1979] IRLR 346). This is not confined to conduct which amounts to a breach of contract or tort, but covers any conduct which was unreasonable in all the circumstances of the case (*Transport & General Workers' Union* v *Howard* [1992] IRLR 170).

It is for the tribunal to assess the extent of the employee's contribution and reduce the award accordingly. The EAT is unlikely to interfere with the tribunal's decision on the extent of the reduction (*Hollier* v *Plysu Ltd* [1983] IRLR 260).

6.3.2 Special grounds for reduction

Under s. 158(5) of the Trade Union and Labour Relations (Consolidation) Act 1992 and ERA 1996, s. 125(5), the special award may be reduced where a tribunal finds that the employee unreasonably:

(a) prevented compliance with an order of reinstatement or re-engagement; or
(b) refused an offer made by the employer other than one which was in compliance with the order which if accepted would have had the effect of reinstating the employee.

It is for the tribunal to assess the amount by which the special award should be reduced in the light of its finding on this point.

6.3.3 Matters to be disregarded

In deciding whether an employee has contributed to his dismissal in 'union related' cases, the tribunal must disregard any conduct which constitutes (TULR(C)A 1992, s. 155(2)):

Unfair Dismissal: the Special Award

(a) a breach, or proposed breach, of any requirement that the employee should
   (i) be or become a member; or
   (ii) cease to be or refrain from becoming a member; or
   (iii) not take part in the activities of any trade union or one of a number of particular trade unions; or

(b) a refusal or proposed refusal to comply with a requirement to make a payment or payments in the event of his failure to become or his ceasing to remain a member of any trade union or particular trade union or one of a number of particular trade unions; or

(c) an objection or proposed objection (however expressed) to the operation of a provision for the deduction of such a sum or sums from his remuneration.

But this does not prevent an industrial tribunal from taking into account the general conduct of the complainant prior to his or her dismissal. For example, in *Transport & General Workers' Union* v *Howard* [1992] IRLR 170, the EAT held that it was open to an industrial tribunal to hold that a former member of the TGWU, who was dismissed in contravention of s. 152 of TULR(C)A when she joined APEX, had contributed to her dismissal by resigning from the TGWU 'without any prior discussion'. The EAT said it was possible to draw a distinction between what was done and the way it was done. The statutory provisions required a tribunal to disregard the former but not the latter.

6.3.4 Joinder provisions

If, in any proceedings before an industrial tribunal, the employer or the employee claims that:

(a) the employer was induced to dismiss the employee by the actual or threatened calling, organising, procuring or financing a strike or other industrial action; and

(b) such pressure was exercised because the employee was not a member of a trade union or particular trade union,

the employer or the employee may ask the tribunal to direct that the trade union be joined as a party to the proceedings (TULR(C)A 1992, s. 160(1)).

6.3.5 Complaint well-founded

In cases where the trade union is joined as a party to the proceedings and the tribunal considers the complaint of pressure well-founded, it may make an order that the trade union pays such amount (which can extend to a full indemnity) as the tribunal considers just and equitable in the circumstances (TULR(C)A 1992, s. 160(3)). Thus trade unions may become liable to pay the enhanced awards of unfair dismissal compensation in closed shop dismissals.

7 A Week's Pay

7.1 PROBLEMS OF DEFINITION

If an employee was asked to define what he thought his week's pay was, he would probably say that it was the amount he earned in the course of a normal working week. In giving that answer he would not be far from identifying the intention underlying the statutory provisions. However, what may appear to be a comparatively simple question is complicated by the different shift patterns and payment structures which exist in industry. For example, there are some workers, e.g., shift workers and piece workers, whose pay varies from week to week.

A further problem arises in relation to the number of hours of employment which count in the calculation of a week's pay; the hours an employee actually works do not necessarily count for the purpose of the statutory provisions. For example, most employees would probably include overtime payments as part of their week's pay, but overtime payments rarely count in the statutory calculation of a week's pay (see 7.2.4.1 below). In order, therefore, to determine what is meant by a week's pay it is necessary to turn to the Employment Rights Act 1996 and its relevant provisions to see how these have been interpreted by the courts and tribunals.

The statutory provisions governing the calculation of a week's pay are to be found in ss. 220 to 229 of the Employment Rights Act 1996. These provisions apply whenever it is necessary to calculate a week's pay for statutory purposes (ERA 1996, s. 220).

Central to the statutory provisions is the distinction between employments with normal working hours and those with no normal working hours, since this determines which of the two basic statutory formulae applies. It should be noted that the formula used to work out a week's pay in cases where there are no normal hours of work is potentially the more generous since it is based on an employee's average earnings over a 12-week period prior to the calculation date (see 7.4 below).

It would seem that the broad object of the statutory provisions is to distinguish between those employments which follow a fixed pattern of work and those where the hours of work fluctuate with the demands of the business. However, the statutory provisions are technical and complex and it is not always easy to determine which formula is appropriate.

7.2 NORMAL WORKING HOURS

There is no general definition of normal working hours in ss. 220 to 229 but some guidance for particular cases is given in s. 234 which provides:

> (1) Where an employee is entitled to overtime pay when employed for more than a fixed number of hours in a week or other period, there are for the purposes of this Act normal working hours in his case.
> (2) Subject to subsection (3), the normal working hours in such a case are the fixed number of hours.
> (3) Where in such a case—
>   (a) the contract of employment fixes the number, or minimum number, of hours of employment in a week or other period (whether or not it also provides for the reduction of that number or minimum in certain circumstances), and
>   (b) that number or minimum number of hours exceeds the number of hours without overtime,
> the normal working hours are that number or minimum number of hours (and not the number of hours without overtime).

Thus the following are all examples of employments with normal working hours:

Example one — hours fixed by contract

An employee whose contract provides for 40 hours a week works a fixed number of hours, i.e., 40 hours, and therefore the employment is one for which there are normal working hours.

Example two — piece workers

Piece workers, whose rate of pay varies with output but who have hours of work which are fixed, are treated as having normal working hours despite the variation in the rate of pay. The particular statutory formula applicable to piece workers takes the variation in pay into account (s. 221(3)).

Example three — rota workers

Less obviously, in the case of persons working on a different shifts in accordance with a rota, provided the shift pattern is fixed in advance, the employment will count as one for which there are normal working hours. Again, the statutory formula takes the different shift patterns into account (s. 222).

7.2.1 Regular overtime no bar to normal working hours

Regular overtime working does not prevent the employment from being one for which there are normal working hours. For example, in one case a group of bakers claimed that they had no normal working hours because the hours they worked depended upon how long the bread took to bake. However, the employers succeeded in their argument that their redundancy payments still fell to be calculated on the basis that the 40 hour week fixed by their contract was their normal working week (*Minister of Labour* v *County Bake Ltd* [1968] ITR 379).

7.2.2 Other employments with normal working hours

The statutory provisions quoted in 7.2 do not purport to give an exhaustive definition of employments with normal working hours and, as the EAT recognised in *Fox* v *C Wright (Farmers) Ltd* [1978] ICR 98, there may be other employments which are capable of being so regarded. In such circumstances, said the EAT, it is necessary to approach the matter 'according to general principles without the benefit of any statutory definition'. However, the EAT failed to spell out what factors tribunals should take into account in the determination of this issue. The matter is further complicated by a number of inconsistent decisions which make it difficult to predict on which side of the dividing line a particular employment is likely to fall.

For example, in *Fox* the EAT held that an agricultural stockman who worked 'as long as the work and the beasts demanded' was nonetheless in an employment with normal working hours because under the relevant order determining agricultural wages he was entitled to overtime pay if he worked more than 40 hours a week. The EAT ruled that those were his 'normal working hours' even though he would often work between 50 and 60 hours a week. The EAT's decision, however, has been criticised on the grounds that the order did not say what the normal hours of work were but simply stated when overtime rates became payable. Moreover, it is clear that the reasoning in *Fox* may lead to arbitrary results. For example, if on the same facts, another stockman had worked only 35 hours a week, he would still be entitled to receive a redundancy payment based on a 40-hour week. Indeed, it may be thought that Mr Fox was a classic example of an employee who had no normal hours of work.

By way of contrast, in *Cooper* v *Secretary of State for Employment* COIT 1717/223, an industrial tribunal found that coach drivers who were on call 24 hours a day, 7 days a week, subject to the limitations of the regulations on drivers' hours, had no normal working hours. The tribunal reached this conclusion despite evidence that the drivers were paid overtime if they were required to work more than 40 hours a week. The EAT's ruling in *Fox* does not appear to have been considered by the tribunal and the two decisions would seem to be irreconcilable.

7.2.3 Employments with no normal working hours

The key feature which would seem to distinguish employment with no normal working hours from employments with normal working hours is that in the former the employee's hours of working fluctuate with the demands of the business, i.e., there is no fixed pattern of work. However, as indicated in 7.2.2 above, the EAT's decision in *Fox* v *C Wright Farmers Ltd* [1978] ICR 98 makes it difficult to say with certainty where the dividing line lies.

A good example of an employment with no normal working hours would be a casual worker who is paid on commission such as an ice cream vendor. There may also be other similar kinds of employment where the employee may be held to have no normal working hours. See *Cooper v Secretary of State for Employment* COIT 1717/223 (see 7.2.1.2 above).

7.2.4 Which hours count as normal working hours

In practice, most employments fall within the concept of normal working hours, so in most cases the real issue is what hours count as normal working hours. However, rather confusingly, the answer to this question is to be found in the same statutory provisions as those which have already been considered in connection with the issue of whether the employment is one with normal working hours.

Thus to paraphrase the statutory provisions (s. 234 quoted in full at 7.2 above) — the number of hours which count as normal working hours is the minimum number of hours of employment as fixed by the contract of employment. Where the contract clearly and unambiguously defines the employee's minimum hours of work, those hours will be the employee's normal working hours for the purpose of calculating a week's pay (*Gascol Conversions Ltd v Mercer* [1974] IRLR 155).

7.2.4.1 Overtime hours
As a general rule, overtime hours do not form part of an employee's normal working hours. This is because normal working hours are defined as the minimum number of hours specified in the contract of employment (s. 234).

Thus where overtime is voluntary on both sides, the normal working hours are the minimum number of hours an employee is required to work under the contract of employment (*Tarmac Roadstone Holdings Ltd v Peacock* [1973] IRLR 157). However, overtime hours do count when they form part of an employee's basic contractual hours. Thus in *The Ouseburn Transport Co Ltd v Mundell* EAT 371/80, Mr Mundell's contract guaranteed a minimum of 45 hours' work a week and the EAT held that his redundancy payment should be calculated on the basis of a normal working week of 45 hours.

A problem arises where the employee is obliged to work overtime but the employer's obligation to provide work is limited to the contractual minimum. This problem was considered by the Court of Appeal in *Tarmac Roadstone Holdings Ltd v Peacock*. Mr Peacock and his colleagues were employed by Tarmac Roadstone as maintenance fitters. Under their contracts of employment they were obliged to work a minimum of 40 hours a week but, in addition, they could be required to work overtime 'in accordance with the demands of the industry during the normal week and/or at weekends'. When they were made redundant. Mr Peacock and his colleagues claimed that their redundancy payment should have been calculated on the basis of the number of hours they regularly worked, i.e., 57 hours a week, but their employers based their calculation on the minimum number of hours as defined by the contract of employment, i.e., 40 hours. The Court of Appeal held that the method used by the employers was correct. The reason, in Lord Denning's judgment, was that the contract did not guarantee work above the minimum, as required by sch. 14, para. 2 (now see ERA 1996, s. 234(3)) and therefore overtime hours were excluded by the wording of para. 1 (now see ERA 1996, s. 234(1)).

An alternative interpretation is that s. 234(3) does not require overtime to be compulsory on both sides — all it requires is that the contract should fix the number of hours of employment including overtime. In *Mundell* the EAT stressed that the crucial factor was whether the contract *fixed* the number of hours, not whether those hours were compulsory. However, the ruling in *Peacock* was confirmed and applied by the Court of Appeal in *Lotus Cars Ltd* v *Sutcliffe* [1982] IRLR 381 (see 7.2.4.2 below) so the present position is that overtime hours will only be included in the calculation of a week's pay where overtime is guaranteed by the employer and is compulsory on the employee.

7.2.4.2 Contracts and particulars of employment and other evidence of normal working hours
Normal working hours may be defined in a formal contract of employment or the statutory statement of written particulars of employment which should state 'any terms and conditions relating to ... normal working hours' (ERA 1996, s. 1(4)(c)). Note, however, that a written statement is not conclusive proof of the terms agreed between the parties and can be challenged if it is inaccurate (*Systems Floors (UK)* v *Daniel* [1981] IRLR 475 and *Alexander & Others* v *Standard Telephone & Cables Ltd (No. 2)* [1991] IRLR 286).

In the absence of a formal written contract or a statement of particulars of employment, the tribunal will have to look at other evidence of normal working hours. Thus, in *Fox* v *C Wright Farmers Ltd* [1978] ICR 98, the EAT relied on the terms of a wages council order to establish Mr Fox's normal working hours.

Where the contractual provisions relating to normal working hours are unclear, the court or tribunal will be required to construe the contract carefully in order to determine the precise nature of the respective obligations of the parties.

For example, in *Lotus Cars Ltd* v *Sutcliffe* [1982] IRLR 381, Mr Sutcliffe's contract included two terms relating to his working hours. His 'basic' working week was 40 hours, but his 'standard' week was 45 hours, the extra being regarded as 'normal extra time' and carrying a supplementary pay increment. The staff handbook also included a profit sharing scheme based on production levels which could only be achieved by working a 45-hour week. When he was made redundant, Mr Sutcliffe argued that his redundancy pay should be calculated on the basis that his normal hours of work were 45 hours a week. However, the company based its calculation on his basic 40-hour week.

Both the industrial tribunal and the EAT agreed with Mr Sutcliffe, but their rulings were overturned by the Court of Appeal who found in favour of the company. The Court said that on a true construction of the contract, the provision of work during 'normal extra time' was at the discretion of the employers.

7.2.5 Variation in normal working hours

Another problem arises where it is alleged that there has been a variation in the terms of the contract. Thus employees who have been required to work overtime over a long period may argue that their contractual working hours are the hours they actually work. In general, tribunals are unlikely to accept this argument.

In *The Darlington Forge Ltd* v *Sutton* (1968) 3 ITR 196, Mr Sutton, a foundry worker, claimed that his normal working hours should be the average number of hours he worked rather than the 40 hours specified by his contract, as it was essential that the furnaces were kept going. However, the High Court said that there had been no variation in his contract of employment and the fact that overtime working was essential to the company did not mean that it was guaranteed by the contract. The employers were therefore correct to calculate his redundancy payment on a basic 40-hour week. Similarly, in *FMC (Meat) Supply Ltd* v *Wadsworth, Dey and Scrimshaw* EAT 20/83, the EAT said that regular working beyond the hours fixed by the contract did not affect normal working hours for the purpose of calculating a week's pay.

7.2.5.1 Agreed variation

In exceptional circumstances, however, courts and tribunals will give effect to an agreed variation in contractual hours where this is clearly established by the evidence (see *Saxton* v *National Coal Board* [1970] 5 ITR 196, where a local agreement was held to take precedence over a national agreement). Such a variation may be shown to have been agreed expressly between the parties or agreement to it may be implied from their conduct.

For example, in *Barrett* v *National Coal Board* [1978] ICR 1101, a national agreement fixed the normal working week for surface workers at 40 hours, but it also provided that an 'arrangement' to work extra shifts could be made locally. Mr Barrett, a fan attendant, worked 56 hours a week in accordance with an informal local arrangement. When he was made redundant, he claimed that his redundancy payment should be calculated on the hours specified by the informal arrangement i.e., that his normal working hours were 56 hours a week. The EAT remitted the case to the industrial tribunal, saying that the absence of a written agreement was not fatal to Mr Barrett's case as there might have been a more informal arrangement to the same effect.

7.2.5.2 Implied variation

A variation may also be implied. *Armstrong Whitworth Rolls Ltd* v *Mustard* [1971] 1 All ER 598 is one of the few reported cases where the argument that there had been an implied variation was successful. In that case, Mr Mustard's contract was subject to a national agreement which specified a 40-hour week. However, after one of his colleagues left, Mr Mustard was told by his foreman to work a 12-hour shift instead of an 8 hour one. The industrial tribunal ruled that the foreman's instruction to work extra hours resulted in a variation in the contract, raising the required minimum to 60 hours a week. However, this decision (although correct on the facts) is very much the exception to the general trend.

7.2.6 Short-time working

Short-time working is all too common a feature of the current industrial climate since it is often seen as preferable to redundancy. In such cases, the general reluctance of courts and tribunals to find a variation in contractual arrangements works to the employee's advantage in relation to short-time working.

Thus, in *Friend* v *PMA Holdings Ltd* [1976] ICR 330, during the 'three-day week', a group of employees came to a temporary arrangement with their employers to work as and when work was available. When they were made redundant, the company said that this arrangement amounted to a variation in their contractual hours of work and therefore their redundancy payment should be calculated on the basis of their average working hours in accordance with ERA 1996, s. 224. The EAT, however, said that the arrangement was designed to meet an emergency, with the result that there was no variation in the contract.

Nonetheless, care should be taken in relation to formal agreements between trade unions and employees on short-time working, since such an agreement which is incorporated into an individual employee's contract may well result in a change to contractual provisions on normal working hours. The status quo may be preserved by including a clause in the collective agreement. For example, the TUC model clause states:

> This agreement is for a temporary period only and is being introduced solely in order to avoid redundancies. This agreement does not affect the existing contracts of employment of any employees: these contracts will remain in force for the duration of short-time working. Should any redundancies still occur during this short-time agreement, then entitlements to redundancy payment shall not be adversely affected by these short-time arrangements and, in particular, the amount of a week's pay used in the statutory calculation for redundancy payments shall be the amount payable under the contract of employment relating to normal working hours.

In essence, this wording preserves the contractual entitlement to a full week's pay during a period of short-time working in the event of redundancy. Where so desired, it should be extended to cover other statutory rights such as the calculation of statutory notice pay which may also be affected by short-time working agreements.

7.3 REMUNERATION

The other key difference between the meaning of a week's pay under statute and the actual amount an employee takes home in his pay packet relates to the statutory definition of 'pay' since some payments received by an employee do not count towards a week's pay. Essentially, a week's pay is the amount of 'remuneration' payable by the employer under a 'contract of employment in force on the calculation date'. The meaning of 'remuneration' is considered below; the meaning of 'calculation date' is dealt with at 7.4 below.

7.3.1 Meaning of remuneration

There is no statutory definition of what payments count as remuneration but, as a general rule, remuneration includes all the contractual payments an employee receives from the employer for work done (*S & U Stores Ltd* v *Wilkes* [1974] 3 All ER 401).

In *S & U Stores Ltd* v *Wilkes* the NICR said that 'any sum which is paid as a wage or salary without qualification is part of an employee's remuneration'. In most cases therefore basic wages or salary will be the main element in a week's pay.

It may also include other payments regularly made to the employee. For example, in *A & B Marcusfield Ltd* v *Melhuish* [1977] IRLR 484, the EAT held that a bonus regularly paid to an employee formed part of her remuneration even though it was not included in her contract of employment. Discretionary payments, such as Christmas bonuses, will not normally qualify as remuneration. Similarly, benefits in kind will not count as they do not qualify as remuneration (see 7.3.10 below). It should be noted that some disparity in tribunal decisions may be explained by the differences in wording under the different statutory formulae, with the result that certain payments may count for some workers but not for others.

A week's pay is calculated on the basis of an employee's gross earnings (*Secretary of State for Employment* v *John Woodrow & Sons (Builders) Ltd* [1983] IRLR 11).

7.3.2 Rate of pay

The rate of pay is the real rate rather than some artificial or notional rate (*Adams* v *John Wright & Sons (Blackwall) Ltd* [1972] ICR 463). For example, an employer who says to an employee that his rate of pay is 50 pence an hour but that he will receive an additional 50 pence for every hour worked is merely using an artificial way of saying that his real rate is £1 an hour (see *Mole Mining Ltd* v *Jenkins* [1972] ICR 282 and 7.3.4 below.)

In employments covered by wages council orders, the minimum rate is that prescribed by the order, even if the employer pays less (*Cooner* v *P S Doal & Sons* [1988] IRLR 338).

7.3.3 Productivity schemes

The principle laid down in *S & U Stores Ltd* v *Wilkes* [1974] 3 All ER 401 (see 7.3.1 above) has been applied to employees who receive incentive payments under productivity schemes. Employees who receive incentive payments over and above certain production levels will normally be able, therefore, to include such payments in their 'week's pay' (*Ogden* v *Ardphalt Asphalt Ltd* [1977] 1 All ER 267).

7.3.4 Bonus payments and commission

For the reason given at 7.3.2 above, bonus payments and commission to which an employee is entitled usually fall to be included in a week's pay. In *Mole Mining Ltd* v *Jenkins* [1972] ICR 282, Mr Jenkins' contract provided that he would be entitled to a shift bonus of one-fifth of a shift for every shift he worked, with the result that if he worked five shifts he would be credited with a payment for an extra shift. When he was made redundant, his redundancy payment did not include his shift bonus. His employers argued that the shift bonus was not a payment for work done, but both the industrial tribunal and the EAT disagreed, ruling that the shift bonus should have been included in the calculation of the redundancy payment. Similarly, in *Weevsmay Ltd* v *Kings* [1977] ICR 244, the EAT ruled that the commission received by a debt collector on the amount he collected, formed part of his remuneration.

7.3.5 Discretionary payments

Discretionary payments do not usually count as remuneration. However, following the Court of Appeal's decision in *Nerva and Ors* v *RL & G Ltd* [1996] IRLR 461, a waiter's tips will normally be included in his week's pay unless the tips are paid in cash direct to the waiter (see *Palmanor Ltd t/a Chaplins Night Club* v *Cedron* [1978] IRLR 303 and *Tsoukka* v *Ptoomac Restaurants Ltd* (1968) 3 ITR 259). In *Tsoukka*, the employers operated a 'tronc' and the employees were held to be entitled to their share of the tips which formed part of their remuneration.

It is also possible that other discretionary bonuses, such as payments under a profit sharing scheme, do not count, though much depends on the contractual nature of the scheme. A discretionary bonus may be included if it is paid regularly (*A & B Marcusfield Ltd* v *Melhuish* [1977] IRLR 484).

7.3.6 Overtime pay

On the face of it, overtime payments clearly fall within the statutory definition of remuneration and therefore prima facie should normally be taken into account in the calculation of a week's pay. However, overtime payments will count towards a week's pay only if overtime hours form part of an employee's normal working hours (see 7.2.4.1 above). Furthermore, in certain circumstances, overtime premia, i.e., additional payments received by an employee for working overtime, are excluded from the calculation of a week's pay. For example, where it is necessary to calculate the 'average hourly rate of pay' (including overtime hours — see 7.5.1.2 below), the calculation should be made as if the work had been done in normal working hours and the amount of that overtime remuneration reduced accordingly. The effect of this provision is that overtime premia are ignored and overtime hours are rated at an employee's ordinary hourly rate.

Note: This exclusion affects employees whose rate of pay varies with output, such as piece workers, and employees whose rate of pay varies with the number of hours they work, such as shift workers or rota workers (see *Example 1* below). It would appear that the statutory exclusion of overtime premia does not apply to employees whose pay is constant (s. 222(1)). Thus, in such circumstances, provided overtime hours form part of such an employee's normal working hours, overtime premia are included in the calculation of a week's pay (see *Example 2* below). Similarly, the statutory exclusion of overtime premia would not seem to apply to employees whose employment is one for which there are no normal working hours (s. 224).

Example 1

An employee works a 40-hour week in week one, a 45-hour week in week two and a 39-hour week in week three. All hours above 39 hours are overtime and are paid at time and a half.

The additional premium rate does not count for the purpose of calculating a week's pay.

Example 2

An employee works a basic 40 hours week with a further 4 hours guaranteed overtime. All hours above 40 hours are paid at time and a half.

The additional premium rate does count for the purpose of calculating a week's pay.

7.3.7 Holiday pay

Holiday pay is normally regarded as part of an employee's remuneration, but payments received in advance of a holiday are excluded. An example of such a practice is the 'stamp system' in the building trade whereby the employer purchases credit stamps from a management company and gives them each week to the employee. The stamps are cashed in when the holiday is taken and therefore do not count as part of the week's pay in the week in which they are given (*Secretary of State for Employment* v *Haynes* [1980] IRLR 270).

7.3.8 Allowances

Allowances cover a wide variety of payments ranging from simple reimbursement of expenses to attendance allowances.

7.3.8.1 Allowances: general principles
In general, where the allowance is intended to be a reimbursement for expenses, it will not count towards the calculation of a week's pay (see 7.3.9 below), but where an allowance is a way of paying additional wages or salary, it will.

For example, an attendance allowance will count as part of an employee's remuneration (*London Brick Company Ltd* v *Bishop* EAT 624/78). Similarly, compensatory payments such as London weighting should be regarded as part of an employee's remuneration, though there is no reported case on this point. An allowance for working anti-social hours or for working in abnormal conditions has been held to count as part of a shift worker's remuneration (*Randell* v *Vosper Shiprepairers Ltd* COIT 1723/13 (IDS 323)).

7.3.8.2 Travelling time
It is more doubtful whether an allowance paid for travelling time counts as part of a week's pay. In *N G Bailey & Co Ltd* v *Preddy* [1971] 3 All ER 225, the High Court ruled that, for the purpose of calculating a redundancy award, it did not, because such payments fell outside an employee's normal working hours. However, this reasoning would not apply to employments with no normal working hours (see 7.3.14 below). Moreover, the wording of the provisions has been slightly amended since the *Preddy* decision and now states that payments received by employees 'throughout normal working hours' are to be included in an employee's remuneration. Thus the better view is that payments for travelling time (as opposed to travel expenses) do count, provided the travelling time is included in the employee's normal hours of work.

7.3.9 Expenses

Sums genuinely paid as expenses do not form part of an employee's remuneration. Thus in *A M Carmichael Ltd* v *Laing* (1972) 7 ITR 1, it was held that a lodging allowance paid to a driver who worked on construction sites in the North of England and Scotland was reimbursement for lodging expenses and therefore did not form part of the driver's remuneration. Similarly, travel expenses will not normally form part of an employee's remuneration because such payments are simply intended to be reimbursement for expenditure incurred by the employee in the course of travelling to and from work (*S & U Stores Ltd* v *Wilkes* [1974] 3 All ER 401).

A payment which exceeds the amount actually spent by the employee is still regarded as expenses, provided it is a genuine pre-estimate of the costs likely to be incurred. In *Josling* v *Plessey Telecommunications Ltd* IRLIB 243, August 1982, Mrs Josling received a weekly travel allowance of £28.41. The rate of her allowance was fixed by a collective agreement. However, because she travelled to work with a friend, she made considerable savings and she argued that those savings formed part of her week's pay. The industrial tribunal disagreed. It said that the allowance was a genuine attempt by her employers to assess her travel costs and that therefore the surplus did not form part of her remuneration (see also *London Borough of Southwark* v *O'Brien* [1996] IRLR 420).

If it is shown that expenses are in reality a disguised form of payment, they will count as part of an employee's remuneration but, in such circumstances, there is a real danger of the payment (and as a result the whole contract) being illegal. (See *Tomlinson* v *Dick Evans 'U' Drive Ltd* [1978] IRLR 77.)

7.3.10 Fringe benefits

Remuneration covers only money payments and not fringe benefits. Tribunals have therefore refused to include the value of a company car as part of an employee's remuneration (*Skillen* v *Eastwoods Froy Ltd* (1966) 2 ITR 112) or the value of free accommodation (*Lyford* v *Turquand* (1966) 1 ITR 554). The rule was confirmed by the NIRC in *S & U Stores Ltd* v *Wilkes* [1974] 3 All ER 401.

7.3.11 Pensions

At one time, a pension was considered to be an ex gratia payment, i.e., a gift to an employee from an employer as a reward for long service. In recent years it has been argued that this view is out of date and that an employer's contribution to an occupational pension scheme should be regarded as part of an employee's remuneration provided the employee has a contractual right to such pension contribution from his employer. Support for the view that pension contributions form part of a week's pay may be found in a number of authorities involving the definition of pay for related purposes. (See *Barber* v *Royal Guardian Exchange Assurance Group* [1990] IRLR 240, where pension contributions were treated as 'pay' under Article 119 of the Treaty of Rome; and *The Halcyon Skies* [1976] 1 All ER 856, where employer contributions to an occupational pension scheme were held to form part of a seaman's wages for the purpose of a claim under section 1(1)(o) of the

A Week's Pay 77

Administration of Justice Act 1956.) It should also be noted that the Inland Revenue treat such contributions as 'remuneration' for tax purposes. However, in *Payne* v *Port of London Authority* 155560/89/LN/C an industrial tribunal has recently held that pension contributions do not count towards a week's pay. The tribunal considered that although pensions contributions might be regarded as pay for some statutory purposes, e.g., for equal treatment of women, pension contributions did not count towards a week's pay for this purpose because:

> they cannot be characterised as sums which an employee is entitled to receive under the contract of employment. They are (commonly) amounts paid by the employer to the pension fund. They may be varied from time to time at the behest of trustees who act on actuarial advice which itself depends on how the fund is prospering. The employee is never entitled to receive the employer's contributions but only the product which they go towards purchasing for him.

7.3.12 Guarantee payments

Guarantee payments are excluded from the calculation of a week's pay by statute. Thus in relation to employees whose pay is constant (see 7.5.1 below) it is provided that remuneration is based on 'the amount payable by the employer ... if the employee works throughout his normal working hours in a week' (s. 221(2)). Similarly, in relation to piece workers and shift workers, it is provided that 'in arriving at the average hourly rate of remuneration, only — (a) the hours when the employee was working, and (b) the remuneration payable for, or apportionable to, those hours, shall be brought in' (s. 223(1)).

However, employees who have no normal hours of work are not covered by the statutory exclusion and it is possible that guarantee payments are included in the employee's remuneration in such circumstances.

7.3.13 State benefits

Remuneration does not cover payments made by a person other than the employer. This means that state benefits do not count as remuneration. Thus in *Wibberley* v *Staveley Iron and Chemical Company Ltd* (1966) 1 ITR 558 it was held that disablement benefit and special hardship allowance did not form part of a week's pay. The position may be different where the payment is made by the employer but is subject to reimbursement by the government. Thus it is possible that statutory sick pay may count as part of an employee's week's pay, but other payments, such as family credit, do not.

7.3.14 Remuneration in employments with no normal working hours

There are some authorities which suggest that some payments which do not count as remuneration for employees with normal working hours do count where the employment is one for which there are no normal hours of work. For example, in *S & U Stores Ltd* v *Lee* [1969] 2 All ER 417 the court held that a £5 car allowance did form part of Mr Lee's remuneration adding that ''remuneration'' is not mere payment for work done, but is what the doer expects to get as a result of the work he does in so far as what he expects to get is quantified in terms of money'. Such a payment would not normally have been included in a week's pay if the employee had normal working hours (see 7.3.8.2 above).

However, in *S & U Stores Ltd* v *Wilkes* [1974] 3 All ER 401 the NIRC thought it 'improbable' that the different method of calculating a week's pay in cases where there are no normal working hours showed that Parliament intended different standards to apply. The better view is that the meaning of remuneration is the same for both.

7.4 THE CALCULATION DATE

A week's pay is defined as the amount of weekly remuneration payable under the contract of employment in force on the 'calculation date'. The 'calculation date' is defined in s. 225; its meaning depends on the particular payment claimed under the statutory provisions.

These provisions were originally introduced by the Redundancy Payments Act 1965 with the object of protecting employees, particularly piece workers, from having their pay artificially reduced in the notice period. The provisions now apply to other statutory awards and are examined below.

7.4.1 Additional award

In relation to the additional award, the 'calculation date' is either the date on which the employee is given notice (s. 226(2)(a)), or the effective date of termination, i.e., the date of dismissal (s. 226(2)(b))).

7.4.2 Basic award

In relation to the basic award, the position is slightly less straightforward since the 'calculation date' depends on whether the notice which the employee gives or receives exceeds or is less than the statutory minimum (see 1.5.1 for the statutory minimum periods of notice). If the notice is less than the employer's statutory minimum, the calculation date is the employee's last day of work (s. 226(3)). However, if the notice is equivalent to or more than the statutory minimum, the calculation date is determined by ascertaining the statutory minimum period of notice applicable and calculating the latest day when the employer would have needed to give notice in order for the employee's contract to have been terminated on the day that he actually left work (s. 226(6)).

Example 1 — summary dismissal

An employee with four years' service is summarily dismissed, i.e., dismissed without notice, or summarily resigns, i.e., resigns without notice.

The calculation date is the employee's last day of employment. The employee's week's pay will therefore be calculated on the rate of pay in force on the last day of employment.

Example 2 — short notice

An employee with four years' service is given three weeks' notice or gives three weeks' notice.

The calculation date is the date on which the notice expires. Thus a week's pay will be calculated on the rate of pay in force on that day.

Example 3 — statutory minimum notice

An employee with four years' service gives or is given four weeks' notice.

The calculation date is the date when notice is given. Thus a week's pay is calculated on the rate of pay in force at the time.

Example 4 — more notice than statutory minimum

An employee with four years' service is given more than four weeks' notice.

The calculation date is fixed by deducting the employer's statutory minimum from the contractual notice. Thus in the case of an employee who is given six weeks' notice, the calculation date is fixed at the beginning of the third week of the notice period.

7.4.3 Special award

There is no statutory definition of the 'calculation date' for the special award, but the definition which applies in the case of the additional award (see 7.4.1 above) would probably apply (see *Port of London Authority* v *Payne & Others* [1992] IRLR 447 at 6.2.5).

7.4.4 Redundancy payment

In relation to a redundancy payment, the calculation date is determined in the same way as for the basic award (see 7.4.2 above) (ERA s. 226(5), (6)). Thus if the employee is dismissed with no notice, or with less than the statutory minimum period of notice, the calculation date is the date the employment ended; but where the notice exceeds or is equivalent to the statutory minimum, the calculation date is found by deducting the statutory minimum from the notice given.

7.4.5 Backdated payments

A week's pay is calculated on the rate of pay in force on the calculation date. This means that any increase in the rate of pay which occurs after that date is ignored, even if it is backdated. Thus in *Leyland Vehicles Ltd* v *Reston* [1981] IRLR 19, the EAT held that Mr Reston's redundancy payment was based on the rate of pay prevailing at the time of his dismissal and therefore he was not entitled to the benefit of a pay increase awarded after his dismissal even though it was backdated.

Similarly, an employee who agrees to a reduction in his rate of pay in order to avoid or defer redundancy, or as part of an agreement on short-time working, runs the risk that a subsequent redundancy payment or other statutory payment will be calculated on the reduced rate of pay in force at the calculation date i.e., the reduced rate (*Valentine* v *Great Lever Spinning Co Ltd* (1966) 1 ITR 71). Some courts and tribunals may be prepared to mitigate the harshness of this rule by holding that a temporary variation does not amount to an agreed variation in the contractual rate of pay, but it should be noted that this is not possible in the face of a clear agreed variation. Thus employees who agree to a reduction in pay in such circumstances should take care to ensure that by so doing they do not prejudice their rights to a full redundancy payment (see 7.2.6 above).

7.5 METHODS OF CALCULATING A WEEK'S PAY

There are four different ways of calculating a week's pay. It is therefore important to identify which method is appropriate for the particular employees concerned. This will depend on their pattern of work.

7.5.1 Employees with normal working hours

The three different ways of working out a week's pay for employees with normal working hours cover workers whose pay is constant (time workers), workers whose pay varies with output (piece workers) and shift or rota workers whose pay varies with the hours they work but whose employment is still one for which there are normal working hours (see 7.2 above).

7.5.1.1 *Time rates*

The formula for workers on time rates is relatively straightforward. A week's pay is simply the remuneration for working the normal working hours in the week (s. 221(3)). If payment is made monthly or yearly, or by reference to a period longer than a week, the tribunal must apportion the payment in the manner it considers just (s. 229(2)).

Example

An employee works a 40 hour week at £5.00 an hour.
   A week's pay is £200 a week.

   Where the payment includes a variable element such as a commission or bonus, one of the other formulae will apply since the amount of pay will vary with the work done. However, where commission or bonus pay is constant it should be added to the basic rate in the normal way. If the period of commission does not coincide with the period of payment, the remuneration or payments should be apportioned in such manner as may be just. Normally this will be a constant rate of commission over the whole period (*J & S Bickley Ltd* v *Washer* [1977] ICR 425).

Example

An employee earns £500 commission in the first and third quarters of a year and £800 commission in the second and fourth quarters. Total commission is £2,600.

The sum of £50 per week which is the average weekly rate of commission, should be added to the employee's basic weekly rate.

7.5.1.2 Pay varying with output

The formula for workers whose pay varies with output is somewhat more complicated as it is necessary to work out their average hourly rate over a period of 12 weeks.

The average hourly rate is worked out by taking the total remuneration for all the hours actually worked including overtime hours (s. 223(1) and (2)) over a period of 12 weeks prior to the calculation date and dividing it by the number of hours actually worked.

Overtime premia are ignored in the calculation of the average hourly rate (s. 223(3)) with the result that overtime hours are rated as basic hours. This can have the effect of artificially depressing the average hourly rate in cases where an employee receives a guaranteed incentive bonus for work done in ordinary hours but receives only an overtime premium for overtime hours. If that premium is ignored in the calculation, the result is that the rate for overtime hours is considerably lower than for ordinary hours and those who work overtime are penalised (see *British Coal Corporation* v *Cheeseborough* [1989] IRLR 148).

If the calculation date (see 7.4 above) does not coincide with the pay day, the period of 12 weeks is the period ending on the last pay day before the calculation date. For weekly employees the 'pay day' is defined as the day on which they are paid; for other employees it is a Saturday (ERA 1996, s. 235(1)).

After establishing the average hourly rate, the week's pay is arrived at by multiplying the average hourly rate by the normal working hours.

Example

An employee receives £170 for working 45 hours in weeks one, two, three and seven, £180 for 45 hours in weeks four, five and twelve, £200 for a 45-hour week in week eleven and £150 for working a 45-hour week in the remaining weeks, six, eight, nine and ten. The normal working week is 40 hours. Hours above 40 hours are rated as normal working hours.

The total remuneration in the 12-week period is £2,020. The total number of hours worked in the 12 weeks is 540. The average hourly rate is worked out by dividing £2,020 by 540, which gives an AHR of approximately £3.75. The normal working week is 40 hours, so a week's pay is approximately £150.

This formula should be used to calculate a week's pay for piece workers or workers whose bonus or commission varies with output.

7.5.1.3 Variable hours

Where the hours of work vary from week to week over a fixed period, it is necessary to work out both the average hours worked in a given period and the average rate of remuneration received in those hours. The average hourly rate is worked out in the same way as for workers whose pay varies with output (see 7.5.1.2 above). The average number of normal working hours is determined by:

(a) ascertaining the pay day (see 7.5.1.2 above);
(b) ascertaining the calculation date (see 7.4 above);
(c) taking a period of 12 weeks prior to whichever of the two is the earlier and adding together the total number of hours worked excluding overtime hours unless these form part of normal working hours;
(d) dividing the total by 12.

Example

An employee works a four week shift. In week one, the employee works 40 hours and is paid £150. In week two, the employee works 60 hours and is paid £300 (including a special bonus). In week three, the employee works 35 hours and is paid £120 and in week four, the employee works 45 hours and is paid £200. The shift pattern is identical for the whole of the twelve week period.

$$\text{Average normal working hours} = \frac{\text{Total hours of shift} \times 3}{12 \text{ weeks}}$$

$$= \frac{540}{12}$$

$$= 45$$

Average hourly rate is calculated as in 7.5.1.2 above (approximately £4.27 per hour) but remember to take the variation in hours into account.

This formula should be used to calculate a week's pay for shift workers.

7.5.1.4 Weeks without remuneration
In calculating a week's pay in the situations covered by 7.5.1.2 and 7.5.1.3 above, a week in which no remuneration is payable is ignored in the calculation and an earlier week is brought into the calculation in its place until the total of 12 weeks is reached (s. 223(1) and (2)). Guarantee payments are ignored in the calculation (see 7.3.12 above).

7.5.2 Employees with no normal working hours

For employees with no normal working hours, such as casual workers, a week's pay is the average remuneration they receive over a period of 12 weeks including overtime hours and overtime rates. (The exclusion of overtime premia does not apply to employees with no normal working hours.)

Again, the average remuneration is taken over the period of 12 weeks immediately before the calculation date or, if that date is not the same as the pay day, the pay day immediately before the calculation date. Weeks in which no remuneration was payable are ignored and earlier weeks brought in to make the total number of weeks up to 12.

Example

An employee with no normal working hours earns £2,000 in 12 weeks. A week's pay is £165.85.

7.5.3 Recent recruits

There is one further statutory formula which applies to recent recruits. This applies to employees who are dismissed shortly after they start a new job but who still qualify for a statutory notice payment. It may also apply to employees who are dismissed shortly after starting work with an associated employer or the purchaser of a business, if continuity of employment is preserved by the statutory provisions or by the Transfer of Undertakings Regulations 1981.

In such circumstances, the tribunal must determine what 'fairly represents a week's pay', applying the statutory rules as it considers appropriate (s. 228(1)). The tribunal may take into account:

(a) any remuneration received by the employee;
(b) any amount offered as remuneration whether it was paid or not;
(c) any remuneration paid by the employer to employees in comparable positions in the same employment or other employments.

If continuity is preserved by statute, as it is where two employers are associated employers, the tribunal must take into account the average remuneration received by the employee from the previous employer which falls within the period of 12 weeks (s. 229(1)). The average rate is calculated in accordance with one of the formulae set out above.

7.6 STATUTORY MAXIMUM

There is a limit to the amount of pay which counts as a week's pay. This is set by the Secretary of State for Employment and is currently fixed at £210. The figure is reviewed annually and the new rate normally comes into force at the beginning of April in the following year. The statutory limit on a week's pay does not apply to the calculation of the special award which is subject to its own maxima (see 6.2 above), or to the calculation of statutory notice pay.

8 The Compensatory Award: General Principles

8.1 INTRODUCTION

The third element in unfair dismissal compensation is the compensatory award. Unlike the basic and special awards, this is not based on a fixed statutory formula but rests on the simple principle that employees should be compensated for the loss caused to them as a result of their dismissal. Thus in most cases (other than those relating to union membership) the compensatory award will be the largest element in the total award. This chapter looks at the general principles which govern the compensatory award. Chapters 9, 10 and 11 consider the types of payment and the benefits for which compensation may be awarded in detail.

The overriding aim of the compensatory award is to compensate employees for the loss caused by their dismissal to the extent that a tribunal considers 'just and equitable', subject to the statutory maximum. To this effect s. 123(1) of the Employment Rights Act 1996 provides that:

> Subject to the provisions of this section and sections 124 and 126, the amount of the compensatory award shall be such amount as the tribunal considers just and equitable in all the circumstances having regard to the loss sustained by the complainant in consequence of the dismissal in so far as that loss is attributable to action taken by the employer.

This provision gives industrial tribunals a wide discretion over the assessment of the compensatory award and they generally approach this task with the minimum amount of technicality. This approach has been encouraged by the EAT and the Court of Appeal. In *Fougère* v *Phoenix Motor Co Ltd* [1976] IRLR 259, for example, the EAT stressed that tribunals are 'bound of necessity to operate in a rough and ready manner and to paint the picture with a broad brush' rather than as skilled cost accountants or actuaries. However, it would be wrong to conclude that the assessment of the compensatory award is an arbitrary exercise since it has been said that a tribunal must exercise its discretion 'judiciously and upon the basis of principle' (per Sir John Donaldson in *Norton Tool Co Ltd* v *Tewson* [1973] 1 All ER 183). Moreover, a tribunal must set out its reasons in sufficient detail to show the principles used in the assessment.

8.2 COMPENSATION, NOT PUNISHMENT

The object of the compensatory award is to compensate employees for loss caused by their dismissal, and not to punish employers for their wrongdoing. The EAT has therefore said that an award should not be increased either out of sympathy for the employee or as a means of expressing disapproval of the employer's industrial relations policy (*Lifeguard Assurance Ltd* v *Zadrozny* [1977] IRLR 56).

8.2.1 Exceptions

However, there are certain well established exceptions to the above principle. The first exception arises in relation to awards of compensation for loss of notice pay. Here, both the NIRC and the EAT have ruled that as a matter of justice and equity, as well as good industrial relations, employees should always recover their lost notice pay either by way of a payment in lieu from the employer or as part of an award of unfair dismissal compensation and do not have to account for earnings received from new employment during the notice period (see *Norton Tool Co Ltd* v *Tewson* [1973] 1 All ER 183; *TBA Industrial Products Ltd* v *Locke* [1984] IRLR 48 and 9.3.2.2 below). These decisions were approved by the Court of Appeal in *Babcock FATA Ltd* v *Addison* [1987] IRLR 173, and it would appear that the principles of good industrial relations referred to by the court cover both contractual and statutory notice pay. However, as Lord Donaldson MR pointed out, the concept of good industrial relations is not a static one and, in the view of Ralph Gibson LJ, there may be circumstances where an employer might not offend good industrial practice by tendering a lesser sum than the full contractual notice entitlement (see 9.3.2.2 below). It should also be noted that this exception does not appear to apply to cases where the employee is employed under a fixed term contract (*Isleworth Studios Ltd* v *Rickard* [1988] IRLR 137).

Another exception to the general principle is the right to receive compensation for the loss of statutory rights (see Chapter 13).

8.2.2 Date of assessment

The normal rule is that, for the purpose of calculating the compensatory award, the employee's loss is determined at the date of the hearing on quantum. This may not be at the same time as the hearing on liability as it is not uncommon for there to be a split hearing, i.e., *Iggesund Converters Ltd* v *Lewis* [1984] IRLR 431.

The normal rule applies even where the assessment of compensation is delayed because of an appeal to the EAT on the question of liability. For example, in *Ging* v *Ellward Lancs Ltd* (1978) 13 IRT 265, following a successful appeal by the employee, the case was remitted to the industrial tribunal. At the rehearing, which took place some 18 months after the date of dismissal, the tribunal found the dismissal to be unfair and proceeded to assess Mr Ging's loss as at the time of the second hearing. The EAT upheld the tribunal's decision. Mr Justice Arnold said:

> It seems to us that for better or for worse, whether it has an effect one way or whether it has an effect another way, the date to be taken must always be the date

at which the assessment actually takes place, all matters which are uncertain then being assessed by the ordinary operation of forming an estimate as to what will happen in the future.

Similarly, in *Gilham* v *Kent County Council* [1986] IRLR 56, following the employer's unsuccessful appeal on liaiblity, the Court of Appeal remitted the case to the industrial tribunal to assess compensation. The hearing on quantum took place two years and nine months after the date of dismissal. The industrial tribunal accepted the employer's argument that its liability to compensate the employees was limited to a period of one year following the date of dismissal (see 14.3.2 below). However, the EAT, allowing the appeal, ruled that the tribunal was entitled to take into account the employees' loss of earnings for the entire period up to the date of the hearing on quantum. However, these decisions should be contrasted with *Qualcast (Wolverhampton) Ltd* v *Ross* [1979] IRLR 98.

8.2.2.1 Implications
In *Gilham* the rule that the loss is determined at the time of the hearing on quantum worked to the employee's advantage, since Mrs Gilham and her colleagues were still out of work at the time of the second hearing. Sometimes, however, it will be to the employee's disadvantage for the hearing on quantum to be postponed — for example, if the employee receives earnings from a temporary job between the date of the first hearing and the hearing on quantum, those earnings will be set off against his loss of earnings claim. For example in *Ging*, Mr Ging's earnings from a temporary job on an oil rig were set off against the loss of earnings he suffered during two periods of unemployment. In such circumstances it may be prudent for the employee to invite the tribunal to assess compensation as soon as liability is established. (This may also be desirable for the purpose of ensuring that interest starts to run from the earliest opportunity.)

From the employer's point of view, it is generally better to seek to get the issue of compensation determined as soon as possible, since, as the decision in *Gilham* illustrates, tribunals are likely to be more sympathetic to the employee in assessing past loss than future loss. Thus awards are likely to be higher if the hearing on quantum is delayed. In such circumstances employers should ask the tribunal to assess compensation as soon as the decision on liability is known or before the 42-day time limit for an appeal has expired.

8.2.2.2 Exception
However the EAT has recently held that where the employee has found a permanent better paid job by the date of the hearing on quantum, the award will be based on the employee's loss up to the date the employee commenced the new job (*Lytlarch Ltd t/a The Viceroy Restaurant* v *Reid* [1991] ICR 216 and *Fentiman* v *Fluid Engineering Products Ltd* [1991] IRLR 150).

8.3 REMOTENESS

Compensation cannot be recovered if the loss suffered by the employee is too remote, i.e., if it does not arise as a 'consequence of dismissal'. For this reason it has been argued that an employer's liability to pay compensation should cease once the employee has started a 'permanent' new job at an equivalent or better rate of pay, even if the employee is later dismissed from the new job or voluntarily leaves the new job, because any subsequent loss is not a 'consequence of dismissal' attributable to the employer's action. The same argument has been relied on to oppose the payment of compensation where, after dismissal, the employee goes on a training course instead of looking for work. The approach of the EAT and industrial tribunals to this question is considered below.

8.3.1 Permanent new employment

It is accepted, as a matter of principle, that an employer's liability to compensate an employee for loss should cease once the employee obtains a permanent new job at an equivalent or better rate of pay. The problem is whether liability continues where what was thought to be a permanent job turns out to be a temporary one.

A strict approach to the issue of causation was adopted by the EAT in *Courtaulds Northern Spinning Ltd* v *Moosa* [1984] IRLR 43. There the EAT held that the employers were not required to compensate an employee beyond the time when he started his new job, even though he had been dismissed from the new job by the time the hearing on compensation took place. The EAT ruled that, where an employee obtained permanent new employment but was later dismissed from his new job, any loss flowing from the dismissal from the new job was not attributable to the original dismissal and therefore was not the responsibility of the original employer. The EAT's decision in *Moosa* was recently followed by the Scottish EAT in *Simrad Ltd* v *Scott* [1997] IRLR 147 where the applicant, voluntarily gave up her new job to retrain as a nurse.

However the EAT's reasoning may be open to criticism on the ground that it introduces the common law concept of causation into the rules on unfair dismissal compensation. If followed, this could lead to complex legal argument as to when a new job can be regarded as sufficiently permanent to break the chain of causation, thereby bringing the old employer's liability to an end. It is not unusual for a job to turn out to be less 'permanent' than was hoped at the time the employee was engaged and the employee may not be to blame for his or her subsequent dismissal. For example, the employee may be selected for redundancy on a 'last in, first out' basis. In *Moosa*, the EAT suggested that a new job should be regarded as permanent if the employment lasts long enough for the employee to requalify for protection against unfair dismissal. But this decision was given before the unfair dismissal qualifying period was raised to two years and therefore offers little current guidance to tribunals as to when they should regard the new job as permanent.

A more pragmatic solution to this question is to consider whether, as a matter of justice and equity, it is reasonable at the time of the hearing on compensation to regard the job taken by the employee as a permanent one. This approach was taken by the EAT in *Morgan Edwards Wholesale Ltd/Gee Bee Discount Ltd* v *Hough* EAT 398/78, which was decided before *Moosa* but was not cited to the EAT in that case. Mr Hough was dismissed on the ground of ill health and was unable to look for a new job until he recovered. Eventually he accepted a lower paid job which he started five months after his dismissal but he was dismissed from the new job three months later.

The industrial tribunal found that Mr Hough had taken the new job on a temporary basis until he was fit enough to return to the same type of work he was doing prior to his dismissal. It therefore awarded compensation for the entire period including the loss following his dismissal from the second job. On appeal the employers argued that the tribunal had failed to consider whether the new job was a suitable permanent job and that a finding to that effect would have put an end to their liability. The EAT, upholding the industrial tribunal's decision, warned that it would be wrong to import into s. 74 (now see ERA 1996, s. 123) 'all the difficult and obstuse propositions of causation that are to be found in the common law'; instead it approved the 'broad common sense' approach to the issue of causation applied by the tribunal saying:

> What an industrial tribunal has to do is to look at the words of the section, to consider justice and equity, and to consider what, in regard to all the circumstances and justice and equity, is the loss sustained by the complainant in consequence of the dismissal.

The pragmatic approach was also applied by the EAT in *Dundee Plant Co Ltd* v *Riddler* EAT 377/88. There the EAT rejected the employer's argument, based on the *Moosa* decision, that an employee who had left his new job because it involved too much travelling was entitled to compensation only up to the time he started the new job. The EAT agreed with the industrial tribunal that Mr Riddler had not acted unreasonably in giving up the new job for another slightly less well paid job closer to home. Moreover, as he had worked there for only three months, the job could not be regarded as permanent. Support for this approach is also to be found in *Fentiman* v *Fluid Engineering Products Ltd* [1991] IRLR 150, where the EAT again emphasised the importance of justice and equity in the assessment of unfair dismissal compensation rather than applying the strict rules of the common law. The same approach has even been adopted where the employee was to blame for his dismissal from the second employment (see *Mabey Hire Co Ltd* v *Richens* IDS Brief 468, May 1992, EAT 207/90 & 54/91). It is submitted that this approach is to be preferred to that suggested by the EAT in *Moosa* and *Scott*, though the outcome in *Scott* could be justified on the basis of either approach.

Finally it should be noted that this issue will only arise where the employee obtains a permanent new job. The chain of causation will not be broken where it is clear that from the outset that the employment is to be on a temporary basis. For example, in *Ging* v *Ellward Lancs Ltd* [1978] 13 ITR 265 (see 8.2.2 above), the industrial tribunal accepted that Mr Ging was entitled to recover compensation for his second period of unemployment because the job on the oil rig turned out to be a temporary one.

8.3.2 Period of training

A similar problem arises where the employee decides to undergo a period of retraining rather than looking for a new job. In such circumstances, a tribunal must consider the question of mitigation (see Chapter 15) as well as whether the employer's liability to pay compensation ceases under s. 123(1). This has led to a conflict of authority.

In *Pagano* v *HGS* [1976] IRLR 9, an industrial tribunal ruled that an employer's liability ceases when the employee starts the training course because any loss

The Compensatory Award: General Principles 89

suffered by the employee during that time is caused by the employee's own actions and not those of his or her former employer. Thus the tribunal limited its award of compensation to the period of 12 weeks before Mr Pagano commenced his course of study. The industrial tribunal's ruling is consistent with the approach taken by the EAT in *Courtaulds Northern Spinning* v *Moosa* [1984] IRLR 43.

By way of contrast, in *Sealy* v *Avon Aluminium* [1978] IRLR 285, an industrial tribunal rejected the argument that an employer's liability under what is now s. 123(1) came to an end in such circumstances pointing out that 'these are hard times even for a young man to find other work and we do not propose to cut short his recoverable loss because meanwhile he has decided to use the time to some purpose'. Similarly, in *Glen Henderson Ltd* v *Nisbet* EAT 34/90, the EAT upheld an industrial tribunal's decision to award compensation to an employee for the time when she attended a five week business enterprise course.

Tribunals seem to prefer this more pragmatic approach to the one based on causation as it accords more with justice and equity. But this does mean that compensation will be awarded in every case. For example, in *Holroyd* v *Gravure Cylinders Ltd* [1984] IRLR 259, an industrial tribunal refused to award compensation for the period during which the applicant attended a one year post-graduate course. Upholding the tribunal's ruling, the EAT took the view that it was the applicant's decision to take himself out of the labour market for 12 months and therefore it was correct not to award him compensation during that period. The EAT considered that as for any loss in the period after the course finished, that was 'so remote as to be ... incapable of calculation'. Compensation therefore may not be awarded where a course is long, is not of a vocational nature or the employee's decision to retrain is taken after having found a new job (*Simrad* v *Scott* [1997] IRLR 147) since the 'loss' is no longer attributable to the dismissal or any action of the dismissing employer.

8.3.3 Consequential loss

The extent of liability imposed by s. 123(1) of the Employment Rights Act 1996 for consequential loss flowing from the dismissal would seem to be substantial. For example, in *Royal Court Hotel Ltd* v *Cowan* EAT 48/84, an industrial tribunal held that compensation could be claimed for the loss to the family's budget arising out of the dismissal of the applicant's spouse who was employed by a 'sister' company. On appeal, the employers argued that the claim should have been disallowed because the loss was too remote. However, the EAT refused to interfere with the industrial tribunal's ruling on the point, although the appeal was allowed on other grounds (see 8.3.4 below). This decision suggests that the employer is liable for any financial loss which flows directly from the dismissal provided it is 'attributable to the employer's action'.

8.3.4 Attributable to the employer's action

The proviso that the loss must be caused by the employer's action, i.e., the dismissal, is an important limitation on the employer's liability under s. 123(1) of the Employment Rights Act 1996.

It was relied on by the EAT when it overturned the industrial tribunal's decision in *Royal Court Hotel* v *Cowan* EAT 48/84 (see 8.3.3 above). The EAT said that the employer could not be held responsible for the actions of its 'sister' company, with the result that the dismissal of Mrs Cowan's spouse was not attributable to action taken by it. (The EAT does not seem to have considered the possibility that the employers could have been liable if the sister company was an 'associated employer'.)

It also means that loss caused by the employee's impecuniosity is unlikely to be recoverable, since it arises from the employee's own action rather than that of the employer. For example, if as a result of dismissal, an employee defaults on a loan, the employer is unlikely to be liable for the costs suffered by the employee in defending any consequential legal proceedings. (The position may be different if the employer knew about the loan or gave the employee financial assistance to pay it off.)

In *McDonald* v *Capitol Coaches Ltd* EAT 140/94, the EAT appears to have extended this reasoning when it upheld an industrial tribunal's decision not to award any compensation to an employee who declined to take up the employer's invitation to discuss the situation surrounding his dismissal with his employer. The EAT held that the industrial tribunal was entitled to conclude that had he taken up the offer, he would have been reinstated and therefore the loss was attributable to his and not his employer's actions. The decision, however, would appear to be inconsistent with the reasoning of the EAT in *Soros and Soros* v *Davison and Davison* [1994] IRLR 264 (14.4.6) and *Lock* v *Connell Estate Agents* [1994] IRLR 444 (see 15.6.3), where the EAT stresses that employers cannot rely on the employee's actions after dismissal to reduce the award of compensation.

In considering the question of remoteness, tribunals should concern themselves only with the actual consequences of dismissal and not hypothetical ones (*Gilham* v *Kent County Council* [1986] IRLR 56). This rule means that if a business is subsequently closed, employees who are unfairly dismissed at an earlier date cannot recover compensation for any loss they suffer beyond the date of closure unless they are able to persuade the tribunal that the closure is not genuine (see *James W Cook & Co (Wivenhoe) Ltd* v *Tipper and others* [1990] IRLR 386).

8.4 HEADS OF COMPENSATION

In *Norton Tool Co Ltd* v *Tewson* [1973] 1 All ER 183, the NIRC said that compensation should be assessed under four main headings:

(a) immediate loss of earnings, i.e., the loss of earnings between the date of dismissal and the date of the hearing;

(b) future loss of earnings, i.e., anticipated loss of earnings in the period following the hearing;

(c) loss arising from the manner of dismissal;

(d) loss of statutory rights, i.e., compensation for being unable to claim unfair dismissal for a period of at least two years.

In *Tidman* v *Aveling Marshall Ltd* [1977] IRLR 218, the EAT said that it was the duty of the industrial tribunal to raise and inquire into each of the four heads of

The Compensatory Award: General Principles

compensation established by *Norton Tool* plus a fifth head, loss of pension rights. The assessment of claims under this last head has proved to be rather complex (see Chapter 11).

8.4.1 Proof of loss

Whilst it is the duty of the tribunal to raise each of the heads mentioned at 8.4 above, it is up to the employee to particularise his claim under each of them. This point was stressed by the EAT in *Adda International Ltd v Curcio* [1976] IRLR 425. In the context of a claim for loss of future earnings, Bristow J said:

> The industrial tribunal must have something to bite on, and if an applicant produces nothing for it to bite on he will only have himself to thank if he gets no compensation for loss of future earnings.

This means that applicants should come to the tribunal well prepared with evidence which shows what their loss is under each head of compensation.

Employers should be requested to disclose any information relevant to the assessment of the employee's compensation claim. This will be particularly important in relation to a claim for loss of pension rights where much, if not all, of the relevant information is likely to be in the employer's possession or control. (See also *Benson v Dairy Crest Ltd* EAT 192/89.) If employers refuse to disclose this information voluntarily, an application should be made to the industrial tribunal for an order of discovery under r. 4(1)(b)(ii) of the Industrial Tribunals (Rules of Procedure) Regulations 1985 (SI 1985 No. 16). Employers may also be penalised if they fail to disclose the details of the new employers' pension scheme (*Bigham v Hobourn Engineering Ltd* [1992] IRLR 298).

Failure to make a claim under one of the heads or to quantify a particular type of loss properly cannot normally be rectified on appeal. For example, in *UBAF Bank Ltd v Davis* [1978] IRLR 442, the industrial tribunal awarded Mr Davis one year's loss of future earnings. On appeal, Mr Davis complained that the tribunal had ignored the fact that his dismissal meant that he would never be able to work in banking again. He argued that consequently the award should be increased. However, the EAT ruled that if Mr Davis had wanted the tribunal to take the point into account he should have raised evidence before it to prove this. See also *Adda International Ltd v Curcio*.

Once an employee has produced evidence of loss suffered under one of the relevant heads of compensation, the evidential burden of proof will usually shift to the employers (*Barley v Amey Roadstone Corporation Ltd* [1977] IRLR 299).

8.4.2 Industrial pressure disregarded

In assessing the compensatory award, industrial tribunals must take no account of 'any pressure which, by ... calling, organising, procuring or financing a strike or other industrial action, or ... threatening to do so, was exercised on the employer to dismiss the employee ...'. The question of compensation must be determined 'as if no such pressure had been exercised' (ERA 1996, s. 123(5)).

8.5 STATUTORY MAXIMUM

The compensatory award is subject to a statutory maximum of £11,300. This maximum is reviewed annually by the Secretary of State for Employment as part of the general review of employment protection payments. Any increase must be approved by Parliament (ERA 1996, s. 124(2)). The new rates normally come into effect on 1 April.

9 Calculating the Compensatory Award: Loss of Earnings

9.1 INTRODUCTION

This chapter looks at the two main heads of compensation established by *Norton Tool Co Ltd* v *Tewson* [1973] All ER 183, which are immediate loss of earnings, i.e., loss of earnings between the date of dismissal and the date of the hearing, and future loss of earnings, i.e., compensation for any continuing loss after the hearing. Tribunals are thus expected 'to glance both backward into the past and forward into the future' (per Waite J in *Thompson* v *Smiths (Harlow) Ltd* EAT 952/83), but before considering how tribunals approach this task, it is necessary to examine what sums count as lost earnings for this purpose.

9.2 WHAT LOSSES COUNT

The object of the compensatory award is 'to compensate, and compensate fully, but not to award a bonus', per Sir John Donaldson in *Norton Tool Co. Ltd* v *Tewson* [1973] 1 All ER 183. Thus in broad terms, an employee may claim compensation for any loss suffered as a consequence of the dismissal provided it is 'attributable to the action taken by the employer' (see 8.1 above). At the same time, it should be remembered that compensation will only be awarded where the tribunal considers it 'just and equitable'. This means that some tribunals may ignore small payments, particularly if they are discretionary, e.g., a Christmas bonus may be disallowed for this reason. For the same reason, tribunals may refuse to award compensation where a claim is made for loss of social security credits (see 9.2.8 below) or may reduce their award to take account of a small tax rebate (9.2.9 below). Bearing this in mind, the first part of this chapter looks at the sort of payments which are included in a claim for loss of earnings.

9.2.1 Pay

As the EAT point out in *Brownson* v *Hire Services Shops Ltd* [1978] IRLR 73 'other things being equal, the first thing you lose in consequence of being dismissed is what you would have got in your pay packet'.

The 'pay packet' in this context includes both the payments which qualify as remuneration for the purpose of calculating a week's pay (see Chapter 7) and payments which are not included in that calculation. Thus it was held in *Brownson* that an employee can claim for the loss of any bonus or productivity payments or any commission received *and* for the loss of overtime payments at premium rates, if appropriate. There is no reason in principle why compensation should not be recovered for profit-related pay or payments due under a profit-share scheme (*Glen Henderson Ltd* v *Nisbet* EAT 34/90). The fact that the employee does not have a contractual right to such a payment is no bar to compensation being awarded so long as it can be shown that the payment is one which the employee might have reasonably been expected to have had but for the dismissal (ERA 1996, s. 123(2)(b)). The loss of regular tips may also be recovered for the same reason (*Palmanor Ltd t/a Chaplins Night Club* v *Cedron* [1978] IRLR 303).

In employments covered by Wages Council orders the calculation will be based on the amount the employer *should* have paid under the relevant order even if the employer was paying less at the time of dismissal (*Senlle* v *G Desai t/a Pizza Express* COIT 29552/85 LN and *Cooner* v *P S Doal & Sons* EAT 307/87).

'Pay' is asssessed as a net figure, i.e., after the deduction of tax and national insurance.

9.2.2 Calculating pay

In contrast to the strict statutory rules which are used to work out the basic and special awards, there is nothing (apart from the words of s. 123 of the Employment Rights Act 1996) to guide tribunals in working out a week's pay for the purpose of calculating the compensatory award. It is therefore up to the tribunal to decide what method of calculation is just and equitable in the particular circumstances.

For example, tribunals may adopt one of the formulae in ss. 221–229 to the Act (see 7.5 above). These formulae set out methods of calculating the weekly earnings of groups of workers like piece workers, whose pay varies with output, or shift workers, whose pay varies with the shifts they work. The problem with this approach, however, is that the formulae in those sections not are intended specifically for the purpose of calculating a 'week's pay' for the compensatory award and ignore certain payments which are included in the compensatory award.

A further problem arises in cases where it is necessary to compensate employees for loss of payments which fluctuate from week to week such as tips, bonuses and commission. In such circumstances, the normal practice is for tribunals to work out the average amount an employee was earning in this way in the 12 weeks prior to dismissal; but there is nothing to prevent employees from arguing that the tribunal should award either a lump sum or use a longer period of time for calculating the average in cases where the work is seasonal or the period of compensation exceeds three months (see 7.5.1.1 as to bonus and commission payments).

The rate of pay should be based on the amount which the employee is entitled to receive under his or her contract. It is for the tribunal to resolve any disputes relating to the correct rate or level of pay to which an employee is entitled. Thus, in *Kinzley* v *Minories Finance Ltd* [1987] IRLR 490 the EAT held that the industrial tribunal had erred in law when it refused to determine whether the applicant was entitled to be compensated on the basis of her actual earnings at the time of her dismissal, or, as she claimed, the earnings which she should have been receiving at that time. The EAT held that loss of earnings should be assessed on what the employee was entitled to receive irrespective of whether the employee was in fact receiving that entitlement at the time of dismissal.

9.2.3 Pay rises

An important difference between the compensatory award and the basic and special awards is the treatment of pay rises.

In *Leyland Vehicles Ltd* v *Reston* [1981] IRLR 19, the EAT ruled that a pay increase awarded after the calculation date could not be included in the basic award even if it was backdated. The same principle applies to the special and additional awards. However, in assessing the compensatory award, a tribunal can take into account any pay increase awarded up to the date of the hearing including a backdated pay rise (*Leske* v *Rogers of Saltcoats (ES) Ltd* EAT 520/82) and 'any benefit which [the employee] might reasonably be expected to have had but for the dismissal' (ERA 1996, s. 123(2)(b)). This may include a future pay rise provided there is a 'high probability that, in conformity with company policy, the company would increase the salary of an employee' in the period of assessment, i.e., during the period covered by the future loss (*York Trailer Co Ltd* v *Sparkes* [1973] IRLR 348).

The size of the award depends on the tribunal's view of the likelihood of the increase. The greater the likelihood, the higher the award — see *Sparkes*.

9.2.4 Notice pay

Section 86 of the Employment Rights Act 1996 sets out the minimum periods of notice to which an employee is entitled on the termination of employment (see 1.5.1 above).

The primary remedy for a breach of these provisions is an action for damages in the ordinary courts (normally the county court) as the tribunal does not have jurisdiction to hear claims arising out of a breach of contract. However, a long line of authority, most recently confirmed in *TBA Industrial Products Ltd* v *Locke* [1984] IRLR 48, has established that such sums may also be included as part of the employee's lost earnings in the compensatory award.

9.2.5 Holiday pay

The primary remedy for loss of holiday pay is an action for damages in the ordinary courts. However, in certain circumstances, employees may be entitled to recover pay for lost holiday leave as part of the compensatory award (*Tradewinds Airways Ltd* v *Fletcher* [1981] IRLR 272). In order to recover compensation it must be shown that the employee has lost a period of paid holiday as a result of dismissal. This commonly occurs where the entitlement to paid holiday at a new job is service-related. For example, in *Wilson* v *Tote Bookmakers Ltd* COIT 15570/81, Mrs Wilson had booked her holiday before she was unfairly dismissed. By the time of the hearing she had found a new job but her new employers would not allow her to go on paid holiday until she had been with them for one year. She therefore claimed compensation for the loss of holiday pay from her old employers. The industrial tribunal upheld her claim.

The same principle would apply to employments where the entitlement to paid holiday increases with length of service. Employees who have acquired extra holiday in such circumstances would be entitled to recover compensation for the loss of their holiday entitlement if the holiday entitlement in their new job is lower. The loss in such circumstances is the difference between the two.

In both these situations the claim is not for loss of holiday pay *per se* but rather the loss of an entitlement to a period of paid holiday consequent upon dismissal. Such a claim will not normally arise where the employee is still out of work at the time of the hearing since the claim for lost holiday pay would be absorbed by the general claim for loss of earnings. However, tribunal practice on this question is by no means universal — some tribunals are willing to ignore the legal niceties and award compensation for loss of holiday pay in itself.

9.2.6 Redundancy payments

The statutory redundancy scheme sets the minimum level of payment which must be made to employees who are dismissed on the grounds of redundancy (see 20.3 below). Many employers simply incorporate these provisions into their employees' contracts of employment. In the event of an employee being unfairly dismissed, the loss of the employee's accrued rights in this respect will be reflected in the basic award.

However, some contractual redundancy arrangements make provision for enhanced redundancy payments, i.e., payments in excess of the statutory minimum, and an employee who is dismissed in circumstances where such arrangements exist may legitimately want to claim compensation for the loss of this benefit. This was recognised by the EAT in *Lee* v *IPC Business Press Ltd* [1984] ICR 306 where it was said:

> ... if it is shown that there was a term in the contract between Mr Lee and the company which was binding on the company and meant that, if Mr Lee was made redundant, he was entitled as a matter of contract to more than the statutory redundancy payment, that is something which he has lost as a result of being unfairly dismissed and it is one of the things which the industrial tribunal should take into account in arriving at their award of compensation if any.

The EAT added that the same principle would apply if the enhanced redundancy payment formed part of a collective agreement which was not incorporated into the individual employee's contract but was honoured in practice.

The EAT's conclusion in *Lee* is supported by the words of s. 123(3) of the Employment Rights Act 1996 which states that an employee's loss under s. 123(1) includes '... any entitlement or potential entitlement to a payment on account of dismissal by reason of redundancy (whether in pursuance of Part XI or otherwise), or ... any expectation of such a payment' to the extent that the entitlement would have exceeded the basic award.

A claim for an enhanced redundancy payment may arise in one of three situations. These three claims are alternatives — the same loss cannot be recovered twice.

(a) An employee who is dismissed is entitled to an enhanced payment for redundancy but does not receive it. Here, assuming that the scheme is contractual, the primary remedy is an action for breach of contract, but the decision in *Lee* shows that, in the alternative, the loss is recoverable as part of the compensatory award. Indeed, this is the only claim which can succeed although there is an expectation of payment, but it is not enforceable in contract.

(b) The employee is dismissed for some other reason but is able to show that he would have been made redundant, and hence would have been entitled to the enhanced redundancy payment, within the period of the award. For example, in *Addison* v *Babcock FATA Ltd* [1986] IRLR 388, the EAT held that Mr Addison was entitled to an enhanced redundancy payment because he would have been dismissed for redundancy 13 months after he was actually dismissed. (The EAT's ruling on this point was not challenged by the employers in the Court of Appeal.) In other cases, the level of the award depends on the likelihood of a redundancy actually occurring.

(c) There is no risk of the employee being made redundant but the employee's claim is based on the loss of the benefit of the additional protection afforded by the enhanced redundancy provisions. Such a claim may arise even if the employee is lucky enough to find a new job with an equivalent scheme because the employee will have lost the value of the years of service with the previous employer and will have to requalify under the new scheme.

The decision in *Lee* above casts little light on how compensation should be assessed in this third situation. One possibility is that the employee should receive compensation for the full loss of the benefits incidental to the old employment, but this takes no account of the fact that the employee was under no risk of redundancy at the time of dismissal. The better view is that this type of compensation is analogous to awards for loss of employment protection rights (see Chapter 13) and so the figure should be based on a proportion of the value of the enhanced benefit, e.g., 50%.

9.2.7 Out of pocket expenses

Genuine tax-free reimbursement for expenses incurred in the course of employment are excluded from the compensatory award.

For example, in *Tradewinds Airways Ltd* v *Fletcher* [1981] IRLR 272. Mr Fletcher claimed compensation for various tax-free allowances he received from his previous employers. Although he also received similar allowances from his new employers, they were at a reduced rate. The industrial tribunal allowed his claim and awarded him the difference between his old allowance and his new allowance. The EAT, allowing the appeal on this point, ruled that the sums claimed represented genuine expenses incurred on the company's behalf and therefore did not form part of Mr Fletcher's pay.

However, the reimbursement of expenses must be distinguished from 'perks', such as a season ticket loan or travel expenses. The loss of the value of such perks could be included in the compensatory award if the new employer either made no provision for such payments or was less generous. Thus, in *Fletcher*, the EAT stressed that the position would have been different if there was an element of profit in the allowance.

Fringe benefits and expenses are considered more fully in Chapter 10.

Note: The payment of 'bogus' expenses to evade tax liability may result in the contract becoming unenforceable on the grounds of illegality, thereby excluding an unfair dismissal complaint altogether (*Tomlinson* v *Dick Evans 'U' Drive Ltd* [1978] IRLR 77).

9.2.8 Loss of social security credits

Compensation may also be recovered for any lost social security credits in the period covered by the compensation claim.

Such claims may arise because of the operation of social security law. Under reg. 9(1) of the Social Security (Credits) Regulations 1975 (SI 1975 No. 556), unemployed persons are generally entitled to a class 1 credit for each week of unemployment. However, this entitlement may be lost for up to a year if a person receives compensation for unfair dismissal during that period (Social Security (Unemployment, Sickness and Invalidity Benefit) Regulations 1983 (SI 1983 No. 1598), reg. 7(1)).

The loss of credited contributions for a short time is unlikely to affect the entitlement to benefit because benefits are assessed on the employee's contribution record over the whole of the relevant contribution year. However, a prolonged period of disqualification is likely to affect an employee's entitlement. This problem may be partially overcome if the employee makes voluntary contributions. In *Allen* v *Key Markets Ltd* COIT 1425/41, the industrial tribunal suggested that compensation for lost credits should be awarded in any case where the employee is unemployed for more than eight weeks. The amount of compensation is fixed by reference to the weekly class 3 contribution rate.

9.2.9 Tax implications

Where, as a result of the dismissal, an employee is entitled to a tax rebate, the employer may argue that the amount of the award should be reduced to reflect this. Conversely, where the dismissal takes place towards the end of the tax year, an employee may argue that account should be taken of the fact that had the correct disciplinary procedure been followed, the dismissal might have occurred in the next tax year leaving him with a larger tax rebate.

Initially, the EAT ruled that this was really a question of 'swings and roundabouts' and therefore tax liability should be completely ignored (*Adda International Ltd* v *Curcio* [1976] IRLR 425). However, more recently, in *Lucas* v *Laurence Scott Electromotors Ltd* [1983] IRLR 61, the EAT ruled to the contrary and decided that the tax implications should be taken into account, although in *MBS Ltd* v *Calo* [1983] IRLR 189, the EAT said that tax implications should be ignored unless the sums involved are large.

9.2.10 Interest

Industrial tribunals have the power to award interest on its award of compensation (see 18.6). It has been argued that interest on loss of earnings may be claimed as part of the compensatory award but, in line with the principles set out above, an award is unlikely unless the sums involved are large.

9.3 CREDITS FOR PAYMENTS RECEIVED

In assessing the loss caused by the dismissal, credit must normally be given for any payments received by the employee both at the time of dismissal and since dismissal. The rules on the treatment of ex gratia payments made by an employer are considered in Chapter 17.

9.3.1 Payments in lieu

In the absence of an express or implied agreement to the contrary, credit should be given for any payment made by the employer to the employee on account of wages or other benefits such as a payment in lieu of notice. This principle was confirmed by the Court of Appeal in *Babcock FATA Ltd* v *Addison* [1987] IRLR 173, which overturned the EAT's ruling that such a payment should be ignored in calculating an employee's loss of earnings. It should be noted however that the EAT's approach in *Addison* may still apply in Scotland as the EAT based its ruling on the earlier decision in *Finnie* v *Top Hat Frozen Foods Ltd* [1985] IRLR 365 which has not been overruled by the Court of Session and therefore may still be good law.

9.3.2 Payments received from a new employer

As a general rule credit must also be given for any payments received from a new employer since dismissal, including income from part-time employment (*Justfern Ltd* v *D'Inglethorpe and Ors* [1994] IRLR 164). There are however two exceptions to this rule. The first is where, prior to the hearing on compensation, the employee has found a permanent new job at an equivalent or better rate of pay. The second relates to earnings received during the notice period.

9.3.2.1 Permanent new employment
It has already been noted that an employer's liability to pay compensation will normally cease once an employee has started a permanent new employment at an equivalent or better rate of pay (see 8.3.1). A related issue is whether in such circumstances, the applicant is required to offset the *additional* earnings received from the new job in the period up to the date of the hearing on compensation against the loss suffered during the period of unemployment.

This point was considered by the EAT in *Lytlarch Ltd t/a The Viceroy Restaurant* v *Reid* EAT 296/90 and in *Fentiman* v *Fluid Engineering Products Ltd* [1991] IRLR 151. In *Fentiman*, the applicant was out of work for 29 weeks after his dismissal. He then found himself a new job which was better paid than his old job. The hearing on compensation took place some 68 weeks after dismissal, i.e., 39 weeks after he had started his new job. The industrial tribunal calculated Mr Fentiman's loss of earnings during the period he was unemployed but set-off against this loss the earnings which he had received from the date he started the new job to the date of the hearing. This produced a net loss of £2,373. The EAT, allowing the appeal, held that Mr Fentiman was entitled to £9,744, representing his full loss of earnings between the date of dismissal and the date when he started the new job and was not required to give credit for the additional earnings which he had received from the new job. (The award of £9,744 was in fact reduced to £8,925 to take account of the statutory maximum which applied at the time.)

The EAT justified its decision on two grounds. First it said that if this were not the case employees would be discouraged from mitigating their loss by finding new employment prior to the tribunal hearing on compensation. Secondly, as a matter of justice and equity, it was unjust that an employer's liability should be reduced to 'a fraction of the loss sustained by the complainant during his period of unemployment' simply because the employee has found a better paid job.

A number of points can be made both for and against the EAT's ruling. On the one hand, the EAT's decision is the mirror image of the ruling in *Courtaulds Northern Spinning Ltd v Moosa* [1984] IRLR 43; just as an employer's liability to compensate an employee will, in general, cease once equivalent employment has been obtained, so an employee will not be required to give credit for payments received from that time onwards. Furthermore, as a matter of justice and equity, it would seem arbitrary that the amount of the award should depend on when the compensation hearing happens to take place as this may well vary from region to region. On the other hand, it may be considered unjust that an employee who obtains a permanent new job which is less well paid is required to give credit for all the earnings he or she receives up to the date of the hearing on compensation whereas one who receives a better paid permanent job does not. Moreover, as has already been noted, sometimes it may be difficult to determine when a new job is permanent.

The ruling in *Fentiman* applies only where the applicant has obtained a permanent new job. The general rule still applies where the job is temporary, part time or, as already noted, is permanent but less well paid than the original employment.

9.3.2.2 Payments during the notice period

The second exception to the general rule relates to payments received during the notice period. Here it is necessary to distinguish between contracts which are terminable by notice and fixed term contracts.

In relation to the former, it was established by the NIRC in *Norton Tool Co Ltd v Tewson* [1973] 1 All ER 183 that, as a matter of good industrial practice, employees should always receive their notice pay either by way of a payment in lieu or as compensation for loss of earnings and further credit need not be given for earnings received from new employment of any nature during that period. This decision was followed by the NIRC in *Hilti (GB) Ltd v Windridge* [1974] IRLR 53 and by the EAT in *TBA Industrial Products Ltd v Locke* [1984] IRLR 48, but departed from in *Tradewinds Airways Ltd v Fletcher* [1981] IRLR 272. The decision in *Norton Tool* was approved by the Court of Appeal in *Babcock FATA Ltd v Addison* [1987] IRLR 173. However, it is not entirely clear whether credit should be given for earnings received in the contractual notice period where this exceeds the statutory notice period. It appears to have been assumed in both *Norton Tool* and *Addison* that this was the case but, if this is so, it conflicts with the earlier decision in *Vaughan* v *Weighpack Ltd* [1974] IRLR 105 and *Hilti (GB) Ltd* v *Windridge*, and the general principle that credit should be given for such payments in assessing damages for breach of contract.

The principle established in *Norton Tool* does not apply to fixed term contracts. Thus, in *Isleworth Studios Ltd* v *Rickard* [1988] IRLR 137, the EAT overturned an industrial tribunal decision to compensate Mr Rickard for his lost earnings during the remaining 29 weeks of his fixed term contract because his earnings from his new business exceeded the loss he had suffered as a result of his dismissal. The EAT was adamant that the *Norton Tool* principle applied only to contracts terminable by notice, and that good industrial relations practice did not require it to be extended to fixed term contracts where compensation should be based strictly on the loss suffered by the applicant. The EAT's reasoning may be open to doubt on the ground that good industrial relations should not distinguish between an employee whose contract is terminable by six months notice and one who is employed under a fixed term contract for six months.

As regards the *Addison* decision itself, it should be noted that both Lord Donaldson MR and Ralph Gibson LJ accepted that the concept of good industrial relations is not a static one and there may be circumstances where the payment (or the award) of some lesser sum may be justified. Ralph Gibson LJ thought that such a departure might be justified either in the case of an employee who was entitled to a long period of notice and stood a good chance of finding a new job within that period, or for 'some other sufficient reason'.

It should also be stressed that this exception applies only to payments received during the notice period. Credit must be given for any payment received outside the notice period (*Vaughan* v *Weighpack Ltd*).

The way in which to ascertain how the EAT will calculate the award is as follows:

(a) calculate the amount of wages lost during (i) the statutory notice period and (ii) the contractual notice period (if any) without making any deductions;

(b) if the claim is for a higher amount than (i) above, then deduct from (ii) all the sums earned since the dismissal. If the balance is still higher than the amount of (i) the tribunal should award the higher sum. If it is less than (i) the tribunal should award the statutory minimum.

Example

An employee, Mr Smith, is dismissed by his employer on 1 November after 2 1/2 years' service. His monthly pay was £1,000 and he was entitled to 3 months' notice. He was employed by a new employer on 1 January at an increased salary of £1,400 per month.

His statutory notice pay is 2 weeks' pay, i.e., £500. His contractual notice pay is £3,000, less the £1,400 he has received from his new job, i.e., £1,600. As this is more than the £500 statutory notice, Mr Smith will be awarded £1,600.

9.3.3 Pay rises in the new job

In working out whether the employee is better or worse off in the new job, the tribunal may take into account likely future increases in earnings in that job (*Gee Walker & Sons Ltd* v *Churchill* EAT 11/84).

This is the converse to the principle examined in 9.2.3 above viz, that tribunals may increase the award by making allowance for possible future pay rises which the employee would have received had he not been dismissed. In theory, tribunals should set off the award they make for one against the other. In practice, tribunals are unlikely to make the deduction unless they are certain that a pay increase is about to be awarded.

In addition, it should be remembered that if the difference between the two sums is small, the tribunal is unlikely to make an award at all. On the other hand, if the evidence shows that the employee would have definitely received an increase, it is unlikely to start weighing up the probabilities of a future pay rise from the new employers and will probably award the difference.

9.3.4 State benefits not deductible

State benefits received during the period of unemployment are not taken into account until after the award has been fixed by the tribunal. The deduction is then made in accordance with the procedures laid down by statutory instrument (see Chapter 18). However, the position appears to be different in relation to other state benefits received by an employee after dismissal and which are not covered by the recoupment provisions. In *Puglia* v *C James & Sons Ltd* [1996] IRLR 70, the EAT ruled that in assessing the loss caused by the dismissal, credit must be given for state sickness and invalidity benefit received by an employee after his dismissal. This contrasts with the EAT's earlier rulings in *Hilton International Hotels* v *Faraji* [1994] IRLR 267, where the EAT ruled that such payments were an 'insurance type' benefit and should be ignored, and *Rubenstein* v *McGloughlin* [1996] IRLR 557, where the EAT rejected the 'all or nothing' approach and suggested that as a matter of justice and equity one half of the amount of the benefit received should be deducted. This issue is likely to be resolved by the Court of Appeal in the near future.

9.3.5 Remoteness

It is open to an industrial tribunal to conclude, as a matter of discretion, that certain benefits an employee receives after dismissal are either too remote or arise independently of the employer's wrong with the consequence that credit need not be given for such payments. For example, in *Justfern Ltd* v *D'Inglethorpe and Ors* [1994] IRLR 164, the EAT upheld an industrial tribunal's decision not to give credit for a £4,000 educational grant received by the applicant in connection with a training course in its calculation of its award of compensatoin. The same principle is likely to apply to payments received by an employee under a private insurance scheme. (See also *Simrad Ltd* v *Scott* [1997] IRLR 147 for a somewhat unusual illustration where an employee was not required to give credit for a loan which was made to her during her employment and was to be repaid by way of work. The EAT took the view that the employee had been denied the opportunity to repay the loan as a result of the actions of the employer and therefore it would not be 'just and equitable' for the employee to give credit for the loan even though it had been waived by the employer on dismissal.)

9.4 ASSESSING LOSS OF EARNINGS

As Lord Donaldson MR pointed out in *Babcock FATA Ltd* v *Addison* [1987] IRLR 173, 'the assessment of any compensation, whether in an industrial relations context or otherwise, must always involve a comparison between what was, is and will be and what would (or should) have been — between the actual past, present and future and the hypothetical past, present and future'.

9.4.1 Immediate loss of earnings

The first head of compensation established by *Norton Tool Co Ltd* v *Tewson* [1973] 1 All ER 183 is the employee's immediate loss of earnings between the date of dismissal and the date of the hearing on compensation. This is calculated by assessing the total loss of earnings and benefits in the relevant period and giving credit for payments received during that time in accordance with the principles outlined above.

Example: Calculating immediate loss of earnings

Mr Jones is unfairly dismissed from his job as an electrician. He takes home £200 a week including overtime and a bonus. He finds a new, slightly better paid, job three months after the dismissal. He worked for his old employer for four years. The hearing takes place four months after the dismissal. The award for immediate loss of earnings is calculated as follows:

	£
Loss of earnings between dismissal and the hearing	2,400
Credit for earnings from new job @ £10 a week for a month	40
Total loss	2,360

9.5 LOSS OF FUTURE EARNINGS

The second head of compensation established by *Norton Tool Co Ltd* v *Tewson* [1973] 1 All ER 183 is loss of *future* earnings. This requires the industrial tribunal to assess the employee's continuing loss and is inevitably a highly speculative exercise. However, so long as the tribunal takes all the relevant factors into account, its decision is unlikely to be overturned on appeal.

The tribunal is always faced with one of the following three situations:

(a) the employee has found a new job by the time of the hearing where he is better paid than, or at least as well paid as, he was in the old job; or

(b) the employee has found a new job by the time of the hearing but he is less well paid than he was in the old job; or

(c) the employee is still out of work at the time of the hearing.

9.5.1 New job — equivalent or better

If the employee has found a new job by the time of the hearing which is at least as well paid as the old job, there will be no continuing loss of earnings and hence no compensatory award for loss of future earnings.

In making the comparison, the tribunal looks not only at pay but also at the fringe benefits in the new job (see Chapter 10).

9.5.2 New job — less well paid

There will, however, be a continuing loss where the new job is less well paid. In such circumstances, the tribunal has to assess how long it will take before the employee earns the same as he was earning in the old job. Again fringe benefits are taken into account.

It is open to the tribunal to conclude that this loss will last indefinitely, i.e., that the employee's earnings in the new job will never match those in the old job. In such circumstances, compensation would be awarded for the remainder of the employee's working life. However, other than in cases where the employee is close to retirement, it is unlikely that the tribunal would reach this conclusion since it fails to take into account the uncertainties of life and also assumes that the employee would have remained in the old job for the remainder of his working life (see 9.4.6 below for the multiplier which may be applied). In most cases, tribunals are likely to place some limit on the length of the continuing loss.

The period of the award may also be limited for other reasons (see Chapter 14 as to limits on full compensation).

9.5.3 Unemployed applicants

At present, it is not uncommon for applicants to be unemployed at the time of the hearing. Here the tribunal is faced with the task of having to decide how long the employee is going to remain unemployed and how long it will be before the earnings from the new job will match those of the old. In theory, for the reasons given above, the period of continuing loss could be indefinite but, in practice, the award will normally be limited because of the various contingencies taken into account by the tribunal (see Chapter 14 as to the limits on full compensation).

9.5.4 Assessing future loss

The tribunal normally takes the personal characteristics of the employee and the state of the labour market into account in assessing future loss.

9.5.4.1 Personal characteristics of employee

In fixing the award for future loss, tribunals will take into account the personal characteristics of the employee such as his age, state of health and other personal circumstances.

This point is illustrated by the EAT's decision in *Fougère v Phoenix Motor Co Ltd* [1976] IRLR 259. Mr Fougère was 58 at the time of his dismissal. Even though he was in a poor state of health, the tribunal based its award on the length of time an average person in his position would have taken to find a new job. The EAT said that this was the wrong approach — the tribunal should have taken his personal circumstances into account.

Similarly, in *Brittains Aborfield Ltd v Van Uden* [1977] ICR 211, the EAT held that an employee who had defective eyesight would be at a disadvantage in the labour market and therefore would find it more difficult to get a new job.

Age is one of the most important factors influencing the tribunal's assessment. Thus an applicant who is close to retirement may recover compensation for the remainder of the applicant's working life. For example, in *Isle of Wight Tourist Board v Coombes* [1976] IRLR 413, the industrial tribunal held that Mrs Coombes, who was dismissed at the age of 58, was entitled to recover compensation for her lost earnings until the date of her retirement, i.e., for two years. Similarly, in *Penprase v Mander Bros Ltd* [1973] IRLR 167, Mr Penprase was three and a half years away from retirement when he was dismissed. The industrial tribunal found that he would have remained in his job until he retired had he not been dismissed and therefore awarded him compensation for the full three and a half years. More recently, in *Sandown Pier Ltd v Moonan* EAT 399/93, the EAT held that an industrial tribunal was entitled to conclude that an employee who was unfairly dismissed at the age of 50 was unlikely to work again given that there was a 20% rate of unemployment in the area where he lived and worked.

Moreover, if the evidence shows that the employee would have been kept on beyond retirement age, additional compensation may be awarded. For example, in *Barrell Plating and Phosphating Co Ltd v Danks* [1976] IRLR 262, the industrial tribunal awarded compensation for an additional six months beyond Ms Danks' retirement age. On appeal, the employers argued that such a claim should be disallowed on the ground that the statutory provisions prevent employees over the normal retiring age from claiming unfair dismissal. Rejecting this argument, the EAT said that such a limitation on an award of compensation could not be implied from the statutory exclusion. On the facts, there was ample evidence to support the tribunal's conclusion that Ms Danks would have been kept on after reaching retirement age.

9.5.4.2 State of the labour market

The state of the labour market obviously has an important bearing on the tribunal's view of how long the applicant is likely to remain unemployed (*Perks v Geest Industries Ltd* [1974] IRLR 228).

In this context, the tribunal will consider the state of the labour market both at a national level and at a local level. It is open to either side to call consultants who specialise in job search to give expert evidence on the applicant's prospects of finding a new job. It is also open to the tribunal to rely on its own knowledge of the local labour market to assess the employment prospects of the applicant and it may even come to a different conclusion from that presented to it by the parties. For example, in *Eastern Counties Timber Co Ltd* v *Hunt* EAT 483/76, the applicant said in his evidence that he thought that he would find a new job in three months but the industrial tribunal thought that this was too optimistic and assessed the future loss at six months. However, in *Hammington* v *Berker Sportcraft Ltd* EAT 344/79, the EAT said that the parties should be given an opportunity to comment at the hearing on an assessment based on the tribunal's own knowledge.

9.5.5 Contingencies

Assessing future loss also involves a consideration of a number of contingencies, such as whether the employee would have left the job voluntarily or would have been forced to retire early. Similarly, if the employee has accepted a new job at a lower rate, the tribunal will have to consider the chances of the employee leaving that job and finding a better job in the future. The tribunal's task in this respect is highly speculative and, provided it considers the point, its decision will normally be final.

In *Cartiers Superfoods Ltd* v *Laws* [1978] IRLR 315, it was argued that the tribunal was wrong to base its award of future loss on a three year period because it had ignored certain factors. These included the chances of Mrs Laws, who was 33 years of age, finding a new job in that period or having a child or being transferred to another part of the country.

The EAT, dismissing the appeal, accepted that these factors were all relevant but held that the tribunal had taken them into account in their decision:

> Nobody could say, of course, how long she would have continued to be employed by Cartiers Superfoods Ltd if she had not been dismissed; partly, it would depend on how long she wanted to work. But, as far as her wishes are concerned, it seems fair to summarise it and to say that the shortest period seems likely to have been two or three years, and the longest about ten; and it does not seem to us that we can say, as a matter of law, that the industrial tribunal misdirected themselves in making the judgment which they did on this point.

9.5.6 The multiplier

The problem of putting a figure on future loss of earnings also arises in claims for personal injuries. In those cases, it is common for the ordinary courts to use a multiplier, i.e., a figure, be it in weeks, months or years, which reflects the employee's likely continuing loss of earnings. Included in the multiplier are the contingencies outlined at 9.5.5 above as well as other factors which actuaries take into account in working out premiums for life insurance policies. Some tribunals use a similar approach in working out the length of future loss of earnings. However, where a multiplier is used, the tribunal need not apply it with the same precision as a cost accountant or skilled actuary (*Fougère* v *Phoenix Motor Co Ltd* [1976] IRLR 259).

9.5.7 Deducting contingencies

The alternative to a multiplier is to decide on the overall figure and then make a deduction based on the various contingencies. Some early authorities suggested that five years was an appropriate starting point for this purpose, but more recently the EAT has suggested one year as a rule of thumb (*Tidman* v *Aveling Marshall Ltd* [1977] IRLR 218).

Example: Calculating future loss of earnings

Mr Jones is unfairly dismissed from his job as an electrician. He takes home £200 a week including overtime and commission. He is unemployed at the time of the hearing which takes place four months after the dismissal. The tribunal finds that he will find a new job in three months and would have received a 5% pay increase three months after his dismissal. The award for loss of earnings is calculated as follows:

	£
Loss of earnings for the first three months	2,400
Loss of earnings for the next four months	3,360
Total loss	5,760

9.5.8 No set amount

It should be stressed that a tribunal has complete discretion to award what it considers to be appropriate in the particular circumstances of the case. Although, in practice, many tribunals limit their awards for future loss to 12 months, they are not required to do so and, subject to the statutory maximum, compensation may be awarded for such period as is considered appropriate in the circumstances (see *Morganite Electrical Carbon Ltd* v *Donne* [1987] IRLR 363, where the EAT rejected the argument that a tribunal's award of 82 weeks' loss of earnings, made up of 30 weeks' loss up to the date of the hearing and 52 weeks thereafter, was excessive).

9.5.9 Power to review

The EAT has emphasised that the speculative nature of the tribunal's task in fixing an award for future loss means that it will rarely overturn its assessment on appeal. However, the industrial tribunal does have a power to review its own decisions if new evidence comes to light which could not have been known or reasonably foreseen at the time of the hearing (Industrial Tribunals (Rules of Procedure) Regulations 1985, r. 10(1)).

This power may be relied on by either the employer or the employee if the forecast which formed the fundamental basis of the tribunal's decision has been falsified to a sufficiently substantial extent so as to invalidate the assessment (*Yorkshire Engineering Co Ltd* v *Burnham* [1974] ICR 77). For example, in *Dicker* v *Seceurop Ltd* EAT 554/84, the employers successfully applied for the award for future loss to be reviewed when Mr Dicker found a new job two days after the hearing. Similarly, in *Cichetti* v *K Speck & Son* COIT 2041/209, the industrial tribunal reviewed its original assessment that it would take Mr Cichetti 13 weeks to find a job when he found a new job with similar pay two weeks later. The same principle applies where there is a fundamental change in the employee's circumstances. In *Bateman* v *British Leyland* [1974] IRLR 101, Mr Bateman successfully applied for a review when he lost his new job two weeks after the hearing on compensation.

An application for review must be made within 14 days of the decision being sent to the parties, although the chairman does have a discretion to allow late applications (Industrial Tribunals (Rules of Procedure) Regulations 1985, r. 12(2)).

10 Calculating the Compensatory Award: Fringe Benefits and Expenses

10.1 INTRODUCTION

Fringe benefits play an ever-increasing part in the employment package, and although the loss of earnings claim is usually the more substantial element in the compensatory award, compensation may also be awarded for the loss of these benefits. This chapter looks at how compensation for the loss of such benefits is assessed and describes the circumstances in which it is possible to recover expenses incurred as a result of the dismissal.

10.2 GENERAL PRINCIPLES

The loss of fringe benefits is included in the assessment of 'loss' under the Employment Rights Act 1996, s. 123.

Section 123(2) states that the employee's 'loss' also includes:

(a) any expenses reasonably incurred by the complainant in consequence of the dismissal, and
(b) subject to subsection (3), loss of any benefit which he might reasonably be expected to have had but for the dismissal.

Taken together these provisions cover the loss of most of the common fringe benefits such as company cars, free or subsidised accommodation, subsidised mortgages, low interest loans and private health insurance. It may also cover the loss of benefits received under a profit sharing scheme or a share option scheme. Some benefits, like travel expenses, depend on the employee continuing to be in work and therefore cannot be claimed while the employee is out of work.

The statutory provisions also cover the loss of any benefit an employee might reasonably expect to receive in the course of employment. However, compensation will be awarded only where the benefit is received on a regular basis (*Mullett* v *Brush Electrical Machines Ltd* [1977] ICR 829). As a result, some ex gratia benefits may be excluded. For example, the loss of a Christmas hamper is not the kind of perk for which compensation would normally be awarded. Moreover, some tribunals may refuse to compensate employees for the loss of benefits where the sums involved are small, although much will depend on the particular circumstances of each case.

The same general principles govern the assessment of loss of fringe benefits as govern a claim for loss of earnings. Thus in *Textet* v *Greenhough Ltd* EAT 410/82, the EAT said that tribunals should first work out the net loss of earnings and then add to that figure the weekly sum awarded for the loss of benefits (in the particular case the loss of a company car).

The award will be calculated up to the date when an employee finds a new job where the package is either as good as or better than the old job. Moreover, credit must be given for the value of additional benefits received in the new job, and may be set off against any loss suffered during the period the employee was out of work.

10.3 MULTIPLIER

Tribunals have to assess the length of time any loss is likely to continue, i.e., future loss. This involves considering a number of contingencies (discussed in greater detail at 9.5 above), such as the chances of the employee having left the old job anyway or finding a better paid job in due course. These contingencies are reflected in the multiplier which is applied to the amount lost (see 9.5.6 above).

It is possible that the period covered by the claim for loss of benefits may exceed that of the loss of earnings claim. For example, in *Morgan Edwards Wholesale Ltd* v *Francis* EAT 205/78, Mr Francis claimed compensation for the loss of his company car. Both sides agreed that this was worth £500 a year. The industrial tribunal held that this loss was likely to continue for a further five years and awarded £2,500. On appeal, it was argued by the company that the five-year period was too long. However, the EAT upheld the award saying that, as Mr Francis did not have a car in his new job, the award was not excessive.

In most cases, however, the period covered by an award for loss of fringe benefits is unlikely to exceed the period covered by the award for loss of earnings, since the loss of fringe benefits must be seen in the context of an employee's overall loss and therefore, in the long run, is likely to be offset by the increase in earnings from the new job.

10.4 VALUING FRINGE BENEFITS

A particular problem in relation to fringe benefits is how to calculate the value of the benefit in cash terms. Providing guidance on this subject is not an easy task since it is relatively uncommon for a tribunal to give reasons as to why it chose one method of valuation rather than another. The EAT has also been reluctant to lay down any guidelines in this area and will not overturn a tribunal's assessment unless it is obviously incorrect or completely unreasonable (see *UBAF Bank Ltd* v *Davis* [1978] IRLR 442). The result is that there are no hard and fast rules on quantifying the loss of particular benefits and much will depend on the nature of the evidence presented to the tribunal. However, there are a number of well-established methods which are often followed by tribunals in practice. These are considered in the context of the particular benefits discussed below.

10.5 COMPANY CARS

Despite recent changes in taxation, the company car remains one of the most common perks received by employees as part of their benefits package. In addition (or sometimes in the alternative), employees often receive financial assistance in the running of the car, such as petrol allowances.

It is important to recognise at the outset that compensation will be awarded only for the loss of the *private use* of the car. If the car is used exclusively for business purposes or if private use is minimal, as may be the case where the employee only has the use of a 'pool' car for business purposes, or if the use of the car is subject to other restrictions, little or no compensation will be awarded. On the other hand, if the car is a 'perk' of the job and business use is minimal, compensation may be substantial. That loss will be greater if, in addition to the use of the car, the employee also receives free maintenance, tax, insurance and petrol.

10.5.1 Valuing use

The biggest problem is to value the use of the car. There is no single or universal method of valuing the loss of the use of a car. Indeed, in many cases, tribunals do not give any clear indication of their reasons for making an award or the method used in choosing a particular figure. For example, in *Gotts* v *Hoffman Balancing Techniques Ltd* 1979 COIT 951/115, Mr Gotts claimed compensation for the loss of a new BMW which he had retained until his notice expired. During that time, the company had levied a charge of £820 per month and Mr Gotts claimed that that was what the benefit was worth. The industrial tribunal disagreed. It pointed out that this was a penal levy which was intended to put pressure on Mr Gotts to return the car. The tribunal considered that £20 a week was a fair sum based on 'their own knowledge in these matters'. (See also *Bowness* v *Concentric Pumps Ltd* 1974 COIT 318/217.) Both these cases were decided some time ago with the result that some allowance must be made for inflation.

Personal injury cases favour a tariff approach to compensation for such claims but yet again the judges' reasons for awarding a particular amount are rather obscure. For example, in *Kennedy* v *Bryan* (1984) *The Times*, 3 May 1984, a victim of a motor car accident received a lump sum of £800 for the loss of her company car. The High Court adopted a tariff approach, saying that the normal range for the loss of such a benefit was between £700 and £1,000. However, the judge gave no particular reason for choosing £800 in the particular circumstances of this case. The tariff approach has also found favour with some industrial tribunals. Recent research by Income Data Services suggests that, in the absence of evidence produced by either party in support of a higher or lower figure, tribunals currently award between £30 and £100 a week for the loss of private use of a car, depending on the type of car and the ratio of private use to business use (IDS 450, p. 7).

10.5.2 Cost of running a car: AA and RAC estimates

One common method of establishing the value of being provided with a company car is to estimate the weekly cost of running a particular type of car. This calculation may be based on the AA's or RAC's estimates which are published annually.

This method was applied by Sheen J in *Shove* v *Downs Surgical plc* [1984] 1 All ER 7, a wrongful dismissal case. The judge awarded £10,000 for the loss of a Daimler motor car over a period of 30 months — the notice period under Mr Shove's contract. In reaching this conclusion the judge relied on the AA estimates and reduced the estimated cost by the ratio of private use to business use.

A further adjustment to these estimates would have to be made if the employee contributes to the running of the car.

This method of assessment normally leads to compensation being assessed on a weekly basis, partly because this makes it easier to calculate the overall loss (see *Textet* v *Greenough Ltd* EAT 410/82). However, where the applicant remains unemployed at the time of the hearing, the tribunal may opt for a lump sum payment instead.

Note: Some employers also have their own motor mileage allowances which are sometimes more generous than the estimates produced by the AA and RAC (see Pay and Benefits Bulletin 288, published by Industrial Relations Services). Where this is the case, it would be open to either the applicant or the employer to base its valuation of the loss on these figures.

10.5.3 Inland Revenue scales

Another method of valuing the benefit of a company car is to rely on the scale charges drawn up by the Inland Revenue for tax purposes. The scale charges are based on the cylinder capacity and age of the car or, in the case of a more expensive car, its original market value and age.

The drawback of relying on the Inland Revenue scales is that they are intended to value the perk for tax purposes and may therefore not give a true valuation of the benefit to the employee. Thus, in *Shove* v *Downs Surgical plc* [1984] 1 All ER 7, Sheen J rejected the employer's argument that he should use the Inland Revenue scales to value Mr Shove's claim for the loss of the company car. Similarly, in *Kennedy* v *Bryan* (1984) *The Times*, 3 May 1984, the judge distinguished the value of the car for tax purposes and the value for compensation purposes. On the other hand, despite recent changes, the Inland Revenue Scales represent a very conservative valuation and may therefore be favoured by employers in settlement negotiations.

10.5.4 Purchase and resale

Another possible way of valuing the loss of a company car is for the employee to buy or hire a car and claim a proportion of the cost from the employer.

This approach was successfully relied on by the applicant in *Nohar* v *Granitstone (Galloway) Ltd* [1974] ICR 273. Following his dismissal, Mr Nohar bought himself a new car which he then resold after he found a new job (where a car was also provided as a perk). In addition to the loss on resale, which was £80, Mr Nohar claimed the cost of insuring the car — a further £20 and £18 for tax making a total of £118. The industrial tribunal rejected his claim but the NIRC, allowing the appeal, held that an award of £100 was 'fair and reasonable'.

Such an approach should, however, be treated with caution because the loss on resale includes the depreciation in the value of the car rather than the 'pure' loss suffered as a direct result of the loss of employment and therefore applicants who go for the 'purchase and resale' option will have to satisfy the tribunal that they acted reasonably.

Similarly, employees who seek to recover the cost of hiring an equivalent car should be aware that the hire charges include the profits of the hire company and therefore a claim for the full amount may be disallowed for this reason. Such a claim may be allowed in exceptional circumstances where the car is necessary to enable the applicant to mitigate his or her loss.

10.5.5 Cars provided on HP

The basis of assessment is different where the benefit takes the form of both the free use of the car and its eventual ownership. This may arise if a car is bought on hire purchase in the employee's name but the employer pays the whole or part of the hire purchase repayments. The assessment of loss in such circumstances raises similar problems to those raised in cases where the employee is claiming compensation for the loss of an interest free loan or a subsidised mortgage (see 10.7).

One method is to award the employee a proportion of the outstanding hire purchase payments. This approach was used by the industrial tribunal in *S & U Stores v Wormleighton* EAT 477/77. The industrial tribunal found that at the time of dismissal £820 was outstanding under the hire purchase agreement. It awarded Mr Wormleighton half this amount. On appeal, the employers criticised the tribunal's assessment, saying that it did not make allowance for the continued depreciation in the value of the car over the remainder of the repayment period. They also challenged the tribunal's calculation of the repayments. Thus they argued that Mr Wormleighton should have received £390 rather than £410. The EAT, dismissing the appeal, said that although the tribunal's approach was rather unscientific, it was not unreasonable in the circumstances.

10.5.6 Calculating the value of the loss of a car: a summary

In summary, the following steps should be taken in assessing the value of a company car:

(a) make sure you know what you are trying to value i.e., the terms on which the benefit was provided;
(b) decide what method of valuation is appropriate;
(c) remember to take into account the ratio of private use to business use;
(d) add the value of the lost benefit to the employee's overall loss.

10.6 ACCOMMODATION

Compensation may be awarded for the loss of rent-free or subsidised accommodation. Here again, the first task is to determine what kind of benefit is being provided, since the award will normally be greater if the accommodation is free than if it is subsidised. Furthermore, no compensation will be awarded if the employee pays the market rent (*Nohar* v *Granitstone (Galloway) Ltd* [1974] ICR 273). Having determined the nature of the benefit, it is then necessary to put a cash figure on it. In practice, tribunals apply a fairly rough and ready approach to the value they place on this benefit.

The most favourable method of assessment from an employee's point of view is the open market value of the accommodation. This method seems to have been used by the industrial tribunal in *Butler* v *J Wendon & Son* [1972] IRLR 15, where the open market rental of a tied cottage was assessed at £3 a week (although clearly this is not a reliable guide to present day values). Employees wishing to rely on this approach should be able to give evidence on the open market value of the accommodation.

The alternative method of assessing the cost of suitable alternative accommodation is more favourable to employers. This method is commonly used where the employee has found new accommodation at the time of the hearing. In *Lloyd* v *Scottish Co-operative Wholesale Society* [1973] IRLR 93, the tribunal awarded the difference between the rent Mr Lloyd paid in the council flat in which he lived at the time of the hearing and the rent he previously paid to his employers for the occupation of tied accommodation. However, it has also been applied where the employee has not found a new place to live. Thus in *Dandy* v *Lacy* EAT 450/77, the tribunal based its award on the difference in rent between a rent-free tied cottage and a council flat in the same area even though Mr Lacy had not found himself a council flat at the time of the hearing. Again, evidence should be presented to the tribunal by employers wishing to rely on this method.

On the other hand, where employees buy accommodation rather than look for suitable rented accommodation, it is arguable that they should be entitled to recover a proportion of the mortgage during the period of assessment. The notional sum should be based on the interest paid by the employee to the building society, thereby excluding the part of the repayment which relates to the purchase of the capital asset. The award will therefore rarely cover the full cost of the mortgage.

10.7 COMPANY LOANS

Many organisations, particularly in the banking and financial sectors, offer their employees the valuable perk of a cheap-rate loan or subsidised mortgage. The loss of such a benefit may be recovered as part of the compensatory award. The problem yet again is how to put a cash value on the benefit. In theory, the assessment should be fairly straightforward — the employee's loss is the difference between the cost of the perk and the comparable market rate for a mortgage or loan — but tribunals often opt for a broad brush approach rather than a mathematical quantification of the award.

For example, in *UBAF Bank Ltd* v *Davis* [1978] IRLR 442, the industrial tribunal awarded Mr Davis £2,000 for all the privileges he had lost as a result of his dismissal. This included a low interest mortgage. Mr Davis had produced evidence to show that he would have to pay a high street building society an extra £675 and argued that this was the annual value of the perk. On appeal, the bank argued that the tribunal's award was excessive because it had failed to take into account the fact that the loan from the bank did not have to be repaid for a year after the dismissal. The EAT said that the bank should have argued this point in mitigation before the tribunal and refused to interfere with the tribunal's award. The fact that the tribunal opted for a lump sum payment does not, of course, mean that it ignored Mr Davis's evidence on quantum. Indeed this evidence would appear to have influenced its decision.

10.8 OTHER BENEFITS

10.8.1 Food

Many companies have their own staff canteens; sometimes the meals are provided free but more often they are subsidised. The loss of this perk has been claimed in a number of cases. For example, in *Fowler* v *Westcliffe* COIT 1001/164, a tribunal estimated that the weekly value of free food and drink was £10. In *Rippa* v *Devere Hotels* COIT 144/83, the value of free meals for one year was held to be £600.

10.8.2 Travel allowances

The loss of a travel allowance or other benefits relating to travel may be recovered as part of the compensatory award. In *Dr Cruz* v *Airways Aero Association Ltd* COIT 6066/72, an industrial tribunal awarded £600 for the loss of a special travel allowance, even though the allowance was a privilege and not a contractual right.

10.8.3 Free telephone

Sometimes, employers pay for an employee's home telephone. Compensation can be recovered for the loss of this benefit (see *Dundee Plant Co Ltd* v *Riddler* EAT 377/88, where £160 was awarded for the free use of a telephone covering both the rental and telephone charges).

10.8.4 Medical insurance

Compensation may be awarded for the loss of private medical insurance, the loss being measured in terms of the cost of providing equivalent or continued insurance cover (*Ross* v *Yewlands Engineering Co Ltd* COIT 17321/83/LN).

10.8.5 Share ownership

Some companies run profit-sharing schemes or encourage their employees to buy shares in the business. The annual value of such benefits may well be considerable and the loss may be claimed as part of the compensatory award.

Compensation may be awarded for the loss of a stock option provided that the industrial tribunal is satisfied that the applicant would have been granted such an option but for the dismissal (*O'Laoire* v *Jackel International Ltd* [1991] IRLR 170). But the loss may be difficult to prove and quantify where there is no more than a mere promise to grant such an option in the future. Another problem may arise where such an option lapses on dismissal and the scheme excludes liability for compensation in such circumstances (see *Micklefield* v *SAC Technology Ltd* [1991] 1 All ER 275). Here, however, it is arguable that an exemption clause would contravene s. 203 of the Employment Rights Act 1996 and therefore has no effect. As to the valuation of lost stock options, see 1.4.2.5.

10.9 EXPENSES

The assessment of loss also includes any expenses reasonably incurred by the employee as a result of the dismissal. However, before such an award is made the tribunal must be satisfied that (ERA 1996, s. 123(2)(a)):

(a) the expenses were incurred as a result of the dismissal;
(b) the expenses were reasonably incurred; and
(c) the sums incurred were reasonable in themselves.

A claim for expenses should therefore be supported by evidence produced at the tribunal hearing.

10.9.1 Cost of finding a new job

The most common kind of expenses allowed under this head are those incurred as a result of looking for a new job. The expenses may include postal costs, phone calls and other costs relating to the application. They also cover the cost of attending interviews (*Leech* v *Berger, Jensen & Nicholson Ltd* [1972] IRLR 58). Such expenses cannot be recovered if the costs are reimbursed by the prospective employer or the Department of Employment.

Tribunals have also allowed employees to claim removal expenses and other costs arising from the need to move home. For example, in *Lloyd* v *Scottish Co-operative Wholesale Society Ltd* [1973] IRLR 93 (see 10.6 above), the tribunal awarded Mr Lloyd £20 for the cost of moving out of the tied accommodation supplied by his employers. A claim for removal costs also succeeded in *Co-operative Wholesale Society* v *Squirrell* (1974) ITR 191. There, the tribunal considered that it was necessary for the employee to move home in order to secure another job. In one case, a tribunal thought that it was just and equitable to award compensation for other expenses connected with the sale of a house such as the conveyancing costs and estate agents' fees (*Daykin* v *IHW Engineering Ltd* COIT 1440/117).

10.9.2 Expenses in starting up a business

In addition, tribunals have allowed employees to recover some of the costs incurred in setting up a business where they considered that this was a reasonable way of mitigating the loss flowing from the dismissal.

In *Gardiner-Hill* v *Roland Berger Technics Ltd* [1982] IRLR 498, Mr Gardiner-Hill claimed £500 worth of expenses which he had incurred in setting up a consultancy service. The industrial tribunal held that Mr Gardiner-Hill had acted reasonably in setting up the consultancy service in mitigation of his loss and allowed his claim in respect of the expenses incurred by him. The EAT agreed, saying that the expenses were reasonably incurred as a result of the dismissal.

Such expenses may include the cost of a car if a car was provided as a perk of the old job (*Sparkes* v *E T Barwick Mills Ltd* 1977 COIT 611/68) and relocation costs. For example, in *United Freight Distribution Ltd* v *McDougall* (S) EAT 218/94, the EAT upheld an industrial tribunal's decision to award £550 to cover the legal fees necessary to sell Mr McDougall's house. The EAT also accepted that in principle an award of compensation could also include a loan to cover relocation expenses provided that the loan was a reasonable estimate of the relocation expenses and was made for that purpose. (See 15.5.4 regarding the issues relating to mitigation.)

10.9.3 Legal expenses

The tribunal is only empowered to award costs in accordance with its own rules of procedure (Industrial Tribunals (Rules of Procedure) Regulations 1985 (SI 1985 No. 16), r. 11). Thus, the legal costs of bringing a complaint of unfair dismissal are not recoverable as part of a compensation claim (*Raynor* v *Remploy Ltd* [1973] IRLR 3). However, the cost of attending the industrial tribunal may be recovered from the tribunal itself.

11 Calculating the Compensatory Award: Pensions

11.1 INTRODUCTION AND GENERAL PRINCIPLES

Potentially, the loss of pension benefits is one of the most serious losses of benefits which may arise on dismissal. The right to recover compensation for loss of pension benefits was established by the NIRC in *Copson* v *Eversure Accessories Ltd* [1974] IRLR 247 as long ago as 1974. The statutory basis for claiming compensation for loss of pension rights is the same as that for other benefits. Section 123(2) of the Employment Rights Act 1996 expressly states that the loss of any benefit which an employee might reasonably be expected to have had but for the dismissal constitutes a loss sustained 'in consequence of the dismissal' under s. 123(1). But, as the EAT observed in *Benson* v *Dairy Crest Ltd* EAT 192/89, it remains one of the most difficult areas of compensation to assess and quantify. As a result tribunals have often applied 'a broad brush' approach to compensation. Inherent in this approach is a risk of inconsistency between cases and over/under-compensation. Accordingly, in more recent times, there has been a trend towards adopting a common approach to assessing compensation, without encouraging the use of elaborate evidence to compute loss. The *Benson* case is a significant judicial reflection of this trend.

In April 1990, a committee of chairmen of industrial tribunals appointed by the President of the Industrial Tribunals (England and Wales), in consultation with the Government Actuary's Department, produced a set of guidelines for assessing pension loss, namely, *Industrial Tribunals: compensation for loss of pension rights*. It built on the Government Actuary's Department guide to tribunals, *A suggested method for assessing loss, which was published of pension rights* in 1980. It is commonly referred to as 'the Blue Book', and is so referred to below. Note that the colour of the book may change in the future.

The Blue Book was described by the EAT in *Benson* as 'an excellent and careful study of the issues with some extremely useful suggestions of how Industrial Tribunals may be helped with the problems that appear before them'. This compliment by the EAT will accelerate the trend for tribunals to assess pension loss in accordance with the terms of the Blue Book. However, as the EAT noted, while the Blue Book 'merits ... careful attention [it is] not by any means laying down rules'. As the EAT stated in *Bigham* v *Hobourn Engineering Ltd* [1992] IRLR 298 there is no duty on industrial tribunals to follow the Blue Book and they will not err in law in failing to give effect to its recommendations. It would therefore be a mistake to view the Blue Book as the answer to all pension loss calculations. Significantly, the EAT's decision in *Benson* was to remit the case to the tribunal that had heard the applicant's case with the suggestion that the tribunal would derive help from using the guidelines.

This chapter starts by explaining the types of occupational pensions likely to be encountered. It then sets out the main principles which have been established by tribunal decisions. Lastly, detailed consideration is given to the guidelines, which understandably will be the first port of call for tribunals and litigants alike.

It should be noted that 'pension benefits' are sometimes taken to include benefits that are occasionally treated by employers as part of a pension scheme although they are not strictly pensions. Such benefits include life assurance and permanent health insurance, but these benefits are not considered in this chapter. They are, however, benefits that might form part of a compensatory award.

It should also be noted that the approach adopted in unfair dismissal cases is not necessarily the same as that applied elsewhere. For example, in sex discrimination cases, the guidelines may not be followed because in unfair dismissal cases 'the statutory ceiling on compensation is such as to cry out for an unsophisticated approach to the computation of pension loss' but there is no ceiling for sex discrimination awards (see *Ministry of Defence* v *Mutton* [1996] ICR 590).

11.2 TYPES OF PENSIONS

In order to assess pension loss in unfair dismissal cases, it is necessary to consider briefly how a pension scheme works.

Occupational pension schemes are, broadly speaking, divided into two types — defined contribution (or 'money purchase') and defined benefits (usually of the 'final salary' type — see below). If under a defined contribution or defined benefits scheme the employee is not obliged to contribute, this is called a 'non-contributory' scheme.

In a defined contribution scheme, the scheme defines the contributions to be made by employer and employee (if any) and on retirement the employee receives whatever pension can be bought by the accumulated contributions.

In a defined benefits scheme the aim is to provide a certain pension benefit on retirement and the level of employer's contribution will be the amount necessary (together with any employee's contributions) to provide that benefit. The level of benefit in a defined scheme is usually expressed as a specified fraction of the employee's salary at or near retirement (often either one-sixtieth or one-eightieth) multiplied by the number of years of pensionable service (usually with an adjustment for additional months). Such a scheme will be known as a 'final salary' scheme. Thus, in a final salary scheme with a one-sixtieth accrual rate, an employee with forty years' service on retirement would be entitled to a pension of two-thirds of final salary.

An employee who leaves service before retirement will usually be entitled to the benefit of the accrued contributions under a defined contribution scheme on attaining the scheme's retirement age or a deferred pension (payable from retirement) under a defined benefits scheme. It will be seen below, however, that notwithstanding the deferred pension the early leaver will suffer a financial loss which tribunals have recognised as compensatable.

The State provides a basic pension (provided certain contribution requirements have been met) and a pension that varies with the amount of National Insurance contributions paid since April 1978 (the State Earnings Related Pension Scheme or SERPS). Some occupational pension schemes are described as 'contracted-out' of SERPS, which means that, in consideration for either agreeing to provide a guaranteed level of defined benefits or paying contributions at a specified level to provide money purchase benefits, the employer and employee pay lower National Insurance contributions.

Reference is often made to the three pillars of pensions. This refers to the three main sources of pensions. The employer and the State are the first two while the third and final source of funding for pensions is the employee. Since 1986 employees may require their employer's occupational scheme to take 'additional voluntary contributions' (AVCs) and provide benefits additional to the basic benefits under the scheme. In July 1988 personal pension plans were introduced. These are money purchase arrangements where employers and/or employees may contribute to a private pension policy with an insurance company or other authorised pension provider. On retirement, the fund so created is used to purchase an annuity for the employee. Employees can use a personal pension plan to 'contract-out' of SERPS, in which case the Department of Social Security will contribute an amount equal to the saving in National Insurance contributions that would have been made if the employee was contracted-out under an occupational scheme (together, as from 6 April 1997, with an additional age-related contribution).

11.3 TYPES OF LOSS

In *Copson* v *Eversure Accessories Ltd* [1974] IRLR 247, the NIRC recognised that compensation for pension loss falls to be considered under two heads, past loss and future loss. However, in some circumstances it may be inappropriate to make an award at all. It is therefore necessary to review separately three situations:

(a) where tribunals take the view there is no compensatable loss;
(b) compensatable past loss; and
(c) cole future loss.

The methods of calculating any loss are looked at subsequently (see 11.4 below).

11.3.1   No compensatable loss

In common with the other heads of compensation, an award will be made only if it can be shown that the employee applicant has suffered loss as a result of the dismissal. Unless the applicant is covered by an occupational pension scheme which confers greater benefits than those guaranteed by the State scheme, there will be no loss.

Even where the applicant is covered by a pension scheme, there may be no compensatable loss if the applicant does not qualify for a pension under the rules of the scheme (see *Jones* v *International Press Institute* EAT 571/81 and *Manning* v *R & H Wale (Export) Ltd* [1979] ICR 433) or if the applicant's rights under the scheme are valueless. In the case of *Samuels* v *Clifford Chance* EAT 559/90, the employer's pension scheme had a qualifying period of five years. Ms Samuels was unfairly dismissed after two and a half years' service. The tribunal concluded that as she would not have stayed with the employer for another two and a half years she would not have qualified for a pension, and therefore no pension loss arose.

11.3.2 Past loss

The first type of compensatable loss is past loss, i.e., loss of all or part of the pension earned at the date of dismissal.

In the case of a defined contribution scheme, the employer's commitment is to contribute to the scheme in accordance with the rules of the scheme. It follows that if the employee receives the full value of those contributions there is no past loss. However if the employee suffers a penalty for early departure from the scheme, then that penalty is the past loss.

In the case of a defined benefits scheme, the employee's entitlement is to a defined benefit so that, at the time of dismissal, the employee will have earned part of the benefit payable on retirement. To the extent that the applicant does not receive the benefit earned, there is clearly a loss but in most cases there is an additional loss (often called 'loss of enhancement of accrued pension rights'). It is common for a defined benefits scheme to offer a pension calculated as a percentage of the employee's 'final salary'. If an employee leaves service early, the pension entitlement on retirement is almost always calculated by reference to the salary at the date of leaving. It follows that, if it is to be expected that the employee's salary would have increased prior to retirement, a loss will arise.

This can be shown by the following example:

Example

X is aged 50 and was employed for 30 years with the benefit of a final salary scheme that promises a pension of two-thirds of final salary after 40 years' service at age 60 (i.e., an accrual rate of one-sixtieth). X was earning £20,000 per annum at the date he left service but, had he worked another 10 years (i.e., until he was 60 and retired), his salary would have been £30,000 per annum immediately before retirement. At the date of retirement his pension would have been £20,000 per annum (40/60 × £30,000).

Looked at another way the amount of pension attributable to his first 30 years of service would have been £15,000 per annum (30/60 × £30,000). However, when X left service at 50 his pension at 60 is calculated by reference to salary at the leaving date. Therefore his pension at 60 will be £10,000 per annum (30/60 × £20,000). Therefore the failure to take account of the prospective increase in salary has produced a pension loss of £5,000 per annum.

In practice the position is more complicated than this. First, part of a member's deferred pension in a contracted-out scheme is a guaranteed minimum pension. This must be revalued in line with statutory requirements and this will reduce the deficit in the above example. Secondly, under the provisions of the Pension Schemes Act 1993, accrued pensions in excess of the guaranteed minimum pension on leaving service (£10,000 per annum in the above example) must be revalued up to retirement by the lower of 5% per year compound and the rise in retail prices (between leaving service and retirement). The extent to which these statutory revaluations increase the pension payable by less than the projected increase in salary is the extent to which the member still suffers a past loss.

The factors which have to be taken into account in assessing past loss are set out below.

11.3.2.1 Transferability

There is no past loss if employees are offered the opportunity of transferring the full value of their pension entitlement to a new fund (provided this takes into account any projected increase in salary). Thus, in *Freemans plc v Flynn* [1984] IRLR 486, the EAT overturned a tribunal award for past loss on the ground that the employee had sustained no loss because the employee could either make such a transfer or leave the contributions in the original scheme so that they would provide him with a pension at 65. See also *Yeats v Fairey Winches Ltd* [1974] IRLR 362, where the fund was frozen and the benefits were therefore preserved.

Until the mid-1980s, it was relatively unusual for employees to be offered the opportunity of transferring the full value of their existing pension entitlement to another fund. Since 1 January 1986, however, employees leaving occupational pension schemes have a statutory right to a 'transfer value' which is at least equal to the cash equivalent of benefits to which the member leaving early would have been entitled had he or she remained in the scheme. Regulations prescribe the types of scheme which are acceptable recipients of transfer values and also set out certain requirements with regard to the calculation of 'transfer values' (see the Occupational Pension Scheme (Transfer Values) Regulations 1985 (SI 1985 No. 1931)). There is no obligation to provide for projected increases in salary (see above).

11.3.2.2 Withdrawal

The possibility that the dismissed employee would have withdrawn from the scheme in any event before normal retirement has to be taken into account in the assessment of past loss. This reflects the chance that the employee would have left the job voluntarily or might have been fairly dismissed due to redundancy or for some other reason before retirement.

It is for the tribunal to assess the chances of withdrawal and reduce the award accordingly. The Government Actuary's Department guidelines of 1980 included a table of percentage deductions based on an 'average' chance of withdrawal. The guidelines deliberately refrain from producing a table on the basis that this is a matter for each tribunal to determine. It is clear that it is open to the parties to call evidence to support a particular level of reduction. For example, in *Manpower Ltd v Hearne* [1983] IRLR 281, the company argued for a greater reduction than that specified in the 1980 Government Actuary's Department guidelines on the ground that the industry had a high labour turnover. The tribunal rejected Manpower's argument and the EAT refused to disturb its ruling on this point but implicitly accepted that it was open to the parties to call evidence in support of a higher or lower figure.

Other factors which may lead a tribunal to increase the percentage reduction for withdrawal include where there is a higher than average chance of resignation (e.g., a 'high flyer' may be considered to have a higher than average likelihood of changing jobs) or where there is a higher than average chance of fair dismissal.

A tribunal's failure to consider the possibility of withdrawal amounts to an error of law (*Manpower Ltd v Hearne* and *Linvar Ltd v Hammersley* EAT 226/83).

11.3.2.3 Deferred pensions

Credit must be given for the receipt of a deferred pension in the calculation of past pension loss. However the acceptance, whether voluntary or otherwise, of a defe for his or her accrued pension. As explained at 11.3.2 above, if an employee stays in service until retirement, the pension would probably have been calculated as a percentage of final salary at retirement but, in leaving early, the deferred pension is likely to be based on the employee's salary at the date of leaving and this is likely to be less. Recent statutory changes go some way to meeting this problem by requiring deferred pensions to be revalued (see 11.3.2 above).

11.3.2.4 Return of contributions

Most schemes give employees the right to a refund of their own contributions if they leave the job before completing two years' service. The return of an employee's contributions does not in itself compensate employees for the pension to which they would have become entitled had they not been dismissed or for the loss of the sums contributed to the fund by the employer on their behalf (*Willment Bros v Oliver* [1979] IRLR 393; *Smith, Kline & French Laboratories Ltd v Coates* [1977] IRLR 220). Nonetheless, some credit must be given for the return of the contributions in the assessment. This will be greater if compound interest is included in the returned contributions.

11.3.2.5 Mitigation of loss

Employees are under a general obligation to lessen the loss flowing from their dismissal (see Chapter 15). The question of whether an employee has taken reasonable steps to mitigate loss is essentially a question of fact. It is therefore, for example, open to tribunals to conclude that an employee is acting unreasonably if he chooses a refund of contributions where he could choose a deferred pension, which is usually more valuable, in the absence of good reason for doing so.

An example of a case where a tribunal decided that an employee was not in breach of the duty to mitigate is *Sturdy Finance Ltd v Bardsley* [1979] IRLR 65. Mr Bardsley refused to accept his employer's offer of a deferred pension and preferred to take a refund of his contributions. Sturdy Finance argued that by taking the less valuable benefit, thereby increasing his loss, Mr Bardsley was in breach of this duty. Mr Bardsley justified his refusal on the ground that the pension would not have been worth very much and he needed the money to set up a new business. Both the tribunal and the EAT accepted that his refusal was reasonable.

11.3.3 Future loss

The second type of pension loss is the loss of future pensions opportunity, i.e., the opportunity to improve on the pension earned at the time of dismissal. In the case of a defined contribution scheme this is the loss of the employer's contribution to the scheme. In the case of a defined benefits scheme, where longer service is likely to lead to increased benefits, the loss is the benefits foregone by reason of the shortened service.

The factors which have to be taken into account in assessing future loss are set out below.

11.3.3.1 Period of unemployment

As is the case with assessing loss of salary, the tribunal has to wrestle with the problem of how long will the applicant be unemployed? Furthermore, where it is thought that the applicant will find new employment, will the employment carry with it pension benefits?

Where an employee finds a new job without an occupational pension scheme, the tribunal will have to assess the chances of the employee finding a job with an equivalent scheme in the future. If the applicant finds a new job and is eligible to join his new employer's occupational pension scheme, the tribunal is faced with the task of comparing the 'old' and 'new' schemes. If the new scheme is broadly the same as the old, there will be no future loss (*Sturdy Finance* v *Bardsley* [1979] IRLR 65). If the new scheme is significantly less beneficial, the tribunal will have to value the consequential loss suffered by the employee. In making this assessment, the tribunal should take into account both the chances of the employee finding a different job with an equivalent pension to the one in the original scheme and the chances of improvements being made to the scheme which he has now joined. It is also possible that, for example, a higher salary reflects the absence of a pension. However, tribunals are likely to adopt a fairly broad brush approach to these matters.

11.3.3.2 Withdrawal

Tribunals must consider the possibility of withdrawal from the 'old' scheme as a result of resignation or fair dismissal. Tribunals often apply the same percentage reduction they apply to past loss (see 11.3.2.2 above and the case of *Manpower Ltd* v *Hearne* [1983] IRLR 281 there noted).

11.3.3.3 Credit for future employee contributions

Allowance must be made for the contributions which the employee would have had to make to the pension scheme had he or she remained in the former employment (see *Pringle* v *Lucas Industrial Equipment Ltd* [1975] IRLR 266).

11.3.3.4 Allowance for accelerated payment

The overall award for loss of pension rights must take into account any accelerated receipt of benefits which would not otherwise have become payable until retirement (see *Smith, Kline & French Laboratories Ltd* v *Coates* [1977] IRLR 220 and *Powermatic Ltd* v *Bull* [1977] IRLR 144). However, the extent to which the award should be reduced for this reason is unclear.

In *Yeats* v *Fairey Winches Ltd* [1974] IRLR 362, the award for pension loss was reduced by approximately 44% to take account of the possibility of withdrawal and to make allowance for the accelerated payment in the form of a lump sum rather than a weekly payment. Unfortunately the tribunal did not specify what proportion of this percentage reduction related to the latter factor. It is arguable that the reduction should be smaller as the employee nears retiring age. Of some interest, therefore, is the recent decision in *Page* v *Sheerness Steel plc* [1996] PIQR Q26where, in determining a discount rate for a lump sum payment of damages for personal injury (which included pension loss), Dyson J applied a rate of 3%, being the rate of return on index-linked gilt securities.

11.4 METHODS OF CALCULATING LOSS

The problem of how to value pension loss was recognised soon after it became a permissible head of compensation (*Scottish Co-operative Wholesale Society Ltd* v *Lloyd* [1973] ICR 137). In later cases, the EAT has said that there is no single correct method of assessing pension loss and the choice of method is essentially a matter for the tribunal to determine. Moreover, provided a tribunal exercises its discretion fairly and reasonably its decision is unlikely to be overturned on appeal.

There are two basic methods of calculating pension loss. These are:

(a) the contributions method — which defines the loss primarily in terms of the employer's contributions to the pension scheme in question; and

(b) various forms of actuarial assessment (sometimes called 'value' or 'benefits' method) — where the loss is assessed in terms of the benefit to which the employee would have become entitled under the relevant pension scheme but for the dismissal.

The guidelines, on the whole, use the contributions methods for future loss and an actuarial method for past loss (see 11.6 below).

11.4.1 Contributions method

The contributions method defines pension loss in terms of the contributions paid by the employer and employee and then applies an appropriate multiplier. An illustration of the use of the contributions method can be seen in the guidelines (see 11.6.2.1 below). The various elements in such an assessment are dealt with below.

11.4.1.1 Contribution rate and interest
If the scheme specifies a contribution rate (usually expressed as a sum equal to a specified percentage of salary), the loss should be determined at that rate. However, if the contribution rate is anomalous (e.g., because the employer is taking a contribution holiday), a notional rate should be found. Consideration ought to be given to whether interest (simple or compound) should be added.

11.4.1.2 Multiplier
The multiplier represents the period over which the applicant's loss should be computed. This is not easy to determine in the case of past loss and therefore the

guidelines do not use the contributions method with a multiplier for this type of loss. As to future loss, the multiplier is likely to be the period during which the applicant, but for the unfair dismissal, might have reasonably expected the employer to contribute to the pension scheme. Account must be taken of the prospect of the applicant leaving the scheme. Thus, in *Powermatic Ltd* v *Bull* [1977] IRLR 144) the applicant had 33 years to retirement at 65. The EAT considered a multiplier of 33 was inappropriate bearing in mind the prospects of Mr Bull leaving the employer's service and therefore substituted a multiplier of 15.

11.4.1.3   Other elements
The prospects of withdrawal must be considered and it may be appropriate to make a discount for accelerated payment as well as giving credit for transfers to another scheme, deferred pension, return of contributions, finding a new job with a pension scheme and the applicant foregoing an obligation to pay contributions to the former employer's pension scheme (see 11.3.2.1 to 11.3.3.4 above).

11.4.1.4   Drawbacks to contributions method
The contributions method is self-evidently easy to apply and therefore has been often used by tribunals. However, its primary drawback is that it is often not an accurate measure of the applicant's loss. In the case of a defined contribution scheme (see 11.3.2 and 11.3.3 above), the contributions method will be appropriate. In the case of a defined benefits scheme, the applicant's loss can be fully provided for only by putting the applicant in the position he or she would have been in but for the unfair dismissal and the contributions method is unlikely to achieve this. In broad terms it can be said that this method tends to favour younger employees with short service and underestimates the value of the benefits of older employees with long service.

11.4.2   Benefits method

The alternative and more accurate method of calculating pension loss is the benefits method. This defines the loss in terms of the pension benefits an employee has earned at the time of dismissal and then seeks to place a value on what is needed to put the applicant in the pension position he or she would have been in had there not been an unfair dismissal. In fact, a number of different benefit methods may be used; some are more generous to employees than others.

Whichever method is adopted, consideration must be given to deductions or discounts for benefits received by the applicant and similar factors as discussed in respect of the contributions method (see 11.4.1.3 above).

11.4.2.1   Cost of annuity
One way of assessing the loss is to work out the capital cost of purchasing an annuity which would yield an equivalent pension to that which the employee would have received but for the dismissal. From this is deducted what the applicant has received (e.g., a deferred pension). In *John Millar & Sons* v *Quinn* [1974] IRLR 107, Mrs

Quinn was dismissed eight years before her sixtieth birthday. The NIRC assessed compensation on the cost of purchasing an annuity which would give her a pension equivalent to the one which she would have received at 60 years of age had she not been dismissed.

However, this approach is likely to be adopted only where the employee is close to retirement. In other cases an adjustment will have to be made to reflect the fact that the loss may not be a continuing one.

11.4.2.2 Effect of pension from new employment

In *Willment Bros* v *Oliver* [1979] IRLR 393, the EAT accepted that it was possible to assess pension loss by comparing the difference in the annual value of the pension which an employee receives in the new job with that in the old. The total loss would then depend on the multiplier adopted in a particular case. However, the EAT warned that it would normally be impossible to make this calculation with any certainty, since there were so many unknown factors to take into account. It would also create difficulties in assessing the possibility of withdrawal.

11.4.2.3 Partial discontinuance method

The Government Actuary's Department guidelines of 1980 were based on the 'partial discontinuance' method. This makes some allowance for inflation and the prospects of an increase in real income before retirement.

The benefits method of valuing pension loss (irrespective of actuarial method used) still requires a tribunal to make:

(a) a discount for the possibility of withdrawal; and

(b) an allowance for the accelerated payment of the benefits (see *Copson* v *Eversure Accessories Ltd* [1974] IRLR 247).

Moreover, if the scheme is contributory, the award must be reduced by the amount of the employee's future contributions (see *Pringle* v *Lucas Industrial Equipment Ltd* [1975] IRLR 266). If the actuarial method adopted takes the salary earned on dismissal rather than the projected final salary, not all the loss referred to at 11.3.2 will have been compensated.

11.5 OTHER PRINCIPLES

11.5.1 Proof of loss

The tribunal must raise pension loss as a head of loss along with the other heads of compensation, but the actual burden of proving loss lies on the employee (*Tidman* v *Aveling Marshall Ltd* [1977] IRLR 218). Thus it is 'for claimants ... to present material to the tribunal upon which they desire an assessment to be made' (*Hilti (GB) Ltd* v *Windridge* [1974] IRLR 53).

The problem is that the relevant information is normally in the hands of the employer with the result that it is up to the employee to get hold of the relevant documentation in advance. If necessary, tribunals may make an order of discovery which compels employers to disclose the information in their possession (see Industrial Tribunals (Constitution and Rules of Procedure) Regulations 1993 (SI 1993 No. 2687), reg. 8(1) and sch. 1, para. 4). Note that employees have the right to extensive information about their pension scheme (see Occupational Pension Scheme (Disclosure of Information) Regulations 1986 (SI 1986 No. 1046), shortly to be revised).

11.5.2 Actuarial evidence

The relevance and admissibility of evidence given by actuaries has been the subject of conflicting judicial rulings. In *Copson* v *Eversure Accessories Ltd* [1974] IRLR 247, the NIRC accepted that evidence from actuaries or pension brokers was relevant and admissible but thought that it would not usually be necessary in the type of case with which tribunals are concerned. On the other hand in *Tradewinds Airways Ltd* v *Fletcher* [1981] IRLR 272, the EAT went so far as to hold that a tribunal was wrong to prefer the evidence of a skilled actuary called on behalf of the applicant to the figures set out in the Government Actuary's Department 1980 paper. The EAT's conclusion is a little surprising. The preferable view is that actuarial evidence is admissible but parties who rely on such evidence do so at their own risk and their own expense (see *Manpower Ltd* v *Hearne* [1983] IRLR 281).

11.5.3 Relationship with other heads of compensation

The award for pension loss must be seen in the context of the applicant's overall compensation claim. Thus, if a former employee's pay and other conditions in a new job either match or are superior to those in the old, there will be no continuing loss and hence no award for future loss will be made. However, an award may be made if the employment package in the new job is as good as the old one in all respects, but inferior in relation to pension.

11.5.4 Contributory fault

The normal rules on contributory fault (see s. 123(6) of the Employment Rights Act 1996) apply to compensation for pension loss.

11.6 THE GUIDELINES

11.6.1 Introduction

As noted at 11.1, in April 1990 a committee of chairmen of industrial tribunals appointed by the President of the Industrial Tribunals (England and Wales), in consultation with the Government Actuary's Department, produced *Industrial Tribunals: compensation for loss of pension rights* (the 'guidelines'). A second and revised edition was produced in 1991 (HMSO 1991, 0-11-361324-5).

The authors, no doubt, hope tribunals will follow the guidelines, but they do warn that they will become 'tripwires if they are blindly applied without considering the facts of each case'. They note that any 'party is free to canvass any method of assessment which he considers appropriate'. The guidelines have no statutory force although, especially in the light of the comments in *Benson v Dairy Crest Ltd* EAT 192/89, tribunals and litigants will increasingly turn to them for guidance. However, the authors unashamedly proclaim that 'where there is a conflict between technical purity and comprehensibility we make no apology for choosing comprehensibility'. They also note that they 'are only dealing with the mainstream schemes'. Litigants therefore need to note that:

(a) simplicity may not always work in their favour, and therefore they need to consider whether they should contend the guidelines do not apply to their case; and

(b) as the guidelines encourage tribunals to determine some elements of pension loss at the first hearing on remedies, the parties should be prepared to argue a departure from the guidelines or risk the tribunal applying them.

The guidelines are examined in detail below.

11.6.2 Types of pension loss

The guidelines recommend that 'the assumption is made that there is no pension loss in respect of a dismissed employee who is not in an occupational pension scheme'. Where there is an occupational pension scheme the guidelines divide pension loss into three heads:

(a) loss of pension rights from the date of dismissal to the date of the hearing (i.e., had the applicant remained in employment the pension rights he or she would have gained the right to additional pension benefits in that period);

(b) loss of future pension rights (i.e., had the applicant stayed in employment beyond the date of hearing he or she would have gained the right to additional pension benefits); and

(c) loss of enhancement of accrued pension rights (i.e., when pension benefits accrued at the date of dismissal would have grown in value had the employee stayed in employment e.g., if pension is computed by reference to final salary at the date of leaving service longer service would mean a higher pension if final salary would have increased).

11.6.2.1 Loss of pension rights from the date of dismissal to the date of the hearing

Money purchase schemes For a money purchase scheme, the applicant's loss in this category is easy to calculate. It is the contributions the employer would have made during the period and although the guidelines do not expressly say so, it would appear to be correct that the same rule must apply to an employer's contribution to a personal pension plan.

While the guidelines do not make the point, it would seem correct to note that regard should be had to any mitigation of loss by the applicant through securing pension benefits from a new employer.

Final salary schemes The guidelines tacitly accept that the technically correct method for computing loss is to value the difference between the pension benefits the applicant is entitled to at the date of leaving employment and the pension benefits the applicant would have been entitled to had employment continued until the date of hearing. The difficulties faced by tribunals and litigants in making this calculation no doubt led the authors to opt for what they describe as 'the fairest method' namely 'the contributions method'. The following formula expresses the method to be applied.

Compensation = weekly pensionable pay × employer's pension contribution rate × number of weeks

Where:
'pensionable pay' is that part of the applicant's pay used for calculating pension or, in the absence of evidence, actual gross pay:
'employer's pension contribution rate' is the figure given in the scheme actuary's report (which members of pension schemes have a right to receive) as the employer's contribution to the scheme expressed as a percentage of total pensionable salary, or if this cannot be easily obtained or is currently anomalous (e.g., because of a contributions holiday) 10% (or 15% if a non-contributory scheme); and
'number of weeks' is the number of weeks from dismissal to the date of the hearing.

Example

A earned £10,000 per annum and his former employer contributed 10% of gross salary to a final salary pension. At the hearing, which occurs 16 weeks after dismissal, A is held to have been unfairly dismissed by the employer.
A's pension loss under this head would be:

$$(10{,}000 \times {}^1/_{52}) \times 10\% \times 16 = £308$$

The guidelines state that one should allow for 'any sums paid in lieu of notice'. It is not entirely clear what this means. It would seem right to make an allowance to the extent that part of any such sums does compensate for loss of pension benefits. As noted in the context of money purchase schemes, it is arguable that one should take into account pension benefits from a new employer.

11.6.2.2 Loss of future pension rights
In assessing loss from the date of the hearing to the date of retirement, the guidelines again recommend the contributions method, although here the authors explicitly recognise the possibility of future employment. Their guidelines concentrate on final salary schemes but the principles should be equally applicable to money purchase schemes.

The authors consider that if a tribunal contemplates new employment within one or two years, it is reasonable to assume that the pension scheme will also be comparable. As to the fact that some pension schemes set down a qualification period before pension benefits are available, the guidelines say this is not only unusual but also that, in such schemes, on qualification entitlement is often backdated to the start of employment. Applicants might in appropriate cases challenge that assumption.

Where the applicant has secured alternative employment the guidelines recommend:

(a) if there is no scheme in the new employment, the employee will be in SERPS and therefore the employer will make a payment which should be deducted at the rate of 3% of gross pay unless there is evidence to the contrary; and

(b) if there is a scheme, the tribunal must assess the difference between the two schemes and here 'a good rule of thumb' is to compare the old and new employer's contribution rates.

Example

B earned £10,000 per annum and his former employer contributed 10% of gross salary to a final salary pension. At the hearing the tribunal determines that B has been unfairly dismissed, that B will find immediate employment but that he will not be entitled to a comparable pension for one year.

Future pension loss would be:

$$(10,000 \times 1/_{52}) \times (10\% - 3\%) \times 52 = £700$$

If the facts were the same but the new employer has expected to provide a pension and contribute to it at the rate of 9% of gross salary for a year and thereafter at 10%.

Future loss would be:

$$(10,000 \times 1/_{52}) \times (10\% - 9\%) \times 52 = £100$$

This method for assessing future loss undoubtedly has the merit of simplicity. However, this can work against the interests of some parties (see, for example, *Ministry of Defence* v *Mutton* [1996] ICR 590, where — although a pregnancy dismissal sex discrimination case — a 'value' method was preferred to the contributions method because of the expected length of the applicant's service but for the dismissal). The guidelines do not consider the possibility of the new employer's scheme being contracted-in where the old employer's scheme was contracted-out. In this case, the old employer's contribution is likely to be a greater percentage of gross salary but the new employer will be paying into SERPS and it would therefore seem just that the SERPS contribution should be added to the new employer's contribution to his scheme. Secondly, account should be taken of any payment made by the new employer to a personal pension plan. Thirdly, to the extent that the period of weeks in the formula is substantial, an employer might argue that there should be a discount for accelerated receipt by the applicant (although a counter-argument is that the contribution rate is a present cost of providing a future benefit).

11.6.2.3 Loss of enhancement of accrued pension rights

Money purchase schemes The guidelines state that in most schemes the applicant suffers no loss of accrued pension rights as the sums accrued continue to be invested for the applicant's benefit. The exception is where the applicant suffers a penalty on leaving the scheme. Here the guidelines recommend compensation equal to the amount of the penalty. Not mentioned is the possibility that a penalty might have been incurred anyway on withdrawal before retirement.

Final salary schemes As previously noted, the applicant who leaves a final salary scheme may suffer a loss of accrued pension benefits where the pension on retirement is calculated as a percentage of final salary. If the applicant's deferred pension (i.e., the pension payable at normal retirement date but calculated on the date of leaving) is not enhanced to reflect increases in salary the applicant might have expected to receive had he or she stayed in employment, there will be a loss if salary would have increased. This potential loss is mitigated to some extent by the statutory obligation to revalue deferred pensions (see 11.3.2 above). However as this revaluation is capped at whichever is the lower of 5% and the annual rise in the retail prices index, an applicant with an expected salary increase in excess of that amount will always suffer a loss.

The guidelines recommend that there be no compensation for this loss where the applicant was a member of a public sector scheme or a private sector scheme but where the applicant is near retirement (e.g., within five years of retirement). They also recommend that there be no compensation where employment would have ended within a year of dismissal.

The recommendation for public sector schemes reflects the authors' assumption that public sector schemes provide cost of living increases broadly in line with salary improvement. As for the other cases, the authors' view is that the difference between cost of living increases (including statutory revaluation) and anticipated salary increases has a less significant effect over a short period. Clearly there will be cases where the applicant will be right to challenge such assumptions.

Assuming that the applicant is not denied compensation for the reasons mentioned above, the guidelines recommend the use of an actuarial method based on a new table prepared by the Government Actuary's Department. The authors hoped that the Department would produce a simplified actuarial method for assessing this loss, albeit on the basis of 'crude assumptions'. In the event the Department has produced a Table that can be used provided four items of information are available, namely the applicant's sex, date of birth, normal retirement age with the employer and the amount of deferred pension at date of leaving service (excluding any anticipated increase in benefit).

The following table, which appears as Appendix 4 to the 1991 paper, sets out the multiplier to be applied to the deferred annual pension to assess compensation for loss of enhancement of accrued pension rights.

Age last birthday	Normal retirement age 60	Normal retirement age 65
Under 35	1.9	1.5
35–44	1.8	1.5
45–49	1.7	1.4
50	1.6	1.4
51	1.5	1.4
52	1.4	1.3
53	1.3	1.3
54	1.1	1.3
55	1.0	1.2
56	0.8	1.2
57	0.6	1.1
58	0.3	1.0
59	0.1	0.9
60	NIL	0.8
61		0.6
62		0.4
63		0.3
64		0.2

Crown copyright. Reproduced with the permission of the Controller of Her Majesty's Stationery Office.

This table is based on a number of assumptions. To the extent that these do not apply in a particular case it might be in the interests of applicant or respondent to challenge the use of the Table (as the employer respondent successfully did in the case of *Bigham* v *Hobourn Engineering Ltd* [1992] IRLR 298). The Department's actuarial assumptions include money can be invested to earn 8½% per annum on average, salaries are assumed to increase by 7% per annum and pensions to increase by 3% per annum. Further assumptions made about the employer's pension scheme are:

(a) the scheme provides a widow or widower's pension at 50% of the member's rate;
(b) there is no lump sum payment on retirement;
(c) the scheme provides 3% per annum increase in most of the pension after retirement; and
(d) the scheme applies equally to men and women (a scheme that does not apply equally to men and women before 17 May 1990 may also raise issues arising from the decision in *Barber* v *Guardian Royal Exchange Assurance Group Ltd* [1990] IRLR 240 and subsequent cases).

However, even where the Table is used, the tribunal must make a further modification. Tribunals are directed to consider an appropriate percentage deduction to represent the likelihood that the applicant could 'have lost his job before retirement' even if he or she had not been unfairly dismissed, for other reasons such as a fair dismissal, redundancy, leaving voluntarily, etc.

This does not include termination of employment through death or disability because this is taken into account in the Department's new Table. Moreover, this is not the same as the percentage likelihood that the applicant would have left employment anyway before retirement. Had the applicant remained in employment for any substantial length of time, accrued pension would have been enhanced. The reduction assessment should reflect the *extent* of loss of enhancement, not whether or not the applicant would have stayed in employment and received full enhancement on retirement. The Department's 1980 paper on pension loss did provide a table showing reduction factors for withdrawal calculated by reference to age, sex and normal retirement age. The authors of the guidelines deliberately refrain from suggesting a new table but consider that it is best left to the discretion of the tribunal. It may be that tribunals will look to the 1980 table for assistance.

Accordingly, the guidelines' formula for loss of enhancement of accrued benefits based on the actuarial method is:

Compensation = (deferred pension) × (multiplier from the new Table) − (percentage for withdrawal)

Example

C earned £10,000 per annum in the private sector. He is unfairly dismissed. His deferred pension is £1,000 per annum. He is 45 with a normal retirement date of 65. The tribunal assesses the withdrawal factor as 25%.

C's loss of enhancement of accrued pension benefits would be:

$$1,000 \times 1.4 - 25\% = £1,050$$

The authors of the guidelines note that the contributions method might in some cases be more appropriate than applying the new Table. This would involve valuing employer and employee contributions to the pension scheme and comparing this value with the value of the applicant's deferred pension. As the authors consider it a most complex calculation to value contributions that might have been paid many years ago their preference is for the new actuarial method. However they say 'if evidence is adduced that the difference between the contributions made and the transfer value is greater than the loss assessed in accordance with (the new Table) the Tribunal may decide to take this into account in assessing a fair and equitable award'.

12 Calculating the Compensatory Award: Manner of Dismissal

12.1 INTRODUCTION

The third head of compensation established by *Norton Tool Co Ltd* v *Tewson* [1973] 1 All ER 183 is compensation for the manner of dismissal. At first, this was thought to include compensation for injured feelings, but subsequent cases have firmly established that, other than in exceptional circumstances, compensation will not be awarded for the distress associated with the dismissal itself. It will, however, be awarded where the manner of dismissal means that the employee is likely to be at a disadvantage in the labour market.

12.2 NO COMPENSATION FOR INJURED FEELINGS

As a general rule, compensation will not be awarded for the distress or emotional upset caused by the dismissal itself. In *Vaughan* v *Weighpack Ltd* [1974] IRLR 105, the NIRC dismissed Mr Vaughan's claim for compensation for the injury to his feelings caused by the distressing circumstances of his dismissal. The NIRC also rejected the idea that his employment prospects would suffer if news of his dismissal spread through the small community in which he lived and worked.

Similarly, in *Brittains Arborfield Ltd* v *Van Uden* [1977] ICR 211, the EAT ruled that a compensation claim would not lie even in cases where gross misconduct had been alleged if the employer's allegation was subsequently shown to be false.

12.2.1 Exceptions

Compensation for injured feelings may be awarded in rare cases where the manner of dismissal is so distressing that it seriously undermines the employee's capacity to look for work, i.e., results in an illness which prevents the employee from looking for work. For example, in *John Millar & Sons* v *Quinn* [1974] IRLR 107, the industrial tribunal awarded Ms Quinn one year's loss of earnings after it had heard that it would take Ms Quinn that length of time before she would be fit to look for work. The NIRC refused to overturn this award on appeal, commenting that the tribunal had heard and seen Ms Quinn in the witness box and was therefore entitled to reach its decision.

Similarly, in *Devine v Designer Flowers Wholesale Florist Sundries Ltd* [1993] IRLR 517, the EAT held that the industrial tribunal was wrong not to award compensation to an employee who, as a result of her dismissal, suffered from anxiety and reactive depression. The EAT held that in such circumstances compensation could be awarded for loss of earnings until such time as the applicant could reasonably be expected to find other employment. However, the EAT warned tribunals against assuming that 'the whole of the period of unfitness thereupon' was attributable to the actions of the employer since 'there may, for example, be questions as to whether the unfitness might have manifested itself in any event'. Furthermore, the EAT pointed out that the fact the employee was not fit to look for work in her former capacity did not mean that she was necessarily unfit for any form of remunerative employment.

Note: The employer's conduct may be taken into account in any event when considering future loss of earnings (see Chapter 12).

12.3 DISADVANTAGE IN THE LABOUR MARKET

Compensation may also be awarded where it is shown that the manner of dismissal gives rise to a risk of financial loss in the future by making it more difficult for the employee to find a new job (*Vaughan v Weighpack Ltd* [1974] IRLR 105) or rendering the employee exceptionally liable to selection for dismissal.

An illustration of a successful claim in such circumstances is *Johnston t/a Richard Andrews Ladies Hairdressers v Baxter* EAT 492/82. Ms Baxter was employed as an apprentice hairdresser. She was dismissed one month before her apprenticeship expired. The industrial tribunal held that she had been unfairly dismissed and awarded her compensation of £765 for loss arising in the period after the expiration of the apprenticeship. The employers appealed, arguing that the tribunal was wrong to award compensation for that period because they were not under an obligation to employ her once the apprenticeship ended. The EAT, dismissing the appeal, ruled that the claim could either be regarded as compensation for consequential loss flowing from the dismissal (i.e., that Ms Baxter's employment prospects might be affected as a result of not finishing her apprenticeship) or that the employer's conduct had actually been the cause of her inability to find a new job and hence it was appropriate to award compensation for the manner of dismissal.

12.4 DISCRIMINATION CASES

An exception to the general rule that compensation will not be awarded for injured feelings exists in sex and race discrimination cases where special statutory provisions apply. (See 20.1.2 below.)

13 Calculating the Compensatory Award: Loss of Statutory Rights

13.1 INTRODUCTION

The final head of compensation established by *Norton Tool Co Ltd* v *Tewson* [1973] 1 All ER 183 is compensation for loss of statutory rights such as the temporary loss of the right to claim unfair dismissal, redundancy or maternity leave in future employment owing to the need to re-qualify for these rights. This head is somewhat inconsistent with the general principle that compensation should only be awarded for financial loss and it would appear from the EAT's decision in *Harvey* v *The Institute of the Motor Industry (No. 2)* [1995] IRLR 416, that industrial tribunals will not err in law if they fail to make such an award or fail to give reasons for not making such an award, though the latter must be open to doubt (*Meek* v *City of Birmingham* [1987] IRLR 250). However, awards under this head are likely to be fairly small. This chapter examines the principles underlying the assessment of compensation under this head.

13.2 REDUNDANCY AND UNFAIR DISMISSAL

In *Norton Tool Co Ltd* v *Tewson* [1973] 1 All ER 183, the NIRC held that an award of two weeks' salary was sufficient compensation for the need to re-qualify for statutory protection against unfair dismissal. In the past, tribunals used to award a nominal sum of £20. However, more recently, in *S H Muffett Ltd* v *Head* [1986] IRLR 488, the EAT ruled that this conventional award should be increased to £100 to reflect the diminution in the value of the pound since 1972. However, as this case was decided more than six years ago, tribunals may well award a higher amount (of around £150) to take account of the loss in the value of the pound since 1986 if they consider it just and equitable to do so.

It is not entirely clear whether this is also intended to cover the need to requalify for redundancy protection. At the time of the NIRC's decision, this was covered by a separate head of claim which was abolished when the basic award was introduced in 1975. It could therefore be argued that a separate award should be made in respect of the need to re-qualify for a redundancy payment but, in practice, this point is ignored.

13.3 OTHER STATUTORY RIGHTS

Additional compensation may be awarded for the loss of other employment protection rights. The most important of these is the right to statutory notice, i.e., the minimum period guaranteed by s. 86 of the Employment Rights Act 1996. This was accepted as a valid category of claim in *Hilti (GB) Ltd* v *Windridge* [1974] IRLR 53 (a case decided under the identical provisions of the Contracts of Employment Act 1972) and was confirmed by the EAT in *Daley* v *A E Dorsett (Almar Dolls) Ltd* [1981] IRLR 385. The EAT suggested that the award should be fixed at half the employee's statutory entitlement to take account of the risk that the employee may be dismissed before requalifying for statutory protection and of other contingencies. So, an employee with six years' service should receive three weeks' net pay. A tribunal which awards more than this conventional sum will err in law (see *Arthur Guinness & Son Co (GB) Ltd* v *Green* [1989] IRLR 288).

Awards may also be made for the loss of other service-related employment protection rights such as the right to maternity leave (*Barnes* v *Gee Hogan (Convertors) Ltd* EAT 198/77).

13.4 NO AWARD

An award of compensation for loss of statutory rights will not be made if the loss is too remote. Thus, in *Gourley* v *Kerr* EAT 692/81, the EAT said that no award should be made unless the applicant satisfies the tribunal both that he will get a new job and that he runs the risk of being dismissed from that job before re-qualifying for statutory protection. For a recent application of this principle, see *S H Muffett Ltd* v *Head* [1986] IRLR 488 and *Puglia* v *C James & Sons Ltd* [1996] IRLR 70.

Of the two conditions put forward by the EAT, the first, that the applicant will get a new job, is the more important since the second, concerning the risk of dismissal, is already taken into account in fixing the conventional award. Thus by awarding only 50% of the lost period of notice, tribunals assume that employees have a fifty-fifty chance of being dismissed from the new job before re-qualifying for their full statutory protection.

As far as the first condition is concerned, tribunals may decline to make an award for loss of statutory rights if it is found that the employee is unlikely to be on the labour market for some time due to illness, or for some other reason. For example, in *Gourley* v *Kerr*, the EAT declined to make an award because it thought that Mr Gourley would not get another job for some while due to the illness which led to his dismissal. Moreover, even if he did find another job, he was close to retirement and therefore would not have been entitled to statutory protection. (The EAT's reasoning on this second point seems unsound because s. 49 of the Employment Protection (Consolidation) Act 1978 (statutory notice) did not contain an age qualification (now see ERA 1996, s. 86).) Similarly, in *Pagano* v *HGS* [1976] IRLR 9, an industrial tribunal also declined to make an award for loss of employment protection rights because Mr Pagano enrolled in a full-time course of study and therefore would be off the labour market for several years. A tribunal may also decline to make an award for loss of statutory rights if an employee becomes self-employed because he will no longer be eligible for statutory protection.

Calculating the Compensatory Award: Loss of Statutory Rights

A further ground for refusing to award compensation for loss of statutory rights is that the employee is unlikely to benefit from the particular form of protection in the future. For example, in *Barnes (Convertors) Ltd* EAT 198/77, the EAT refused to make an award for the right to maternity pay because Mrs Barnes was aged 44 at the time of the hearing and was unlikely to have another baby. The claim was therefore considered to be too remote.

13.5 REDUCED AWARD

The conventional figure may be reduced in the light of uncertainties surrounding the employee's future employment prospects. For example in *Arthur Guinness & Son Co (GB) Ltd* v *Green* [1989] IRLR 288, the EAT limited its award to four weeks' net pay because of the uncertainty as to when Mr Green would be fit to return to work.

14 Reducing Unfair Dismissal Compensation: Justice and Equity

The grounds upon which an award of unfair dismissal compensation may be reduced or limited are regulated, like the awards themselves, by statute (*Cadbury Ltd* v *Doddington* [1977] ICR 982).

In summary, the *basic award* may be reduced where:

(a) the industrial tribunal considers it just and equitable to reduce the award because of the conduct of the employee before the dismissal (ERA 1996, s. 122(2)); or

(b) the employee unreasonably refuses an offer of reinstatement (s. 122(1)).

In addition, any redundancy payment made to the employee, whether under the statutory scheme or otherwise, is set off against the employer's liability to pay the basic award (s. 122(4)).

The *compensatory award* may be reduced where:

(a) the tribunal finds that the conduct of the employee caused or contributed to the dismissal (ERA 1996, s. 123(6));

(b) the employee is shown to have failed to mitigate his or her loss (s. 123(4)); or

(c) the industrial tribunal considers it just and equitable to limit its award for some other reason (s. 123(1)).

Moreover, if the employee has received a redundancy payment, any part of it which has not been set off against the basic award will be set off against the compensatory award (s. 123(3)).

The *special award* for union-related dismissals and health and safety related dismissals may be reduced where:

(a) the industrial tribunal considers it just and equitable to reduce the award because of the conduct of the employee before dismissal (ERA 1996, s. 125(4)); or

(b) the employee unreasonably prevents a re-employment order from being complied with; or

(c) the employee unreasonably turns down an offer of reinstatement (s. 125(5)).

Reducing Unfair Dismissal Compensation: Justice and Equity

This chapter considers the circumstances in which it may be just and equitable to limit the compensatory award. Chapters 15 to 17 look at the other factors which may give rise to a reduction in compensation.

14.1 LIMITING THE COMPENSATORY AWARD

The statutory provisions recognise that a compensatory award will be made only where it is 'just and equitable' to do so. The breadth of discretion conferred on tribunals by this provision was recognised by the House of Lords in *W Devis & Sons Ltd* v *Atkins* [1977] IRLR 314, where Viscount Dilhorne noted that the relevant provision (now s. 123(1) of the Employment Rights Act 1996) 'does not... provide that regard should be had only to the loss resulting from the dismissal being unfair. Regard must be had to that, but the award must be just and equitable in all the circumstances, and it cannot be just and equitable that a sum should be awarded in compensation when in fact the employee has suffered no injustice by being dismissed'. This principle has become particularly important since the House of Lords' ruling in *Polkey* v *A E Dayton Services Ltd* [1987] IRLR 503, where their lordships approved the ruling of Browne-Wilkinson J in *Sillifant* v *Powell Duffryn Timber Ltd* [1983] IRLR 91 to the effect that, although the so called 'any difference' rule did not apply in determining liability for unfair dismissal, the degree of injustice suffered by the applicant was relevant to the issue of compensation. It has therefore been accepted that there may be circumstances where it is just and equitable to make no award at all or to limit the compensatory award to a specific period of time.

14.2 GENERAL PRINCIPLES

14.2.1 No injustice, no award

In *Tele-Trading Ltd* v *Jenkins* [1990] IRLR 430, the Court of Appeal stated that the authorities established that it may be just and equitable to make no award where:

(a) at the time of the application to the industrial tribunal, the employer can show that the employee is in fact guilty of the misconduct alleged against him, or some other serious misconduct (see *Polkey* v *A E Dayton Services Ltd* [1987] IRLR 503 per Lord Mackay at pp. 506-8); or

(b) the employer would or might have fairly dismissed him if a thorough and just investigation had been conducted prior to the dismissal, whether or not the employee is in fact guilty of the alleged misconduct (see *Polkey* v *A E Dayton Services Ltd* per Lord Bridge at pp. 508-9).

14.2.1.1 Category (a)
The facts in *W Devis & Sons Ltd* v *Atkins* [1977] IRLR 314 are a classic illustration of a case falling within category (a). Mr Atkins, was the manager of Devis & Sons' abbatoir in Preston. He was dismissed for his persistent refusal to obey directions from his employers in relation to the purchase of livestock. After his dismissal, information came to light which showed that, during his employment, Mr Atkins had been involved in dishonest dealing in live animals. The House of Lords remitted the

case to the industrial tribunal to consider whether any compensation should be awarded in the light of Mr Atkin's gross misconduct which, had in fact been known at the time of his dismissal, would have been a fair ground for dismissal in the first place.

14.2.1.2 Category (b)

The more recent decision of the EAT in *Parker* v *D & J Tullis Ltd* EAT 306/91 illustrates the kind of case which falls within category (b). Mr Parker was dismissed for allegedly stealing scrap metal. The main evidence against him was from two other employees who had witnessed the incident. However, the names of the witnesses were not disclosed to Mr Parker in the course of the disciplinary proceedings and the industrial tribunal held that his dismissal was unfair for this reason. Nevertheless, a majority of the tribunal considered that it was not just and equitable to make a compensatory award because the employers would have been entitled to prefer the evidence of the two witnesses to that of Mr Parker and therefore Mr Parker suffered no injustice as a result of the procedural irregularity. The industrial tribunal's decision was upheld by the EAT. For another illustration see *Martin* v *British Railways Board* [1989] ICR 198. It follows that, although a procedural irregularity will normally lead to the dismissal being held unfair, it is open to tribunals to award no compensation where employers can show that they would have been justified in dismissing the employee had they followed a fair procedure.

14.2.2 Insufficient evidence of an employee's guilt

This argument will not be successful if the employers are unable to satisfy the tribunal on that there is sufficient evidence that the employee was in fact guilty of the alleged misconduct. For example, in *Tele-Trading Ltd* v *Jenkins* [1990] IRLR 430, the company was unable to satisfy the tribunal that it had reasonable grounds for suspecting Mr Jenkins of dishonesty. At the hearing on compensation, it sought to rely on police evidence which was not available at the time of dismissal, but the tribunal considered that this evidence was inconclusive and accordingly made a full award of compensation. The Court of Appeal upheld the industrial tribunal's ruling on the grounds that the tribunal was entitled to conclude on the evidence before it that the employers did not have reasonable grounds for their belief in the applicant's guilt and therefore the tribunal was justified in making a full award.

14.2.3 Distinction between procedure and substance?

It is clear that it will be easier for employers to show that a particular defect made no difference to the decision where the defect is characterised as purely procedural, i.e., where redundancy was inevitable despite a failure to consult. Conversely, it will be more difficult for employers to show that a particular defect made no difference to the decision where the defect was one of substance, i.e., where the employer applied the wrong redundancy selection procedure. However, in *Steel Stockholders (Birmingham) Ltd* v *Kirkwood* [1993] IRLR 515, the EAT went further than this and suggested that, as a matter of law, it would not be 'just and equitable' to limit compensation in cases where the defect in procedure related to the 'substance of the decision'. So, for example, in the *Kirkwood* case, it was not open to the employers to argue that Mr Kirkwood would have been selected for redundancy if the employers had used the correct pool for redundancy selection purposes as this related to the substance of the decision and was not a matter of mere procedure.

It must be doubted, however, whether the House of Lords in *Polkey* (and Lord Bridge's judgment in particular) intended to limit its decision to procedural defects alone, and there is nothing to support such a distinction in the statute itself. Moreover, as the EAT recognised, in both *Boulton & Paul Ltd v Arnold* [1994] IRLR 532 (another redundancy selection case involving the misapplication of redundancy selection criteria) and *Highfield Gears Ltd v James* EAT 702/93 (a misconduct case involving a number of procedural errors), the distinction suggested by the EAT in *Kirkwood* is often very difficult to apply in practice. More recently, in *O'Dea v ISC Chemicals Ltd* [1995] IRLR 599, Peter Gibson LJ, giving the judgment of the Court of Appeal, said that he did not regard it as 'helpful to characterise the defect as procedural or substantive', nor, in his view, 'should the industrial tribunal be expected to do so'.

It would therefore seem that the EAT's ruling in *Kirkwood* is incorrect in so far as it purports to establish a general principle that awards cannot be limited where the defect is regarded as one of substance as opposed to procedure. It follows that it is still open to a tribunal to limit its awards where the defect is one of substance if it considers this to be just and equitable in the particular circumstances. On the other hand, it may also, as a matter of discretion, refuse to limit its award in such cases.

14.2.4 Is dismissal inevitable?

A tribunal must be satisfied that dismissal was inevitable or at least 'likely' on a balance of probabilities, i.e., the employer's must satisfy the 'any difference' test that the procedural omission made no difference to the decision to dismiss and that an employer would have been reasonable in so concluding. For example, in *Townson v The Northgate Group* [1981] IRLR 382, the EAT held that a tribunal was wrong to limit compensation to four weeks' loss of pay since it thought that Mr Townson's attendance might have improved if he had been given a warning, so dismissal was not inevitable. On the other hand, in *Highfield Gears Ltd v James* EAT 702/93, the EAT held that the tribunal should have considered whether Mr James would (or might) have been dismissed if the employers had conducted a proper investigation and had not taken into account a spent disciplinary warning.

Moreover, it is open to the tribunal to conclude that, although the procedural omission made no difference to the substantive decision, it did make a difference to its timing. In such circumstances, the award of compensation may be limited to the period between the actual dismissal and the time when a fair decision to dismiss could have been taken. This principle is particularly important in redundancy dismissals where there has been a failure to consult (see below).

14.2.5 Degrees of injustice: limiting the award

In other cases, tribunals may be required to weigh up the degree of injustice suffered by the applicant (*Townson v The Northgate Group Ltd* [1981] IRLR 382). This may involve considering the likelihood of dismissal and limiting compensation accordingly. This principle is again particularly important in redundancy and ill health cases where it may be necessary to consider whether the employee would in fact have been made redundant if consultation had taken place (see *Airscrew Howden Ltd* v *Jacobs* EAT 773/82 and the other cases referred to in 14.3.1 below).

Unlike its role in determining the reasonableness of dismissal, a tribunal is under a duty to consider for itself whether or not to reduce or limit its award in accordance with these principles based on the evidence presented to it (*Fisher* v *California Cake & Cookie Ltd* [1997] IRLR 212). Failure to do so may be grounds for appeal even if the issue is not raised by the parties (*Hepworth Refractories Ltd* v *Lingard* EAT 555/90) but see *Wolesley Centres Ltd* v *Simmons* [1994] ICR 503, but they will not be required to speculate as to the possible outcome if evidence is not placed before them (*Boulton & Paul Ltd* v *Arnold* [1994] IRLR 532).

The reduction should be made after the complainant's loss has been calculated (see *Cox* v *London Borough of Camden* [1996] IRLR 389 and *Digital Equipment Co. Ltd* v *Clements (No. 2)* [1997] IRLR 140).

14.3 ILLUSTRATIONS OF THE PRINCIPLES

14.3.1 Redundancy dismissals

The application of these principles is particularly relevant to the assessment of compensation in redundancy dismissals where the dismissal itself is held unfair on the grounds that the employers should have warned or consulted the employee prior to dismissal. A tribunal will have to weigh the consequences of the failure to consult or give prior notice of redundancy in the particular circumstances of the case.

14.3.1.1 Procedural defects
It is open to a tribunal to hold a dismissal fair where dismissal is inevitable and consultation would have been 'futile' or 'utterly useless' (*Polkey* v *A E Dayton Services Ltd* [1987] IRLR 503). But an industrial tribunal is more likely to hold that the dismissal was unfair and that, at the very least, consultation would have led to the dismissal being postponed for a short period of time (*Abbotts* v *Wesson Glynwed-Steels Ltd* [1982] IRLR 51). It may therefore limit its award of compensation to the period of time it would have taken for the employer to go through the process of consultation (*Mining Supplies (Longwall) Ltd* v *Baker* [1988] IRLR 417). The award for a failure to consult where dismissal is inevitable is normally between 14 days (*Abbotts*) and one month (*Castleman & Patterson* v *A & P Appledore (Aberdeen) Ltd and Hall Russell Ltd* SEAT 478/90, a case which involved a failure to consult in the context of a business transfer). A period of six*Mining Supplies (Longwall) Ltd* v *Baker*.

On the other hand, a full award of compensation should be made where it is clear that the employee would have been retained had proper consultation taken place, e.g., where the failure to consult has led to the wrong employee being selected for redundancy or where consultation would have resulted in the employee being offered alternative employment (see *Guest* v *A & P Appledore (Aberdeen) Ltd and Hall Russell Ltd* SEAT 503/90).

The position becomes more complicated where dismissal would have been a possible but not inevitable outcome, e.g., where the employee might have come up with an alternative proposal to avoid the redundancy or where the employee might have been offered suitable alternative employment. In such circumstances, tribunals will consider the likelihood of redundancy and limit their awards accordingly. For example, in *Hough* v *Leyland DAF Ltd* [1991] IRLR 194, the EAT upheld an industrial tribunal's ruling that compensation should be reduced by 50% to take account of the chances of the employees being retained had the employers consulted them prior to making them redundant. Similarly in *Moran* v *A D Hamilton* EAT 509/89, the EAT held that if there had been consultation, the applicant might have been offered alternative employment with an associated company. Unlike the tribunal, it considered that there was a 50% chance of this happening because the applicant would have been willing to accept a drop in salary. It accordingly limited the award to 50% of the full award. (See also *Airscrew Howden Ltd* v *Jacobs* EAT 773/82, where the EAT remitted the case to the tribunal to 'attempt the assessment, difficult though it may be, of deciding the chances of Mr Jacobs getting another job within the group', *Rao* v *Civil Aviation Authority* [1992] IRLR 203 below, where the Court of Appeal made a similar assessment in the context of an ill health dismissal and *O'Dea* v *ISC Chemicals Ltd* [1995] IRLR 599, where the Court of Appeal upheld an industrial tribunal ruling that the applicant would have had a one in five chance of not being selected for redundancy had he been given the opportunity of being considered for a new post, and accordingly reduced his award of compensation by 80%.) Where a tribunal concludes that the applicant would or might have been offered alternative employment, compensation for loss of earnings should be assessed on the earnings the employee would have received in that new job (*Red Bank Manufacturing* v *Meadows* [1992] IRLR 209). So, for example, if an employee would have been earning £200 a week in the new job instead of £250 in the old job and there is an even chance of the employee getting the job, the award of compensation for continuing loss of earnings should be assessed at £100 a week, i.e., that there was a 50/50 chance of the employee being offered the alternative job (see *Weston* v *Metzler (UK) Ltd* EAT 303 and 304/91).

A tribunal will err in law if it fails to assess the chances of success in accordance with the principles outlined above, (see *GEC Energy Systems Ltd* v *Gufferty* EAT 590/87, where the tribunal failed to assess the chances of alternative employment).

Example: Limits on full compensation

Mrs James, a school cleaner, is found to have been unfairly dismissed. However, the industrial tribunal accepts the employer's evidence that it is going to privatise the school cleaning service in three months. The hearing is held three months after dismissal.

(a) Assuming that Mrs James could not have been redeployed, compensation is limited to six months' loss of earnings.
(b) Assuming that Mrs James could have been redeployed and would have accepted the job, she is entitled to *full* compensation; but if she would have rejected the job, the tribunal may refuse to make an award for future loss, or limit its award, on the ground that she would have failed to mitigate her loss.

14.3.1.2 Substantive defects
The position may be even more complicated where the defect is regarded as substantive rather than procedural. For example, in *Steel Stockholders (Birmingham) Ltd* v *Kirkwood* [1993] IRLR 515, the EAT ruled that an industrial tribunal had not erred in refusing to assess the chance that Mr Kirkwood would still have been dismissed if the employers had identified the correct pool of employees for redundancy selection purposes. Similarly, in *Boulton & Paul Ltd* v *Arnold* [1994] IRLR 532, the EAT ruled that the industrial tribunal had not erred in law in failing to raise and consider the question of whether the employee's compensation should be reduced to reflect the possibility that she would have been made redundant if the employers had correctly applied the agreed redundancy selection criteria. The EAT stressed that the onus of adducing such evidence is on the employer and the tribunal was not obliged to raise the issue itself.

However, as the EAT pointed out in *Arnold*, the distinction between substance and procedure is often hard to draw and, for the reasons given above, it may well be open to tribunals to apply the 'any difference' approach even where the defect is regarded as one of substance. In such circumstances, the tribunal would have to consider whether, in the light of the evidence, it was inevitable, likely or unlikely that the employee would have been selected for redundancy had the correct redundancy selection procedure been followed, and limit (or not limit) its award accordingly. It would also be open to a tribunal to conclude that it was unwilling to speculate as to the outcome and accordingly make a full award.

14.3.2 Future risk of redundancy

Compensation may also be limited where the tribunal finds that the employee's job was insecure because of impending redundancy. Thus in *Youngs of Gosport Ltd* v *Kendell* [1977] IRLR 433, the EAT reduced the amount of the compensatory award from 12 months to 9 months because it found that Mr Kendell was likely to be made redundant in 9 months' time.

However, employers wishing to pursue this line of argument must show that the employee would have been made redundant, or at least was among the group of employees who could reasonably have been selected for redundancy. It is not enough to show that the employee might have been made redundant if other factors had remained the same. An interesting application of this principle arose in *Gilham* v *Kent County Council* [1986] IRLR 56. The council argued that compensation should be limited to one year because if the vast majority of staff employed in the school dinner service had not agreed to new terms of employment, it would have had to close the service within a year, thereby making all the employees redundant (including those who claimed that their dismissals were unfair). The EAT rejected this argument, saying that the tribunal should have assessed compensation on the basis of what actually happened. Thus, as the service had not closed, the employees were entitled to full compensation.

14.3.3 Capability

Capability dismissals generally fall into two categories. The first concerns cases where employees are to blame for their lack of ability (which may be viewed as a dismissal for 'misconduct'), and the second, cases where they are not to blame, i.e., where the dismissal flows from an innate lack of ability due to ill-health or some other reason beyond their control.

In most cases, tribunals will be required to consider whether the employee should have been given an opportunity to improve, and if so, whether any improvement was likely (*Winterhalter Gastronom Ltd* v *Webb* [1973] IRLR 120). If the tribunal concludes that the warning would or may have resulted in an improvement, the loss flowing from the dismissal is substantial since it would not accord with justice and equity to limit the compensatory award.

On the other hand, if the tribunal finds that an improvement is unlikely, it may hold that dismissal was in all probability inevitable and limit compensation accordingly. For example, in *Mansfield Hosiery Mills Ltd* v *Bromley* [1977] IRLR 301, an industrial tribunal found that Mr Bromley's dismissal was unfair because of inadequate warnings and lack of supervision. However, it also found that he would probably not have come up to scratch even if he had been given a further opportunity to improve and he was therefore awarded limited compensation on the ground that he would have been fairly dismissed a short time later. The EAT upheld the decision. Similarly, in *Webb* the NIRC ruled that Mr Webb's compensation should be limited to three months because it was by no means certain that 'even if Mr Webb had received a warning, he would have been able to hold down the job in future'. See also *Plumley* v *A D International Ltd* EAT 591/82, where compensation was limited to two months' loss of earnings because Ms Plumley was 'constitutionally unable to rectify her conduct'. The EAT observed that 'had she been given the necessary warnings, it would not have been long before her employment would have been terminated'.

Where the tribunal concludes that the dismissal was inevitable, it may award no compensation at all (see 14.2.4 above).

14.3.4 Ill-health dismissals

The principles set out above in relation to redundancy dismissals may also apply in ill-health dismissals. Thus, a tribunal may decline to make a compensatory award where medical evidence obtained after the dismissal shows that the employee was incapable of doing the job and therefore dismissal was inevitable (*Slaughter* v *C Brewer & Sons Ltd* [1990] IRLR 426, *Gowland* v *BAT (Export) Ltd* IRLIB 269 and *Gourley* v *Kerr* EAT 692/81). But, as in cases of redundancy, it will normally be appropriate to award somect the length of time it would have taken to obtain a medical report and, therefore, to consult the employee in accordance with the 'guidelines' established for ill-health dismissals (*East Lindsey District Council* v *Daubney* [1977] IRLR 181). A full compensatory award is likely where the employee should have been offered suitable alternative employment or retained for some other reason.

In some cases, however, the position may not be so clear cut and it will be necessary for a tribunal to assess, in percentage terms, the chances of the applicant being retained. For example, in *Rao* v *Civil Aviation Authority* [1992] IRLR 203, the EAT and the Court of Appeal ([1994] IRLR 240) upheld an industrial tribunal's ruling that there was only a 20% chance that Mr Rao would have kept his job if the employers had postponed their decision on his future pending the outcome of further treatment for a recurring back problem and accordingly reduced the award by 80%.

14.3.5 Breach of disciplinary procedures

Similar considerations apply in considering whether the compensatory award should be limited as a result of a failure to follow a disciplinary procedure. For example, it may be necessary to decide whether, as a matter of justice and equity, the employee should have been given a warning and, if so, whether compensation should be limited in the light of its likely effect.

As noted at 14.2.1 above, it is open to tribunals to award no compensation at all where the employee's dismissal is held unfair on procedural grounds but the employee suffers no injustice as a result. Moreover, in *Mining Supplies (Longwall) Ltd* v *Baker* [1988] IRLR 417, the EAT indicated that the argument that compensation should be awarded for the period during which it would have taken to handle the matter fairly will not apply where there is an internal appeal because this will have already been taken into account. The EAT, however, appeared to overlook the fact that the employee will often not be paid in the intervening period.

14.3.6 Alternative reason for dismissal

In a number of cases, it has been suggested that it is 'unjust' to award compensation where an employer can show that the employee who was unfairly dismissed for one reason could have been fairly dismissed for another reason, which existed at the time of dismissal. In support of this argument it is said that if employers are entitled to rely on information which comes to light after a dismissal which would have justified dismissal, as in *W Devis & Sons Ltd* v *Atkins*, why should they not be entitled to rely on another reason which existed at the time of dismissal and which, if relied on, would have amounted to a fair dismissal?

This argument appears to have been accepted by the EAT in *McNee* v *Charles Tenant & Co Ltd* EAT 338/90, where an industrial tribunal, having held that a dismissal on health grounds was unfair, refused to make a compensatory award on the ground that the employee could have been fairly dismissed on the ground of his unsatisfactory attendance record. The industrial tribunal's decision was upheld by the EAT.

However, in the earlier case of *Trico-Folberth Ltd* v *Devonshire* [1989] IRLR 396, on almost identical facts to those in *McNee*, the Court of Appeal rejected this argument: May LJ considered that it was none the less 'just and equitable to award the employee compensation since, put simply, she no longer had the job that she would have had but for the dismissal which the industrial tribunal had held to be unfair'. Nourse LJ had different reasons. He said 'it cannot be just and equitable for an employee to be deprived of the compensation to which she would otherwise be entitled if the employers themselves would not have relied on that other ground'.

This leaves open the possibility that compensation may be so reduced where, as a matter of evidence, employers can persuade the tribunal that they would have dismissed on the alternative ground. They were unable to do this on the particular facts of *Devonshire*. Indeed, the evidence was to the contrary. The Court of Appeal's decision does not appear to have been cited in *McNee* and, in the face of conflict, its ruling is likely to prevail at least in England and Wales.

14.4 OTHER REASONS FOR LIMITING COMPENSATION

It may be just and equitable to limit the compensatory award in a number of other situations.

14.4.1 Loss of secondary employment

In *Bakr* v *Sade Bros Ltd* EAT 470/83, the EAT upheld a tribunal's decision to limit to six weeks the amount of compensation received by an employee for the loss of his second job. Mr Bakr was unfairly dismissed from his part-time job as assistant chef in a restaurant which he held in addition to a full-time job in an hotel. The tribunal held that compensation should be limited to six weeks' loss of earnings. He appealed on the ground that the tribunal should have awarded him 11 months' loss of earnings because he had not been able to find himself a new secondary job. The EAT, dismissing the appeal, said that the decision lay within the discretion of the tribunal and that it was entitled to conclude that Mr Bakr could reasonably have been expected to find himself a new job within the six week period.

It may be queried whether the EAT in *Bakr* confused the power to reduce compensation on the grounds of 'justice and equity' with the employee's duty to mitigate and would appear to be inconsistent with the EAT's decision in *Soros and Soros* v *Davison and Davison* [1994] IRLR 264 (see Chapter 15).

14.4.2 Dismissal during notice period

In certain circumstances, it may be just and equitable to limit the amount of the compensatory award to the unexpired period of notice due under the contract, e.g., where the employer commits a fundamental breach of contract in the notice period after an employee has handed in his resignation. In such circumstances, the employee could claim constructive dismissal but it would be unjust to award compensation beyond the expiry of the notice period (see *Ford* v *Milthorn Toleman Ltd* [1980] IRLR 30).

14.4.3 Other inequitable conduct

It would appear that the compensatory award may also be limited where an industrial tribunal is critical of other 'inequitable' conduct on the part of the employee. For example, in *Cullen* v *Kwik Fit Euro Ltd* EAT 483/83, the EAT upheld an industrial tribunal's decision not to make a compensatory award to an employee who failed to answer an allegation that he had been involved in 'private trading'. The tribunal considered that the resultant dismissal was attributable to the employee's own action. More recently, in *Onions* v *Apollo Design and Construction (Scotland) Ltd* EAT 156/88 the EAT upheld an industrial tribunal's decision that compensation should be reduced by 50% under s. 74(1) of the Employment Protection (Consolidation) Act 1978 (now s. 123(1) of the ERA 1996) on account of the employee's 'obstructive' conduct in response to his employer's decision to impose a pay cut. It is submitted that in both these circumstances, a tribunal could have made a reduction for contributory fault and that unless such conduct merits a reduction for contributory fault (see Chapter 16), it should not be open to a tribunal to make a reduction under s. 123(1). For this reason the correctness of these decisions is open to doubt.

14.4.4 Onus on employers

The onus is on the employer to satisfy the tribunal that compensation should be limited to a certain period, though in practice some tribunals will bring the question to the employer's attention at the hearing (*Boulton & Paul Ltd* v *Arnold* [1993] IRLR 532).

14.4.5 Post-dismissal conduct

The power to limit compensation under ERA 1996, s. 123(1) cannot be relied on where the employee's conduct takes place after dismissal. So, for example, in *Soros and Soros* v *Davison and Davison* [1994] IRLR 264, the EAT held that the industrial tribunal was correct in refusing to limit its award on account of the fact that the applicants had sold allegedly confidential information about their employment to national newspapers after their dismissal.

14.4.6 Failure to appeal

The Conservative Government has proposed that tribunals should be given the power to reduce compensation where an employee unreasonably refuses to pursue an internal appeal (see clause 13(1) of the Employment Rights (Disputes Resolution) Bill). There is an equivalent provision to increase compensation where the employer unreasonably refuses to allow an employee to appeal (see clause 13(2) of the Employment Rights (Dispute Resolution) Bill). It remains to be seen whether these provisions will be implemented after the 1997 General Election.

15 Mitigation of Loss

15.1 INTRODUCTION

This chapter looks at the circumstances in which compensation may be reduced as a result of an employee's failure to mitigate the loss caused by the dismissal.

15.1.1 Statutory provisions

In determining the loss suffered by the employee, a tribunal is under a duty to 'apply the same rule concerning the duty of a person to mitigate his loss as applies to damages recoverable under the common law of England and Wales or (as the case may be) Scotland' (ERA 1996, s. 123(4)). The intention of the statutory wording is that the common law rules on mitigation should apply to unfair dismissal (*Fyfe* v *Scientific Furnishings Ltd* [1989] IRLR 331).

The common law duty to mitigate actually embodies two ideas. The first is that a plaintiff should not recover damages for any loss which could reasonably have been avoided. The second is that a plaintiff must give credit for benefits received in consequence of the defendant's breach. Sometimes the first duty is described as the 'duty to mitigate in law' and the second as 'the duty to mitigate in fact', but not too much importance should be attached to this terminology as it does not affect the basic principles outlined above. The distinction is used here purely as a matter of convenience.

In the context of unfair dismissal law, the first duty requires an employee to take reasonable steps to minimise the loss by, for example, finding a new job. The first part of this chapter looks at what steps applicants are expected to take in this respect. The second aspect of the duty requires employees to bring into account the benefits they have received since dismissal, thereby reducing the overall loss. This aspect, which has already been discussed in detail in Chapter 9, is briefly summarised at the end of this chapter.

15.2 DEFINING THE DUTY TO MITIGATE IN UNFAIR DISMISSAL CASES

In *Archbold Freightage Ltd* v *Wilson* [1974] IRLR 10, Sir John Donaldson gave the following definition of the duty to mitigate: 'It is the duty of an employee who had been dismissed to act as a reasonable man would do if he had no hope of receiving compensation from his previous employer'. But in *Fyfe* v *Scientific Furnishings Ltd* [1989] IRLR 331, Wood J suggested that the standard of reasonableness is not appropriate as it is the respondent employer who is the wrongdoer. Moreover, in *Johnson* v *The Hobart Manufacturing Co Ltd* EAT 210/90, the EAT held that the test is a subjective one rather than an objective one, i.e., has the particular applicant taken reasonable steps to mitigate his loss. This may be particularly important when considering whether an employee acted reasonably in turning down an offer of reinstatement or re-engagement.

15.2.1 Question of fact or law?

Despite some differences over the precise formulation of the duty itself, the essence of the duty is clear, namely that an industrial tribunal will need to be satisfied that the applicant has taken positive steps to minimise the loss caused by the dismissal. In most cases this will involve taking reasonable steps to find a new job but in some cases employees may be penalised if they unreasonably turn down an offer of re-employment from their former employer (see 15.3 below).

The question 'what is reasonable' is essentially one of fact and one pre-eminently to be decided by industrial tribunals *as industrial juries*. The tribunal's decision will only be overturned on appeal if it is shown that it misdirected itself in law (i.e., by failing to consider the question at all) or the decision is perverse in the sense that it is one to which no reasonable tribunal could have come. The citation of authority in this context in particular is principally of illustrative value (*Yetton* v *Eastwoods Froy Ltd* [1966] 3 All ER 353; *Bessenden Properties Ltd* v *Corness* [1974] IRLR 338).

A failure to consider the issue of mitigation will amount to an error of law and will be grounds for appeal (*Morganite Electrical Carbon Ltd* v *Donne* [1987] IRLR 363).

15.3 RE-EMPLOYMENT ORDERS

Where an industrial tribunal orders reinstatement or re-engagement and an employee unreasonably prevents such an order from being complied with, the employee's conduct may be failure to mitigate for the purpose of assessing the compensatory award (ERA 1996, s. 117(8)).

15.4 OFFERS OF RE-EMPLOYMENT

The idea that employees might be under a duty to accept an offer of re-employment in mitigation of their loss is well established at common law (see 1.7.2.1 above) and was held by the EAT to apply to cases of unfair dismissal in *Martin* v *Yeoman Aggregates Ltd* [1983] IRLR 49, *Sweetlove* v *Redbridge and Waltham Forest Area Health Authority* [1979] IRLR 195 and *Fyfe* v *Scientific Furnishings Ltd* [1989] IRLR 331.

15.4.1 Reasonableness test

The test under s. 123(4) of the Employment Rights Act 1996 is whether the employee acted reasonably in turning down the employer's offer. Thus an offer of re-employment may be considered reasonable even though it does not amount to full reinstatement. For example, in *Smith v N E Transport & Plant Hire (Broughty Ferry) Ltd* EAT 402/83, the EAT held that Mr Smith was unreasonable to turn down a job as a DAF lorry driver when he had previously been employed as an HGV driver. The EAT said that Mr Smith had acted unreasonably even though he was not being offered his old job back. (Contrast this decision with the EAT's ruling in *Artisan Press Ltd v Srawley and Parker* [1986] IRLR 126.)

The reasonableness of the offer appears to be judged subjectively; the fact that 'a particular job is satisfactory for nine men out of ten' does not necessarily mean a failure to mitigate if it is 'unsuitable for the man in question' (per Ian Kennedy J in *Johnson v The Hobart Manufacturing Co Ltd* EAT 210/89. It is therefore necessary for a tribunal to consider both the reasonableness of the offer itself and of the reasons for the employee's refusal.

15.4.1.1 Reasonableness of the employer's offer

Where the employer offers re-engagement, as opposed to reinstatement, the tribunal will normally first consider the reasonableness of the employer's offer. The test applied by tribunals is not dissimilar from that used to determine whether alternative employment is suitable in redundancy dismissals. Thus tribunals will look at the terms of the offer, such as pay, hours of work, status, responsibility, location etc. and decide whether it is suitable for the employee, in the light of his training and other qualifications.

15.4.1.2 Reasonableness of the employee's refusal

If the employer's offer is considered reasonable, tribunals must then go on to consider the reasons for the employee's refusal of the employer's offer. These may relate to the terms of the offer (as in 15.4.1.1 above) or the idea of being re-employed by the employer in the light of the circumstances surrounding the dismissal. As a rule of thumb, applicants will not normally be penalised for turning down an offer of re-employment if it involves significant changes in the terms of employment. However, where the job is virtually the same, the burden will be very much on the applicant to show why it was reasonable to turn it down.

In determining 'reasonableness', tribunals take account of the following factors.

(a) *Timing of the offer*. An employee is more likely to be found to have acted reasonably if the offer is made at the 'eleventh hour', i.e., just before the hearing, than if it is made shortly after the dismissal, since in the latter situation the employee might be found to have 'closed his mind' to the employer's offer (per Kilner Brown J in *Martin v Yeoman Aggregates Ltd* [1983] IRLR 49).

(b) *Clarity of the offer*. An employee might not be unreasonable in rejecting an offer which is vague or unclear as to its terms (*John Crowther & Sons (Milnsbridge) Ltd v Livesey* EAT 272/84).

(c) *Reason for dismissal*. The grounds of dismissal may justify the employee's rejection of the offer, e.g., where the employer makes an unjustified allegation of dishonesty.

(d) *Reasonableness of the dismissal*. The manner of dismissal may justify the employee's refusal of an offer, in *Livesey* for example, where the employee was held to have acted reasonably because he had lost his confidence and trust in management as a result of the manner of dismissal.

In the following instances the employee was held to have acted reasonably in refusing a re-employment offer.

(a) Employee failed to ask for reinstatement following an industrial dispute (*Courtaulds Northern Spinning Ltd* v *Moosa* [1974] IRLR 101).
(b) Employers trying to ascertain whether police were still considering prosecuting the employee for a till offence (*How* v *Tesco Stores Ltd* [1974] IRLR 194).
(c) Employee feared that there would be a bad atmosphere at work if he returned (*Dobson, Bryant, Heather* v *K P Morritt Ltd* [1979] IRLR 101).
(d) Humiliating manner of dismissal or other humiliating treatment of the employee at the hands of the employer (*Simmonds* v *Merton, Sutton and Wandsworth Area Health Authority* EAT 789/77; *Farrell* v *Exports International Ltd* EAT 569/89; *Fyfe* v *Scientific Furnishings Ltd* [1989] IRLR 331).
(e) Employee had found a new job (*Yetton* v *Eastwoods Froy Ltd* [1966] 3 All ER 353).

However, much will depend on the particular circumstances of the case. For example, in *Gallear* v *J F Watson and Son Ltd* [1979] IRLR 306, the EAT held that Mr Gallear had acted unreasonably in turning down two offers of re-employment even though they were made after he presented his originating application and the dismissal had been handled in a manner which contravened the ACAS code of practice.

15.4.2 Offers of alternative employment

In principle, it is open to an employer to argue that there has been a failure to mitigate loss where the applicant turns down an offer of alternative employment. As above, this argument is more likely to succeed where the terms of employment on offer are similar to the original terms than where the new job involves a substantial deterioration in the terms and conditions of employment.

In *Baillie Brothers* v *Pritchard* EAT 59/89, an employee was held to have acted reasonably in turning down an offer of alternative employment made to him some months after the dismissal where the new job involved a reduction in pay of £13 a week and the loss of a van which he had previously used for travelling to and from work. On the other hand, in *Plewinski* v *McDermott Engineering London* EAT 465/88, an employee was held to have acted unreand, for a short time become self-employed, rather than accept a cut in overtime in his old job.

An employee may be held to have acted unreasonably in turning down the same job in a different location (see *Pearson* v *Leeds Polytechnic Students' Union* EAT 182/84); but in judging reasonableness, tribunals will take account of the amount of travelling involved and the personal circumstances of the employee.

Tribunals may take a more lenient view if the employee has already found another job (*How* v *Tesco Ltd* [1974] IRLR 194). Consideration will also be given to other reasons why the applicant turned down the job offer and whether he or she was reasonable to do so (see 15.3.1.2 above).

Mitigation of Loss

15.4.3 Offers of early retirement

In principle, it is open to employers to argue that employees who unreasonably turn down an offer of early retirement on generous terms in redundancy or ill-health cases have failed to mitigate their loss by so doing. But employees will not necessarily act unreasonably in turning down such an offer.

For example, in *Fyfe v Scientific Furnishing Ltd* [1989] IRLR 331, the employers failed to show that the applicant had failed to mitigate his loss when he turned down an offer of early retirement made shortly after his dismissal for redundancy. The early retirement package, on its face, appeared to be extremely generous when compared to the redundancy payment to which the applicant was entitled. The tribunal found that Mr Fyfe was unreasonable in turning down the offer and held that he had failed to mitigate his loss. But the EAT, allowing the appeal, held that Mr Fyfe had not acted unreasonably because his employers had failed to set out the full implications of their offer and had failed to give Mr Fyfe more time to make up his mind. The employers had therefore failed to discharge the burden of proving that Mr Fyfe had failed to mitigate his loss.

15.5 DUTY TO FIND EMPLOYMENT

Offers of re-employment are comparatively uncommon. Normally, the duty to mitigate will require the employee to look for a new job. 'Signing on' is not normally enough (*Burns v Boyd Engineering Ltd* EAT 458/84) but two visits a week to the local job centre were considered reasonable in *British Garages Ltd v Lowen* [1979] IRLR 86.

Many tribunals, however, expect applicants to cast their net more widely than the vacancies advertised at the job centre. Applicants may be asked if they have looked at adverts in the trade press or local newspapers. For example, in one case an employee was held not to have mitigated his loss because he had sought employment from only one agency rather than approaching other agencies which might have had appropriate vacancies on their books. The employee was also criticised for not having taken up a reference that had been promised by his old employers (*Field v Leslie & Godwin Ltd* [1972] IRLR 12).

15.5.1 State of the labour market

Tribunals will take their knowledge of the local labour market into account in deciding whether the employee has made reasonable efforts to find a new job. Tribunals are also influenced by the current levels of unemployment. For example, in one case, a London tribunal regarded 30 weeks' loss of earnings as 'a medium period' (*Plessey Military Communications Ltd v Bough* IDS 310) and in *Scottish & Newcastle Breweries plc v Halliday* [1986] IRLR 29, the EAT suggested that 'with mass unemployment' it is frequently 12 months or even more. See also 9.4.4.2 above.

15.5.2 Personal characteristics of the applicant

Tribunals will also take account of any personal characteristics of the employee which put him or her at a disadvantage in the labour market. For example, an employee who is elderly or in poor health may experience particular difficulty in finding a new job. In *Bennett* v *Tippins* EAT 361/89, the EAT recognised the difficulties pregnant women have in finding employment and a similar principle may well apply to mothers with child care responsibilities.

15.5.3 Reasonable offers of employment

A further aspect of the duty to mitigate is that employees should not turn down a reasonable offer of employment. Thus as Sir John Donaldson said in *Archbold Freightage Ltd* v *Wilson* [1974] IRLR 10, a complainant should 'accept alternative employment if, taking account of the pay and other conditions of that employment, it is reasonable to do so'.

However, this does not mean that employees have to accept the first job that is offered to them. As the NIRC said in *A G Bracey Ltd* v *Iles* [1973] IRLR 210:

> It may not be reasonable to take the first job that comes along. It may be much more reasonable, in the interests of the employee and of the employer who has to pay compensation, that he should wait a little time. He must, of course, use the time well and seek a better paid job which will reduce his overall loss and the amount of compensation which the previous employer ultimately has to pay.

It should be observed that this statement was made at a time when unemployment was relatively low and it is possible that at the present time tribunals are likely to react less favourably if an employee turns down a comparable job, particularly in an area of high unemployment. In general, tribunals are likely to be sympathetic to employees who, in the short term, turn down jobs which are lower paid or offer other less favourable terms and conditions of employment.

15.5.3.1 Flexibility
However, applicants who have been out of work for some time may be required to accept lower-paid jobs in mitigation of their loss. In extreme cases, applicants have been penalised for turning down jobs where the pay offered in the new job was less than the amount they were receiving as unemployment benefit, though the EAT has warned tribunals that they should be 'slow' to reach this conclusion (*Daley* v *A E Dorsett (Almar Dolls) Ltd* [1981] IRLR 385).

Flexibility may also be required in relation to other conditions of employment. Thus in *Lloyd* v *The Standard Pulverised Fuel Co Ltd* [1976] IRLR 115, it was held that an employee who had previously worked during the day was unreasonable to turn down night work. Similarly, employees may be expected to be prepared to more to a new location where suitable work is available. Thus in *Collen* v *Lewis* IDS 390 an industrial tribunal held that a language teacher who had previously been employed in London should have accepted a job in Wales even though the job offer involved a reduction in pay and the loss of a London weighting allowance. The tribunal awarded the net difference in earnings between the two jobs for one year (see also *O'Reilly* v *Welwyn and Hatfield District Council* [1975] IRLR 334). But in other cases, tribunals have been reluctant to penalise employees who refuse to move away from their home town particularly where this involves moving home and uprooting their family (see *Ramsay* v *W B Anderson & Sons Ltd* [1974] IRLR 164).

Some applicants may be required to accept temporary work or part-time work iunals for giving up a temporary job when there is no prospect of finding a more permanent one (*Hardwick* v *Leeds Area Health Authority* [1975] IRLR 319). But tribunals may take a more lenient view if there are good reasons for so doing (see *Dundee Plant Co Ltd* v *Riddler* EAT 377/88, where the applicant gave up a permanent job for another permanent but less well paid job as the first job involved too much travelling, and *Wilson* v *Gleneagles Bakery Ltd* EAT 40/88, where the EAT held that an applicant had not acted unreasonably when she gave up her new job on the ground that she could not cope with her new responsibilities).

15.5.4 Setting up business

It is possible to mitigate loss by setting up a business or becoming self-employed but it is for the tribunal to decide whether an applicant was reasonable in doing this rather than looking for employment elsewhere.

In the past, tribunals tended to regard self-employment as an unreasonable way of mitigating loss due to the length of time it normally takes for a business to become profitable. However, high levels of unemployment have led to a more sympathetic response from tribunals, particularly in cases where the applicant is at a disadvantage in the labour market because of age or the limited employment opportunities available to someone with the applicant's particular skills.

The leading case on this point, *Gardiner-Hill* v *Roland Berger Technics Ltd* [1982] IRLR 498, is a good illustration of the sort of situation where setting up a business in mitigation may be considered reasonable. Mr Gardiner-Hill was dismissed from his post as managing director of a consultancy service after 16 years of employment at the age of 55. He decided to set up his own business. In the six and a half months between his dismissal and the tribunal hearing he had spent some 80-90% of his time starting up and running the business, but had received only £1,500 from his new employment. His former employers argued that this had prevented him from looking for alternative employment and that he had therefore failed to mitigate his loss. The EAT disagreed. It held that Mr Gardiner-Hill had acted reasonably because it was 'at least as prudent of him to seek to exploit his own expertise by conducting his own business and gaining an income from his own business to replace the income which he had previously received from his employment'. The EAT also permitted him to recover £500 for the expenses he incurred in setting up the business (see *Glen Henderson Ltd* v *Nisbet* EAT 34/90 for a more recent illustration).

Furthermore, provided the decision to set up the business was a reasonable one, the employee will not be penalised if the business subsequently fails (see *Blick Vessels & Pipework Ltd* v *Sharpe* IRLIB 274, February 1985).

15.5.5 Re-training as mitigation

Another possible way of mitigating loss is for the applicant to undergo a period of training, thereby increasing the chances of finding alternative employment.

For example, in *Sealy* v *Avon Aluminium Co Ltd* EAT 516/78, the EAT rejected the argument that the applicant had failed to mitigate his loss by attending a college course for part of the time covered by the compensatory award, and in *Glen Henderson Ltd* v *Nisbet* EAT 34/90, the EAT held that the applicant had not failed to mitigate her loss by attending a business enterprise course for five weeks before starting up her own business.

Here again, in determining the question of reasonableness, tribunals are likely to be influenced by levels of unemployment and the state of the labour market in the locality. There is also some evidence that tribunals take a more sympathetic attitude to short term vocational courses than longer academic ones (see *Holroyd* v *Gravure Cylinders Ltd* [1984] IRLR 259).

15.5.6 'Signing on' for sickness benefit as mitigation

A similar problem may arise where an employee who is unfairly dismissed on health grounds elects to receive sickness benefit and invalidity benefit rather than to look for alternative employment. Depending on the circumstances, it may not be unreasonable for an employee to 'sign on' sick if the employee reasonably believes that this is the best way of securing an income. In *Wilson* v (1) *Glenrose (Fishmerchants) Ltd* and (2) *Chapman and others* (EAT/444/91) an industrial tribunal ruled that it was not just and equitable to award compensation in such circumstances because the applicant had voluntarily taken himself out of the labour market. Allowing the appeal, the EAT held that the crucial issue was whether the applicant had acted unreasonably in signing on sick rather than waiting for a job to turn up. This involved considering the reasonableness of his conduct at the time he signed on (including the fact that his previous applications for employment had all been unsuccessful), and whether it was reasonable for him to continue to receive benefit rather than look for work at any time during the period he received benefit. However it should be noted that in this case the applicant was fit enough to carry out duties he had been required to do prior to his dismissal and there was a clear finding that the applicant would have been likely to continue in his employment until his retirement but for his dismissal. Both these factors are critical if the applicant is to have a claim for loss of earnings in the first place.

15.5.7 Pregnancy dismissals

The duty to mitigate applies where a dismissal is found to be automatically unfair under ERA 1996, s. 104 for pregnancy or pregnancy-related reasons. However, in *MOD* v *Sullivan* [1994] ICR 193, a sex discrimination claim brought under the Equal Treatment Directive, the EAT ruled that a woman could not reasonably be expected to mitigate loss in the period immediately after childbirth and that the duty would not arise until her physiological and mental functions had returned to normal. The EAT also held that an employee who was dismissed in such circumstances was entitled to compensation for loss of earnings for a period of up to six months whilst she decided whether or not to return to work. (For compensation in pregnancy sex discrimination cases see 20.1.2).

Mitigation of Loss

15.6 LIMITS TO THE DUTY TO MITIGATE

The duty imposed on employees by statutory provisions is simply to take reasonable steps to lessen their loss. Ultimately, it is up to the tribunal to decide whether the employee's efforts in this respect are sufficient. However, in the following circumstances, employees will not be held to be in breach of the statutory duty as a matter of law.

15.6.1 Duty arises after dismissal

The duty to mitigate arises only after the dismissal. This means that an offer of re-employment made by employers before the employee is dismissed cannot be relied on as evidence of a failure to mitigate. For example, in *Gilham v Kent County Council* [1986] IRLR 56, the council argued that the applicants should have lessened their loss by accepting the new terms the council were offering to their dinner ladies. The industrial tribunal, following *Trimble v Supertravel Ltd* [1982] IRLR 451, ruled that as the council's offer was made before the dismissal, it could not be said that the employees had failed to mitigate their loss. Similarly, in *McAndrew v Prestwick Circuits Ltd* [1988] IRLR 514, the applicant was held not to have failed to mitigate his loss when he turned down an offer to work in a nearby factory because the offer was made prior to his dismissal. The lesson for employers is that an offer made before dismissal should be renewed after the dismissal.

15.6.2 Failure to use grievance procedure

It follows that in constructive dismissal cases, employees will not be penalised if they fail to pursue a grievance under their employer's grievance procedure before they resign (*Seligman & Latz Ltd v McHugh* [1979] IRLR 130), though this may amount to contributory conduct (see Chapter 16).

15.6.3 Internal appeals

In law an internal appeal normally takes place after the date of dismissal (*J Sainsbury Ltd v Savage* [1981] ICR 1); therefore in principle it should be open to employers to argue that there is a failure to mitigate when an employee fails to appeal against dismissal where the appeal would have been successful and the employee would have been reinstated or re-engaged.

This view was supported by the EAT in *Hoover Ltd v Forde* [1980] ICR 239, where the EAT ruled that a failure to appeal may be a breach of the employee's duty to mitigate loss for the reason given above and reduced compensation by 50%. The decision in *Forde* was followed in *Ever Ready v Foster* EAT 310/81, where the employers persuaded the EAT that the appeal would almost certainly have been successful. However, in *William Muir (Bond 9) Ltd v Lamb* [1985] IRLR 95, the EAT considered that a failure to appeal could not be regarded as a failure to mitigate because there were too many 'imponderable factors' and therefore an employee who failed to appeal could not be regarded as having acted unreasonably. The EAT's decision in Lamb was followed and approved of by the EAT in *Lock v Connell Estate*

Agents Ltd [1994] IRLR 444. Overturning its earlier ruling in *Hoover Ltd v Forde*, the EAT stated that 'it is one thing to say that a plaintiff is required in certain circumstances to consider an offer by a wrongdoer; it is quite another to say that if no such offer is made, then the plaintiff is under a duty to solicit the wrongdoer to change his mind'. This reasoning is far from persuasive in an employment context and the Conservative Government has proposed a provision which would give tribunals the power to reduce compensation in these circumstances (see 14.4.6 above). It remains to be seen whether these provisions will be implemented after the 1997 General Election.

At the time of writing the position is that employees will not be in breach of the duty to mitigate if they fail to pursue an internal appeal. On the other hand, it would appear that a complainant who unsuccessfully pursues an internal appeal, will not be held to have acted unreasonably in not looking for alternative employment until the appeal has been determined (*Williams v Lloyds Retailers Ltd* [1973] IRLR 262).

15.6.4 Compensation negotiations

Employees will not normally be penalised for dragging their feet or being inefficient or muddled in compensation negotiations because this will not in itself have caused the loss (*Blick Vessels & Pipework v Sharpe* IRLIB 274, February 1985). Negotiations conducted on a 'without prejudice' basis are inadmissible in any event.

15.7 ONUS OF PROOF

In *Fyfe v Scientific Furnishings Ltd* [1989] IRLR 331, the EAT confirmed that the burden of proving that the employee has failed to lessen the loss flowing from the dismissal is on the party alleging it, i.e., the employer. This is the same as the rule that exists at common law (per Roskill LJ in *Bessenden Properties Ltd v J K Corness* [1974] IRLR 338 and per Browne Wilkinson J in *Daley v A E Dorsett (Almar Dolls) Ltd* [1981] IRLR 385.

Strictly speaking this means that an employee should not be held to be in breach of the duty to mitigate unless the issue is both raised by the employer and some evidence to that effect is produced by the employer. However, in practice tribunals tend to disregard the technicalities of the legal burden of proof and raise the issue of mitigation themselves. This means that applicants should come to the tribunal prepared to show what steps they have taken since dismissal to mitiey should be ready to offer copies of adverts, job applications, replies etc. and give reasons for not applying for vacancies. This also applies to applicants who wish to argue that it was reasonable for them to set up a business since they must still show that they acted reasonably in mitigating their loss in this way.

From the employer's point of view, it is important to find out before the hearing what steps the former employee has taken to lessen his loss. This can be achieved by requesting the applicant to disclose information as to the steps he has taken to find a new job prior to the hearing. The request for information may be made in the form suggested below. If the applicant refuses to supply the information voluntarily, the employer may apply to the tribunal for an order to compel disclosure (Industrial Tribunals (Rules of Procedure) Regulations 1985, reg. 4). Doubt has been cast on the employer's right to obtain such an order before the issue of liability has been determined as a result of the EAT's decision in *Mutual Life Assurance Society Ltd* v *Clinch* [1981] ICR 752. The EAT reasoning, which assumes that the information can be obtained before the hearing through a conciliation officer, is open to question and would probably not preclude an order from being made after liability had been established. Employers who wish to challenge the reasonableness of the employee's action may produce evidence of their own, for example, details of local vacancies and advertisements in the press. This evidence should normally be disclosed to the employee before the hearing.

The burden of proof is likely to come into play only in borderline cases where the applicant's evidence is either unchallenged or unsuccessfully challenged or the employer is shown to have acted unreasonably in some other way, as in *Fyfe* itself (see 15.3.3 above).

15.7.1 Mitigation of loss: discovery

The following letter may act as a precedent when acting for an employer who is seeking information as to the steps a dismissed employee is taking to find a new job.

Dear Mr Brown

Would you please send me details of any steps you have taken since your dismissal to find a new job including:

Re: Brown v *Discoveror Ltd*

   (a)   a list of all job applications you have made;
   (b)   any job offers that have been made to you; and
   (c)   any jobs you have rejected.

If you fail to send me these particulars within 14 days I will apply to the tribunal for an order to compel disclosure under Regulation 4 of the Industrial Tribunals (Rules of Procedure) Regulations 1985.

Yours sincerely

cc ROIT

Note: These particulars may be requested at the same time as making an application for disclosure of documents relating to liability.

15.8 ASSESSING THE DEDUCTION

There is no specific statutory guidance on how the deduction for failure to mitigate is to be calculated. The normal approach is to decide when the employee would have found other work or set up a reasonably secure business and limit the compensatory award accordingly. This is similar to the principle applied in wrongful dismissal cases (see 1.7.5 above).

The approach which tribunals ought to apply was described by the EAT in *Ladbroke Racing Ltd* v *Connolly* EAT 160/83. The EAT said that tribunals should forecast the date when the employee would have been re-employed and award the net loss of earnings between the date of dismissal and the date when the employee ought, in the tribunal's view, to have found a new job.

If the tribunal concludes that the new job would be less well paid, this will be reflected in its award for continuing loss (*Smith, Kline & French Laboratories Ltd* v *Coates* [1977] IRLR 276; *Peara* v *Enderlin Ltd* [1979] ICR 804). Tribunals should not however reduce the compensatory award on a percentage basis as they do in assessing contributory fault.

15.9   MITIGATION IN FACT

The second aspect of the duty to mitigate requires employees to give credit for any income received since dismissal including income from self-employment (but excluding unemployment benefit and other social security benefits which are dealt with separately by the regulations providing for recoupment — see Chapter 18). These amounts may therefore be set off against the loss suffered by the employee between the dismissal and the date of the hearing (see 9.3.1 above).

16 Contributory Fault

16.1 INTRODUCTION

All awards of unfair dismissal compensation except the additional award (*City and Hackney Health Authority* v *Crisp* [1990] IRLR 47) may be reduced for contributory fault by such amount as the industrial tribunal considers just and equitable in the circumstances. This chapter looks at the circumstances in which an award may be reduced.

In relation to the compensatory award it is provided that where the tribunal finds that the dismissal was to any extent caused or contributed to by any action of the complainant, it shall reduce the amount of the compensatory award by such proportion as it considers just and equitable having regard to that finding (ERA 1996, s. 123(6)).

Originally the wording of the statutory provisions relating to the basic award was identical to that of the compensatory award but it was changed following the House of Lords' ruling in *W Devis & Sons Ltd* v *Atkins* [1977] IRLR 314 that a reduction in accordance with these provisions would be justified only where the conduct relied on was known to the employer at the time of dismissal. It is now provided that the basic and special awards may be reduced for any conduct of the complainant before dismissal irrespective of whether this conduct is known or unknown to the employer at the time of dismissal.

This means that the basic or special awards can be reduced where, for example, an employee has been stealing money from his or her employers, although this was not known to the employer at the time of dismissal, whereas the compensatory award cannot be reduced for contributory fault in such circumstances. However the practical effect of the difference in wording is very much reduced as a result of the House of Lords' acceptance in *W Devis & Sons Ltd* v *Atkins* that, in such circumstances, it is possible for an industrial tribunal to make no compensatory award at all on the alternative basis that, under s. 74(1) (now see ERA 1996, s. 123(1)), it was not just and equitable to do so (see 14.2.1 above).

A possible consequence of the difference in the wording of the statutory provisions arises in relation to the nature of the conduct which can be taken into account by an industrial tribunal. Thus, it could be argued that the wider wording in relation to the basic and special awards would entitle a tribunal to reduce these awards on account of any conduct on the part of the employee throughout the duration of the employment, whereas in relation to the compensatory award a reduction is justified only if the conduct complained of causes or contributes to the dismissal. There is some support for this view in the Court of Appeal's decision in *Parker Foundry Ltd v Slack* [1992] IRLR 11 on the decisions of the Northern Ireland Court of Appeal in *Morrison v Amalgamated Transport and General Workers' Union* [1989] IRLR 361 and the EAT in *Polentarutti v Autokraft Ltd* [1991] IRLR 457 that tribunals can take a fairly broad view of contributory conduct under ERA 1996, s. 123(6) and therefore the distinction may not matter much in practice. Moreover, a reduction is unlikely to be considered just and equitable if the conduct is only remotely connected with the events that led to the dismissal.

It should be noted that, although the same general principles apply to all three awards, special statutory provisions apply where dismissals are found to be unfair for trade union reasons (see 5.3.1 and 6.3.1).

16.2 GENERAL PRINCIPLES

Three conditions must be met before a reduction for contributory fault is justified:

(a) there must be culpable or blameworthy conduct on the part of the employee;
(b) subject to the point made above in relation to the basic and special awards, the conduct complained of must have caused or contributed to the dismissal;
(c) it must be just and equitable to reduce the award.

Whether each of these conditions is met is essentially a question of fact to be determined by the industrial tribunal. As such it lies very much at the heart of the fact finding role of an industrial tribunal whose decision will not be overturned unless the tribunal misdirects itself in law or reaches a perverse decision on the facts, i.e., a decision to which no reasonable tribunal could have come (*Hollier v Plysu Ltd* [1983] IRLR 260). It follows that the EAT is extremely reluctant to overturn an industrial tribunal's decision provided the relevant principles of law have been taken into account.

16.2.1 What conduct is considered culpable or blameworthy?

The requirement that the employee's conduct must be blameworthy was established by the Court of Appeal in *Nelson v BBC (No 2)* [1979] IRLR 346, where it was held that this requirement was implicit in the provision that the conduct itself should have caused or contributed to the dismissal. Alternatively, the court considered that it would not be just and equitable to make a reduction unless the employee's conduct was shown to be blameworthy.

In *Nelson*, Brandon LJ sought to describe the sort of conduct which could be regarded as blameworthy:

> The concept does not, in my view, necessarily involve any conduct of the complainant amounting to a breach of contract or a tort. It includes, no doubt, conduct of that kind. But it also includes conduct which, while not amounting to a breach of contract or a tort, is nevertheless perverse or foolish, or, if I may use

Contributory Fault

the colloquialism, bloody minded. It may also include action which, though not meriting any of those more perjorative epithets, is nevertheless unreasonable in all the circumstances. I should not, however, go as far as to say that all unreasonable conduct is necessarily culpable or blameworthy; it must depend on the degree of unreasonableness involved.

Most, if not all, misconduct would therefore be regarded as blameworthy conduct. The following have all been so regarded: dishonesty (*Gaskin* v *MSW Business Systems Ltd* IDS 309); breach of company rules (*McNicholas* v *AR Engineering* IDS 309; going on holiday or returning late from holiday without permission (*Allen* v *N E Lancashire Dairies Ltd* EAT 230/83 and *Hall* v *Vincemark Ltd* COIT 2029/54); soliciting customers for a rival business or working for a rival outside normal working hours (*Baxter* v *Wreyfield* EAT 9/82 and *Fraser* v *Tullos Business Services* EAT 655/87); setting up a rival business (*Connor* v *Comet Radiovision Services Ltd* EAT 650/81); poor attendance record (*McNicholas*); conduct setting back recovery from an illness (*Patterson* v *Bracketts* EAT 486/76); failing to reply to a letter requiring an employee to attend a disciplinary interview or to undergo a medical examination (*Slaughter* v *C Brewer & Sons Ltd* [1990] IRLR 426); negligence (*Coalter* v *Walter Craven Ltd* [1980] IRLR 262). Employees have also been penalised for other unreasonable conduct such as a refusal to disclose the names of employees who had been involved in acts of misconduct (*Simpson* v *British Steel Corporation* EAT 594/83), a failure to use an internal grievance procedure to resolve a pay dispute (*Walls* v *Brookside Metal Co Ltd* EAT 579/89) and, more recently, a failure to abide by an agreement with the company regarding time spent on union duties (*Dundon* v *GPT Ltd* [1995] IRLR 403).

On the other hand, compensation will not be reduced for contributory fault if the employee's conduct is not regarded as blameworthy in the sense described by the Court of Appeal in *Nelson*. For example, a refusal to obey an instruction to falsify records (*Morrish* v *Henlys (Folkestone) Ltd* [1973] IRLR 6); a refusal to disclose a criminal conviction which is spent under the Rehabilitation of Offenders Act 1974 (*Property Guards Ltd* v *Taylor* [1982] IRLR 175) and a failure to call witness at a disciplinary hearing (*British Steel Corporation* v *Williams* EAT 776/82) have all been held *not* to justify a reduction in compensation.

Moreover, a reduction will not be justified if there is insufficient evidence of such conduct before the industrial tribunal. For example, in *Tele-Trading Ltd* v *Jenkins* [1990] IRLR 430, the Court of Appeal upheld an industrial tribunal's refusal to make a reduction for contributory fault where the tribunal was not satisfied that there were reasonable grounds for believing that the employee was guilty of the conduct alleged by the employers either at the time of dismissal or at the hearing itself. It is also doubtful whether every breach of contract would justify a reduction for contributory fault since liability for breach of contract can arise without any fault on the part of the employee and a reduction in such circumstances would be contrary to the underlying principle that the conduct in question must be of a blameworthy nature.

16.2.1.1 Industrial action and contributory fault

Following a series of conflicting EAT decisions, the Court of Appeal in *Crossville Wales Ltd* v *Tracey and Ors* [1996] IRLR 91 confirmed that tribunals should not reduce compensation for contributory fault where an employee is dismissed for taking part in industrial action and the dismissal is found to be unfair under s. 238 of the Trade Union and Labour Relations (Consolidation) Act 1992, which deals with the discriminatory re-engagement of strikers. In support of its decision, the Court endorsed the views expressed by the EAT in *Courtaulds Northern Spinning Ltd v Moosa* [1984] IRLR 43, that the general immunity from claims in such circumstances is an indication of Parliament's intention that tribunals should not seek to weigh up the rights and wrongs of a particular industrial dispute and that therefore mere participation in industrial action could not be regarded as blameworthy conduct justifying a reduction in compensation for contributory fault. However, the Court said that a reduction for contributory fault might be justified if the employee went beyond mere participation by, for example, acting over-hastily or in an inflammatory manner. The same may also apply if strikers behave in an intimidatory manner.

Similar principles would probably also apply where employees were unfairly dismissed for threatening industrial action. For example, in *Adapters and Eliminators v Paterson* EAT 801/82, the EAT doubted whether a threat of industrial action by itself amounted to blameworthy conduct.

16.2.2 Contributory fault and dismissals for incapability

In general, compensation will be reduced in capability dismissals only if the employee is to blame for the actions which led to the dismissal, but should not be reduced where the employee's lack of ability cannot be regarded as blameworthy conduct.

The distinction between these two types of capability dismissal was considered by the EAT in *Kraft Foods Ltd v Fox* [1977] IRLR 43. Mr Fox was dismissed from his job as a sales manager after he had failed to meet the high standards set by his predecessor. The industrial tribunal held that the dismissal was unfair but reduced the award by 50% on the grounds of contributory fault. The EAT allowed the employer's appeal against the tribunal's finding that the dismissal was unfair, but it also held that the tribunal had erred in law on the issue of contributory fault because Mr Fox was not to blame for lacking the ability of his predecessor. The EAT said that:

> If an employee is incompetent or incapable and cannot, with the best will in the world, measure up to the job, it seems to us to be wrong to say that that condition of incapacity is a contributory factor to his dismissal.

It drew a distinction between actions over which an employee has control and those outside his control. In the former situation, the employee is guilty of misconduct and compensation may be reduced, but in the latter situation the employee cannot be blamed and therefore compensation should not be reduced.

However, some doubt has been cast on this principle in the subsequent case of *Moncur v International Paint Co Ltd* [1978] IRLR 223. Here again, Mr Moncur's dismissal arose as a result of his lack of managerial ability. In particular it was alleged that he was not good at getting on with his superiors and fell short of the required standards of administrative control. The industrial tribunal, having found the dismissal unfair, reduced compensation by 40%. The EAT, upholding this decision, said that the tribunal had not erred in law and that it was entitled on the facts to make such a reduction. The decision in *Moncur* was followed by the EAT in *Finnie* v *Top Hat Frozen Foods Ltd* [1985] IRLR 365. However, the EAT's approach in *Fox* appears to be more consistent with the underlying principle that compensation should not be reduced unless the employee's conduct is shown to be blameworthy.

This, of course, does not mean that a reduction in capability dismissals will never be justified. For example, in *Sutton & Gates (Luton) Ltd* v *Boxall* [1978] IRLR 486, the EAT said that an industrial tribunal was wrong to refuse to reduce the award where an electrician was dismissed for poor performance. The EAT said that the ruling in *Fox* applied only to what it called 'true' capability dismissals, i.e., cases where the employee's dismissal was due to a lack of ability beyond his control. It did not apply to cases where the dismissal was brought about by the employee's laziness, idleness, or negligence as these were matters which lay within the employee's control and therefore were matters which could justify a reduction for contributory fault. See also 14.3.3 above.

16.2.3 Contributory fault and ill-health dismissals

Compensation should not be reduced for contributory fault in ill-health dismissals unless the applicant is shown to be guilty of blameworthy conduct. This principle was reaffirmed by the EAT in *Slaughter* v *C Brewer & Sons Ltd* [1990] IRLR 426 when it overturned an industrial tribunal's decision to reduce its award by 80% because of the applicant's incapacity for work at the time of his dismissal. However the EAT recognised that there may be circumstances where a reduction for contributory fault would be appropriate, e.g., where an employee refused to obtain a medical report or to attend a medical examination. A reduction may also be justified if an employee acts in a manner which was detrimental to his or her recovery (*A Links Ltd* v *Rose* [1991] IRLR 353).

16.2.4 Conduct judged objectively

The test for determining whether or not the conduct is blameworthy is objective. Therefore, it is irrelevant, for the purpose of determining blameworthiness, for the tribunal to consider whether the employee knew that the conduct complained of was wrong. See *Ladbroke Racing Ltd* v *Mason* [1978] ICR 49, where two employees' involvement in negotiations for their employers' betting shops was held to be a gross breach of trust even though the employees did not know that their conduct was wrong.

Nevertheless, an employee's state of mind may be relevant for the purpose of determining the degree of blameworthiness since, once it has been established that blameworthiness exists, the extent of the deduction may be determined by reference to the employee's knowledge of the wrongfulness of the action. Thus, where an employee knew that the conduct was wrong the deduction may be larger than would otherwise be the case to reflect this knowledge (see *Washbrook* v *Podger* EAT 123/85, where the employee's contribution was increased from 40% to 80% because he knew that he was acting contrary to his employer's instructions).

16.2.5 Conduct of agents

Employees may be responsible for the actions of those acting on their behalf if the agent's conduct causes or contributes to the dismissal. Similarly it is no defence for employees to say that their act based on advice from a third party if that advice is negligent or unreasonable (see *Allen* v *Hammett* [1982] IRLR 89, where the applicant was held responsible for the negligent advice given to him by his solicitor).

16.2.6 Employee's conduct alone relevant

Tribunals may take into account only the conduct of the employee (or the employee's agents) in deciding whether or not to make a reduction for contributory fault and are not entitled to consider how the employer treated others involved in the same incident (*Allders International Ltd* v *Parkins* [1981] IRLR 68). This principle has recently been confirmed by the Court of Appeal in *Parker Foundry Ltd* v *Slack* [1992] IRLR 11, where the court upheld an industrial tribunal's decision to reduce compensation by 50% for contributory fault where the applicant had been dismissed for fighting. The court rejected the argument that the tribunal should have taken account of the fact that the other employee who had been involved in the fight had only been suspended without pay for two weeks ruling that the statutory provisions are concerned only with the conduct of the applicant and not the conduct of others. However, it is submitted, that a tribunal is entitled to consider the conduct of others in order to determine the extent to which the applicant was to blame for the dismissal, e.g., in *Slack* it is clear that the tribunal did have regard to the extent to which Mr Slack was to blame for the fight.

16.2.7 Conduct linked to the dismissal

As far as the compensatory award is concerned, the satutory provisions make it clear that compensation may be reduced only where the conduct genuinely causes or contributes to the dismissal. For example, in *Smith & Smith* v *McPhee and Stewart* EAT 338/339/89, the EAT held that an industrial tribunal was correct not to make a reduction for contributory fault where it was found that the cause of the dismissal was that the employer was trying to save face over an embarassing incident for which he was partly responsible. In these circumstances, the applicants carelessness had not itself caused or contributed to the dismissal. Similarly, in *Hutchinson* v *Enfield Rolling Mills* [1981] IRLR 318, the EAT held that the industrial tribunal had erred in law when it took into account the unrelated factors such as the employee's political views or its adverse view of him as a trouble maker. The EAT said that the only relevant matters were those which led to the dismissal and all other factors should be ignored. Tribunals should not therefore 'simply point to some bad behaviour of employees and say that by reason of that matter they are going to reduce compensation' (*Steer* v *Messrs Primlock Ltd* EAT 687/85).

On the other hand, employers are not confined to relying on the conduct which constitutes their principal reason for dismissal — they can also rely on other subsidiary reasons for dismissal provided that those reasons contribute to the decision to dismiss (*Robert Whiting Designs Ltd* v *Lamb* [1978] ICR 89). For

Contributory Fault 169

example, in *McNicholas* v *AR Engineering* IDS 309, a tribunal thought that Mr McNicholas's poor record for absence and time-keeping contributed to his dismissal.

As noted in 16.1 above, the power to reduce the basic and special awards is somewhat wider than the power to reduce the compensatory award since tribunals may take account of 'any conduct' of the complainant. Some tribunals have held that this includes conduct which is unrelated to the employer's reasons for dismissal. For example, in *Artisan Press Ltd* v *Srawley and Parker* [1986] IRLR 126, an industrial tribunal reduced Mr Parker's special award by 10% because of his persistent lateness even though this had nothing to do with the reason for dismissal, as found by the tribunal. However, it must be doubted whether the amendment made by s. 9(2) of the Employment Act 1980 was intended to change the test of causation. The better view is that it is not just and equitable to reduce the basic and special awards unless there is some link between the employee's conduct and the dismissal.

16.2.8 Conduct in the notice period

Industrial tribunals have no power to reduce compensation for contributory fault if the misconduct occurs during the notice period. Thus, in *Bell* v *Service Engines (Newcastle) Ltd* IDS 309, an industrial tribunal held that it was not entitled to reduce the basic award where thefts occurred during the employee's notice period.

In relation to the compensatory award, compensation may be limited on the alternative ground of 'justice and equity' under s. 123(1) of the Employment Rights Act 1996 (see Chapter 14). Thus in *Bell* above, the tribunal held that it was inequitable to make a compensatory award in the light of the employee's conduct during the notice period.

16.2.9 Internal appeals

An employee's failure to lodge an internal appeal does not justify compensation being reduced for contributory fault. An internal appeal is an event after the dismissal takes effect, so the employee's failure to appeal does not contribute to the dismissal and does not justify a reduction in either the basic or special awards (ERA 1996, s. 122(1)) or the compensatory award (ERA 1996, s. 123(6)). See *Hoover Ltd* v *Forde* [1980] ICR 239 and *Ever Ready Co (GB) Ltd* v *Foster* EAT 310/81. However, a reduction for contributory fault may be justified for failing to use the grievance procedure prior to dismissal.

The position in relation to the duty to mitigate is discussed in Chapter 15.

16.2.10 Constructive dismissals and contributory fault

The same general principles apply irrespective of whether the dismissal is direct or constructive. So provided the employee's conduct is blameworthy in the sense described by Brandon LJ in *Nelson* v *BBC (No 2)* [1979] IRLR 346 (see 16.2.1 above) and can be said to have caused or contributed to the dismissal, there is no reason in principle why a reduction for contributory fault should not be made simply because the dismissal is constructive rather than direct (see *Garner* v *Grange Furnishing Ltd* [1977] IRLR 206).

In *Holroyd* v *Gravure Cylinders Ltd* [1984] IRLR 259, the EAT ruled that compensation should be reduced for contributory fault in constructive dismissals only in 'exceptional circumstances', by which the EAT appears to have meant cases involving a variation in contract. The EAT's ruling was subsequently given a wider interpretation which suggested that a reduction for contributory fault should not be made in 'constructive dismissal' cases. However in *Morrison* v *Amalgamated Transport and General Workers Union* [1989] IRLR 361, the Northern Ireland Court of Appeal ruled that, insofar as *Holroyd* purported to lay down a rule of law, it was wrongly decided and that it was not necessary to show 'exceptional' circumstances before a reduction for contributory fault would be justified in constructive dismissal cases. This decision has now been followed and approved by the EAT in *Polentarutti* v *Autokraft Ltd* [1991] IRLR 457.

Tribunals have also been encouraged to take a 'broad common sense' approach to issue of causation in constructive dismissal cases. So, although the immediate cause of the dismissal is the employer's repudiatory conduct, tribunals are entitled to consider the extent to which the employee's own behaviour caused or contributed to the situation which led to the constructive dismissal. For example, in *Morrison* the Northern Ireland Court of Appeal held that a tribunal was entitled to consider the reason why the applicant had been suspended without pay which resulted in her being constructively dismissed. See also *Polentarutti*, where the EAT said that the tribunal was entitled to take into account the applicant's bad workmanship which led to his constructive dismissal.

16.2.11 Relationship with power to limit compensation

In principle, it is open to tribunals both to limit the period over which compensation is awarded (see Chapter 14) and reduce the award for contributory fault. For example, where the principal reason for dismissal is ill-health, a tribunal might conclude that dismissal would have been fair within a month and therefore limit the award to a month's compensation. It may also reduce the award for contributory fault on the grounds that the employee had retarded recovery by gardening or playing a sport (see *Rao* v *Civil Aviation Authority* [1994] IRLR 240).

However, if the reason for limiting the compensatory awarno further reduction under s. 123(6) of the Employment Rights Act 1996. For example, in redundancy dismissals, although compensation may be limited to the period it would have taken the employers to consult the employees, a further reduction for contributory fault would not normally be justified (see *Abbotts* v *Wesson-Glynwed Steel Ltd* [1982] IRLR 52). The same applies to capability dismissals where the employee is not to blame for the dismissal (see 16.2.2 above). Moreover, some tribunals are unwilling both to limit compensation and reduce the award for contributory fault if this means penalising the employee twice for the same conduct. For example, in *Vildung* v *Ocean Electronics Ltd* EAT 295/79, a case of gross negligence, the EAT thought that both to limit and reduce the award was 'unjust and the application of a double penalty'.

Contributory Fault

16.3 AMOUNT OF REDUCTION

Once the employee's conduct is shown to be blameworthy, the tribunal has to go on to decide whether it is just and equitable to reduce the award, and if so, by how much.

In *Hollier* v *Plysu Ltd* [1983] IRLR 260, the Court of Appeal gave some guidance to industrial tribunals on how they should approach the issue of apportioning blame for the dismissal. As a rule of thumb the EAT suggested that there were four types of cases as follows:

(a) the employee is wholly to blame for the dismissal and compensation could be reduced by 100%;

(b) the employee is largely to blame and nobody would quarrel with a reduction of 75%;

(c) both parties are equally to blame and compensation should be reduced by 50%;

(d) the employee is slightly to blame and compensation should be reduced by 25%.

In *York* v *Brown* EAT 262/84, the EAT added a fifth category, namely cases where the employee's degree of blame is so small that it would not be worth making a reduction at all. The EAT suggested that this would apply to reductions of 10% or less.

Though subsequently endorsed by the Court of Appeal in the same case, these 'guidelines' should be treated with some caution since the court stressed that the question of apportionment is a matter for the tribunal which should adopt 'a broad commonsense view of the situation'. It follows that a failure to apply the 'guidelines' is not in itself sufficient grounds for appeal unless it can also be shown that the tribunal made an error of law, i.e., misunderstood or misconstrued its statutory powers, or came to a decision which no reasonable tribunal could have reached.

Thus sometimes tribunals reduce awards by less than the recommended 25%. For example, in *Artisan Press Ltd* v *Srawley and Parker* [1986] IRLR 126, the industrial tribunal reduced Mr Parker's award by 10% because of the persistent lateness. At the other end of the spectrum tribunals have been known to reduce compensation by 90%. For example, in *Gibson and Others* v *British Transport Docks Board* [1982] IRLR 228, a case where nine employees were dismissed for allegedly intimidating two colleagues, the EAT substituted a reduction of 90% for 100% because 'the overwhelming blame for the dismissal lies in this case at the door of these applicants'. For a further example see *Thompson* v *Imperial College of Science and Technology* IDS 309.

16.3.1 No reduction

In the overwhelming majority of cases, the tribunal will make some reduction if it finds the employee to blame for the dismissal. However, it is open to a tribunal not to reduce compensation at all where it regards the employee's conduct as falling within the *'de minimis'* principle, as suggested by the EAT in *York* v *Brown* EAT 262/84 (see 16.3 above), or where it considers that it would not be just and equitable to make a reduction (see *Central Nottinghamshire Health Authority* v *Shine* EAT 562/82).

16.3.2   100% reduction

At one time it was thought that it was wrong in principle for a tribunal to hold a dismissal unfair and reduce compensation by 100%. However, in *W Devis & Sons Ltd* v *Atkins* [1977] IRLR 314, the House of Lords approved earlier EAT decisions to the effect that such a reduction is possible where the employee's conduct was the sole cause of the dismissal.

An illustration of such a case is *Maris* v *Rotherham Borough Council* [1974] IRLR 147. Mr Maris, who worked in the council's cleaning department, was dismissed as a result of being convicted of submitting fraudulent expenses. The decision to dismiss was finally taken after industrial pressure from the workforce and the dismissal was found to be unfair for this reason. However, the industrial tribunal awarded no compensation because it thought that such an award was not just and equitable in the circumstances. The NIRC affirmed this decision on different grounds. They said that no award should be made to Mr Maris because he was the sole author of his own misfortune.

The right to make a 100% reduction for contributory fault in appropriate cases was recently confirmed by the EAT in *Chaplin* v *Rawlinson* [1991] ICR 553 where the dismissal was held unfair on procedural grounds but a 100% reduction was justified as the employee had been dismissed for urinating on a consignment of wheat before delivering it to a customer. Other cases where 100% reductions have been upheld include *Baxter* v *Wreyfield* EAT 9/82 — soliciting customers for a rival company and *Allen* v *NE Lancashire Dairies Ltd* EAT 230/83 — going on holiday without permission.

However, before reducing compensation by 100%, a tribunal must be satisfied that the employee was wholly to blame for the dismissal. Thus in *Trend* v *Chiltern Hunt Ltd* [1977] IRLR 66, the EAT said that it thought that a 100% reduction would be appropriate only where 'a dismissal has been found to be unfair on technical grounds or where later ascertained facts had they been known at the date of the hearing would have amply justified it' (see 16.5 below). Similarly, in *Gibson* v *British Transport Docks Board* [1982] IRLR 228, the EAT held that a reduction of 100% was inconsistent with the industrial tribunal's ruling that the employers were at fault for not investigating the circumstances of Mr Gibson's particular case. It therefore said that a 90% reduction was appropriate (see also *Thomas* v *Gauges North West (Scientific Instruments)* IRLIB 277, March 1985).

16.3.3   Industrial pressure and contributory fault

Tribunals must ignore industrial pressure in deciding whether the dismissal is fair or unfair (ERA 1996, s. 107). Similarly, once a dismissal is held to be unfair, in assessing compensation, no account is taken of industrial pressure (ERA 1996, s. 123(5) — see 8.4.2 above).

This rule does not prevent tribunals from reducing the award for contributory fault where the employee was to blame for the actions which led to the industrial pressure

Contributory Fault

to dismiss. For example, in *Colwyn Borough Council* v *Dutton* [1980] IRLR 420, Mr Dutton's colleagues in the refuse collection service refused to work with him because his driving was so bad. The EAT held that Mr Dutton's conduct contributed to the dismissal. In some cases like *Maris* v *Rotherham Borough Council* [1974] IRLR 147, a reduction of 100% may be justified where it is shown that the employee was wholly to blame for the dismissal.

16.3.4 Reduction not proportional to employer's loss

The amount of the reduction need not be proportional to the loss to the employer caused by the employee's conduct. For example, in *Acorn Shipyard Ltd* v *Warren* EAT 20/81, the company lost £8,500 as a result of Mr Warren's underestimation of the length of time and the cost of building a ship. It was argued that the reduction in the award should reflect the loss suffered by the company. The EAT, however, refused to interfere with the industrial tribunal's decision that compensation should only be reduced by 25%. It said that the tribunal had taken this factor into account in making its assessment and concluded that the responsibility for the error was not entirely Mr Waat the reduction in the award should be proportional to the financial loss suffered by the company.

16.4 CONSISTENT REDUCTIONS OF AWARDS

The general rule is that both the basic and compensatory awards should be reduced by the same amount. Thus, in *G M McFall & Co Ltd* v *Curran* [1981] IRLR 455, the Court of Appeal in Northern Ireland overturned an industrial tribunal's decision to reduce the compensatory award by 40% and not to reduce the basic award at all. The court said that both awards should be reduced by the same amount. See also *RSPCA* v *Cruden* [1986] IRLR 83.

However, in exceptional circumstances, the EAT has upheld decisions to reduce the awards by different amounts. For example, in *Les Ambassadeurs Club* v *Bainda* [1982] IRLR 5, the EAT upheld an industrial tribunal's decision to reduce the compensatory award by 70% but not to reduce the basic award at all. Similarly, in *Thompson* v *Woodland Designs Ltd* [1980] IRLR 423, the EAT upheld a decision to reduce the basic award by 85% and the compensatory award by 100%.

Another situation where it might be considered just and equitable to reduce the awards by different amounts is where the tribunal has limited the compensation award under s. 123(1) and also decided to reduce the award for contributory fault (see 16.2.1.1 above). Here, a tribunal might decide that it is just and equitable to reduce the compensatory award by a lower or higher amount than the basic award (*Rao* v *Civil Aviation Authority* [1994] IRLR 240 and *Charles Robertson (Developments) Ltd* v *White and another* [1995] ICR 349).

It is also possible that an inconsistent reduction could be applied on the grounds that the power to reduce the basic and special awards is wider than the power to reduce the compensatory award (see 16.1 above).

The reduction for contributory fault is made after the applicant's loss has been quantified but before applying the statutory ceiling on the compensatory award

(*Walter Braund (London) Ltd* v *Murray* [1991] IRLR 100). See also 17.3.2 below as to the treatment of ex gratia payments.

16.5 NEW EVIDENCE AFTER THE HEARING

A further reduction in compensation may be made if new evidence of misconduct comes to light after the hearing. This arose in *Ladup Ltd* v *Barnes* [1982] IRLR 8. Mr Barnes was dismissed after being charged with growing and possessing cannabis. His dismissal was found to be unfair on the grounds that the company had failed to carry out an independent investigation into the allegation. The tribunal refused to reduce the award of compensation because it considered that Mr Barnes was not to blame for the dismissal. About a month after the hearing, Mr Barnes was convicted of possessing cannabis and the company applied to the tribunal for a review. Its request was turned down by the tribunal but the tribunal's decision was overturned by the EAT on appeal. The EAT said that the tribunal's refusal to reduce the award in the first instance was correct, but the position had changed in the light of Mr Barnes' conviction. This new evidence meant that the decision should be reviewed in the interests of justice and that compensation should be reduced by 100%.

The EAT's decision in *Ladup Ltd* v *Barnes* is open to doubt for two reasons: First, it would appear to conflict with the principle in *W Devis & Sons Ltd* v *Atkins* [1977] IRLR 314 that information coming to light after the dismissal is not relevant to the issue of contributory fault. (The same objection would seem to apply to reducing basic and special awards in such circumstances even though statutory powers to reduce those awards for contributory fault are wider.) Secondly, the decision is open to the more general criticism that by allowing the award to be reviewed outside the 14-day period provided for by the industrial tribunal rules, the EAT has created a degree of uncertainty in an area where finality should be the guiding principle. On the other hand, if *Ladup Ltd* v *Barnes* is correct, the same principle should apply to an employee who is subsequently acquitted or whose conviction is quashed on appeal (see Industrial Tribunals (Constitution and Rules of Procedure) Regulations 1993, r. 11(1)(e)).

Note: Where there is a split hearing, the Chairman should make it clear to the parties whether the issue of contributory fault is to be dealt with at the hearing on liability or at the remedies hearing (*Dundon* v *GPT* [1995] IRLR 403).

17 Ex Gratia Payments and Other Deductions

Redundancy and ex gratia payments are liable to be deducted from an award of unfair dismissal compensation. This chapter looks at the circumstances in which such payments are deducted.

17.1 DEDUCTING REDUNDANCY PAYMENTS FROM UNFAIR DISMISSAL COMPENSATION

The primary purpose of the statutory provisions is to prevent employees from receiving both a basic award and a redundancy payment. However, where an employee receives an enhanced redundancy payment, i.e., a payment over and above the statutory maximum, this may be set off against the compensatory award, but this applies only where redundancy is found to be the true reason for dismissal (*Boorman* v *Allmakes Ltd* [1995] IRLR 553). The relevant statutory provisions are examined in greater detail below.

17.1.1 Statutory redundancy pay

It is provided that where an employee receives a redundancy payment, 'The amount of the basic award shall be reduced or further reduced by the amount of ... any redundancy payment' (ERA 1996, s. 122(4)).

This provision applies irrespective of whether the payment is made by the employer or awarded by the tribunal.

Example

An employee aged 28 who earns £120 a week with four years' service is made redundant. The employer gives him a redundancy payment of £360. The dismissal is found to be unfair.

The employee would be entitled to a basic award of £480, but he has already received £360 so that the balance payable is £120.

17.1.2 Enhanced redundancy payments and the compensatory award

It is provided that, if the amount of any payment made by an employer on the ground that the dismissal was by reason of redundancy exceeds the amount of the basic award which would be payable but for s. 122(4) of the Employment Rights Act 1996, the excess shall go to reduce the amount of the compensatory award (s. 123(7)). This provision may be relied on by employers where the basic award is reduced for contributory fault (a redundancy payment being irreducible), and where the redundancy payment exceeds the minimum payment provided for under the statutory redundancy payment scheme. So, if the facts in the example given at 17.1.1 were varied so that a payment of £800 was made under a company redundancy scheme, there would be a reduction in the compensatory award of £320.

Note: Where a '*Polkey*' reduction is made to the compensatory award (see Chapter 14), the correct approach is:

(a) to calculate the loss;
(b) to set off the excess contractual redundancy payment against the loss; and
(c) to reduce the balance by 'a proportionate *Polkey* reduction' per Mr Justice Morison (see *Digital Equipment Co. Ltd* v *Clements (No. 2)* [1997] IRLR 140).

17.1.3 Relationship with compensation claim for enhanced payment

Section 123(3) of the Employment Rights Act 1996 allows an employee to recover compensation for the loss of an enhanced redundancy payment as part of the compensatory award (see 9.2.6 above). It is unclear whether any sum *awarded by the tribunal* under s. 123(3) should then be set off against the rest of the award of compensation, thereby putting an employee in the same position as if the employer had made the payment at the time of dismissal; or whether it should only be set off *where the payment is made by the employer*. It would seem from the wording of s. 123(7) that it is only intended to apply in this latter situation. If this interpretation is correct, s. 123(7) will not apply where the compensation for the loss of an enhanced redundancy payment is awarded by the tribunal as part of the compensatory award, with the result that employees who receive their redundancy payments from their employers at the time of dismissal will be worse off than those who recover such payments as part of their claim for unfair dismissal compensation.

Note: These provisions apply only where the dismissal is both 'by reason of redundancy' and unfair. Thus they will not affect employees who claim compensation for the loss of an enhanced redundancy payment in a non-redundancy dismissal (see *Addison* v *Babcock FATA Ltd* [1986] IRLR 388).

17.2 EX GRATIA PAYMENTS

It is not uncommon for employers to make an ex gratia payment in addition to any payment which an employee is entitled to receive on dismissal such as a payment in

Ex Gratia Payments and Other Deductions 177

lieu of notice. For this purpose, an ex gratia payment may be defined as any sum paid to an employee without any legal liability to do so.

17.3 EX GRATIA PAYMENT AS A DEFENCE

In *Chelsea Football Club & Athletic Co Ltd* v *Heath* [1981] IRLR 73, the EAT ruled that in principle there was no objection to employers relying on an ex gratia payment as a defence to the statutory liability to pay compensation.

Mr Heath was dismissed from his job as Chelsea Football Club's chief talent scout as a result of the appointment of a new manager. After his dismissal, he was sent a cheque for £7,500 by the club. Mr Heath subsequently successfully claimed that he had been unfairly dismissed. When it came to assessing compensation, the club argued that the tribunal should take the ex gratia payment into account. The industrial tribunal accepted this argument and declined to make a compensatory award, though they did make a basic award of £1,920.

On appeal, the club argued that as the ex gratia payment exceeded the statutory maximum (which at that time was £5,200) the balance should be set off against the basic award. The EAT agreed, saying that although the payment did not specifically refer to the basic award, there was a presumption that the club were really offering to pay the full statutory compensation 'without prejudice' to the issue of liability.

In *Horizon Holidays Ltd* v *Grassi* [1987] IRLR 371, it was held that, following the Court of Appeal's decision in *Babcock FATA Ltd* v *Addison* [1987] IRLR 173, an ex gratia payment should normally be deducted from an award of unfair dismissal compensation (see also *Rushton* v *Harcross Timber & Building Supplies Ltd* [1993] IRLR 254, where the EAT appears to have treated an ex gratia payment made to the employee at the time of his redundancy as an enhanced redundancy payment falling within EPCA 1978, s. 74(7), and *Boorman* v *Allmakes* [1995] IRLR 553, where Lord Justice Evans suggested that where an enhanced redundancy payment is paid by mistake, the payment can be deducted from the compensatory award).

17.3.1 Payments which count

Not all post-dismissal payments are regarded as ex gratia payments. For example, a payment in lieu of notice will not be considered to be an ex gratia payment and credit for such a payment will be given in calculating the applicant's loss under s. 123(1) of the Employment Rights Act 1996. The same applies to other payments made on account of wages or salary, e.g., any back pay in compliance with a re-engagement order. These should be taken into account in calculating the applicant's loss and not treated as an ex gratia payment (see *Butler* v *British Railways Board* EAT 510/89).

However, in *Chelsea Football Club & Athletic Co Ltd* v *Heath* [1981] IRLR 73, the EAT said that an ex gratia payment could be a defence to statutory liability if the payment itself was made with reference to the statutory awards. It said that this will often be implied since an employer and employee who are negotiating this kind of agreement must be taken to know that, if unfair dismissal is shown, there is an entitlement to a basic award and to a compensatory award if loss is established. It is then a question of whether the amount which was paid is sufficient to cover both the basic award and the compensatory award to which an employee would be entitled.

In *Heath*, the EAT held that the reference in the employer's covering letter to the payment being 'as a result of your termination of employment' was sufficient to make it referable to the statutory provisions. Moreover, in *Horizon Holidays Ltd* v *Grassi* [1987] IRLR 371, the EAT held that such a payment should be deducted from the compensatory award even though there was no reference to the payment being made in discharge of statutory liabilities. On the other hand, in *Darr* v *LRC Products* [1993] IRLR 257, the EAT indicated that such an inference would not necessarily be drawn in relation to the discharge of liability to pay an additional award and therefore recommended that if the intention was for the ex gratia payment to cover potential liability for such award, this should be expressly stated.

Similarly, in *Ladbroke Racing Ltd* v *Mesher* EAT 375/83, the EAT rejected Ladbroke's argument that a payment which was expressed to be in lieu of notice (but which exceeded the employee's notice entitlement) was really an ex gratia payment and therefore could be off-set against the statutory liability to pay compensation. The EAT, referring to the express terms of the letter said that 'the payment of £992 was a pure payment in lieu of notice and nothing more'. In the light of this decision, employers should ensure that any payment is linked to the statutory provisions.

Finally, certain 'ex gratia' payments, which would have been payable to the employee in any event, should not be deducted. For example, in *Addison* v *Babcock FATA Ltd* [1987] IRLR 173, the applicant recovered compensation for the loss of an ex gratia payment he would have received it had been dismissed at the same time as his colleagues some 15 months later when the employer's business was closed. Similarly, in *Roadchef Ltd* v *Hastings* [1988] IRLR 142, the EAT held that the industrial tribunal was correct not to deduct an ex gratia payment which the employee would have received even if he had not been dismissed. The same reasoning was held to apply to the non-deduction of a bonus payment which an employee would have received had he remained in employment during the period covered by the award in *Quiring* v *Hill House International School* EAT 500/88.

Doubt has been cast on the correctness of these decisions by the EAT in *Rushton* v *Harcross Timber & Building Supplies Ltd* [1993] IRLR 254, where the EAT declined to follow its earlier ruling in *Hastings* and ruled that an employer always should be given credit for an ex gratia payment made to a redundant employee, adding that such a payment should always be set off against an employer's liability to make a compensatory payment. In support of its decision the EAT relied on the 'meaning and intent of s. 74(7)' (now ERA 1996, s. 123(7)), i.e., that in the calculation of a compensatory award an employer should receive credit for any redundancy payment he makes since 'the manifest purpose of that subsection was to encourage employers who find it necessary to dismiss for redundancy to be generous in making ex gratia payments'. However, the EAT appears to have misunderstood Mr Rushton's argument, namely that he would have received such a payment in any event, though no evidence in support of this argument was placed before the industrial tribunal. The EAT also appears to have failed to distinguish between an 'ex gratia' payment and a payment under s. 123(7), as such payments may be made for different reasons. The decision therefore may be open to doubt.

17.3.1.1 Illustration
The following wording in a letter enclosing an ex gratia payment is likely to have the effect that the payment is deducted from any entitlement to compensation which the recipient may have:

> We are making the above payment in discharge of any liability to pay compensation under current employment legislation.

17.3.2 Deduction from total loss or final award

Assuming that the ex gratia payment is deductible, the next question is whether it should be included in the assessment of overall loss under s. 123(1) of the Employment Rights Act 1996 or whether it should be deducted from the final award. The point is important, because if the former approach is correct, the ex gratia payment will be brought into the assessment before compensation is reduced for contributory fault, whereas if the latter approach is correct, the payment will be deducted from the final award. Until the recent decision of the EAT in *Digital Equipment Ltd* v *Clements (No. 2)* [1997] IRLR 140, there was a conflict of authority on this point.

In *UBAF Bank Ltd* v *Davis* [1978] IRLR 442, Mr Davis was given the sum of £3,156 on dismissal from his job at the bank. This was equivalent to six months' pay even though he was entitled to only three months' notice. The industrial tribunal held that the correct approach was to deduct the ex gratia payment from its assessment of Mr Davis' loss and then reduce the award for contributory fault which it found to be 50%. On appeal, the bank argued that this was wrong and that the tribunal should have first given credit for the part of the payment which was referable to the notice period and included that in the overall assessment of loss, they should then have reduced the award by 50% and, finally, deducted the balance of the ex gratia payment from the final award. Rejecting the argument, the EAT said that the tribunal's approach was correct on the ground that the employee could not be said to have suffered loss during a period for which compensation had been paid.

However, in *Clement-Clarke International Ltd* v *Manley* [1979] ICR 74 (a case decided a few days after *Davis* but before it was reported), the EAT came to the opposite conclusion and held that an ex gratia payment should be deducted from the final award, because otherwise employers would not be given the full credit for the payment they had made. In another case, *Parker & Farr Ltd* v *Shelvey* [1979] IRLR 434, the EAT followed *Davis*, although it reached the rather surprising conclusion that there was no conflict between the two decisions.

More recently, in *Derwent Coachworks* v *Kirby* [1994] IRLR 639, the EAT came down firmly in favour of the approach taken in *Clement Clarke International Ltd* v *Manley*, arguing that justice and equity required the award to be reduced for contributory conduct before any payments made by the employer are deducted (though it should be noted that the *Kirby* case involved a payment in lieu, the reasoning would apply more strongly to an ex gratia payment). The significance of the point is illustrated by the example given below.

Example One

Applying *Davis*, the calculation is as follows:

An industrial tribunal assesses compensation at £3,500 but says that the award should be reduced by 50% for contributory fault. In addition, the employers have made an ex gratia payment of £1,500.

	£
Award of compensation	3,500
Less ex gratia payment	1,500
Balance:	2,000
Less 50% reduction for contributory fault	1,000
Total award	£1,000

Applying *Kirby*, the calculation is as follows:

Example Two

	£
Award of compensation	3,500
Less 50% reduction for contributory fault	1,750
Balance:	1,750
Less ex gratia payment	1,500
Total award	£ 250

The EAT in *Digital Equipment Co. Ltd* v *Clements (No. 2)* [1997] IRLR 140 has now endorsed the approach in *Davis* and *Shelvey* (Example One) confirming that the reduction for a failure to mitigate and for contributory fault should be made *after* taking into account any payments made by the employer, thereby overturning its earlier rulings in *Kirby* and *Manley* (Example Two). The EAT reasoning applies to all post-termination payments received by the employee including an enhanced redundancy payment (see 17.1.2 above). At the time of writing, it is unclear whether Digital intend to appeal to the Court of Appeal but there are two cases dealing with this issue which are due to be heard by the Court of Appeal in the summer of 1997.

17.3.3 Ex gratia payments and the statutory maximum

A related issue is whether an employer is given credit for an ex gratia payment before or after the statutory maximum is applied. On this point, the statutory provisions give a clear answer. Section 124(5) of the Employment Rights Act 1996 provides as follows:

(5) The limit imposed by this section applies to the amount which the industrial tribunal would, apart from this section, award in respect of the subject matter of the complaint after taking into account—

(a) any payment made by the respondent to the complainant in respect of that matter, and

(b) any reduction in the amount of the award required by any enactment or rule of law.

The effect of this provision was considered by the EAT in *McCarthy v British Insulated Callenders Cables plc* [1985] IRLR 94. In that case the tribunal assessed the total compensatable loss at £15,820. It then applied the statutory maximum (which at that time was £7,000) and deducted an ex gratia payment received by Mr McCarthy from the maximum, leaving a balance of £5,726.

On appeal, the EAT said that this was wrong — the industrial tribunal should have first assessed the loss, then deducted the ex gratia payment and then applied the statutory maximum. This meant that although the ex gratia payment was taken into account in working out Mr McCarthy's overall loss, it had no impact on the final award, as his loss, even allowing for the payment, far exceeded the statutory maximum.

The decision in *McCarthy* was followed by the EAT in *Milnbank Housing Association v Murphy* EAT 281/85 and was confirmed by the EAT in *Walter Braund (London) Ltd v Murray* [1991] IRLR 100, where it held that for the same reason the statutory maximum should be applied after making the deduction for contributory fault.

Thus employers will only obtain a financial advantage by making an ex gratia payment in discharge of their statutory liability to pay the compensatory award if that liability, i.e., the total loss suffered by the employee as a result of the dismissal (as determined by the tribunal), is likely to be less than the maximum which a tribunal may award as a compensatory award.

Example

The employee's loss is £10,000 and it is thought that the tribunal is likely to reduce compensation by 25%.

As the law stands, if an employer made an ex gratia payment of £2,000, the award would be calculated as follows:

	£
Total loss	14,000
Less ex gratia payment	2,000
Balance	12,000
Less 25% reduction for contributory fault	3,000
Apply statutory maximum £11,300	
Tribunal award	£ 9,000

Note: It is impossible for employers to overcome the problem raised in *McCarthy*, as the deduction in relation to the compensatory award is governed by the express wording of the statutory provisions. However, there is no equivalent provision in relation to the basic award. It is therefore possible that if the ex gratia payment was made in discharge of the liablity to pay the basic award, it would count. However, to do this, it would be necessary to link the payment expressly to the basic award by stating that 'the above payment is made in discharge of any liability to pay a basic award under current employment protection legislation'.

18 Recoupment Regulations, Tax and Miscellaneous Matters

18.1 RECOUPMENT OF BENEFITS FROM TRIBUNAL AWARDS

The amount of unemployment benefit or income support received by employees between the date of dismissal and the hearing is disregarded for the purpose of assessing the compensatory award. However, such payments are deducted by the employer from the final award and must be paid directly to the Secretary of State under The Employment Protection (Recoupment of Jobseeker's allowance and Income Support) Regulations 1996 (made pursuant to the Industrial Tribunals Act 1996, ss. 16 and 17), referred to below as 'the regulations'.

The regulations preserve the fundamental principle that an employee should recover compensation only for the loss suffered as a result of the dismissal whilst at the same time ensuring that the State and not the employer is the beneficiary from the operation of this principle. They only apply where the employee has been in receipt of one or more of the recoupable benefits since dismissal (reg. 4(8)).

18.2 THE MONETARY AWARD

In assessing a monetary award of compensation, a tribunal must disregard any amount of jobseeker's allowance or income support which may have been paid to or claimed by the employee (reg. 4(1)). The tribunal must state the amount of the award to which the recoupment rules apply. This is known as 'the prescribed element'. In relation to awards of unfair dismissal compensation, the prescribed element is based on the employee's past loss of earnings between the date of dismissal and either the date on which the employee has or should have found an equivalent job, or (if the employee is still out of work), the date of the hearing. So, for example, if an industrial tribunal awards six months' loss of earnings between the date of dismissal and the date of the hearing which takes place 10 months later, the prescribed element should be based on the six-month period (*Howman* v *A1 Bacon Ltd* [1996] ICR 721). It does not cover sums awarded for loss of future earnings or loss of fringe benefits (reg. 3 and para. 7 of the schedule).

If the monetary award is reduced for contributory fault or on account of a statutory limit to the amount of the award, the prescribed element is reduced proportionately (reg. 2)). In *Tipton v West Midlands Co-operative Society (No. 2)* EAT 859/86, the EAT held that the correct procedure is for an industrial tribunal first to assess the compensatory award, then reduce it to the statutory minimum and finally reduce the prescribed element by the same proportion as it has reduced the overall award to bring it down to the statutory maximum (see also *Mason v (1) Wimpey Waste Management Ltd and (2) Secretary of State for Employment* [1982] IRLR 454 which is to the same effect).

18.2.1 Particulars of award

The tribunal's decision must contain certain particulars and must inform the parties about the effect of regulations 7 and 8 (see 18.3 below), unless the tribunal is satisfied that the employee did not receive or claim jobseeker's allowance or income support during the period to which the claim relates. In addition to stating the monetary award, the particulars must state:

(a) the amount of the prescribed element;
(b) the dates of the period to which the prescribed element relates;
(c) the amount, if any, by which the monetary award exceeds the prescribed element.

Similar particulars must be sent by the Secretary of Tribunals to the Secretary of State (reg. 4(3)).

To effectuate this procedure, the applicant must, within certain time limits, give the tribunal clerk the address of the office of the Department of Social Security or Department of Employment from which the benefits were received. The employer also has to provide certain information to the Department of Employment direct. This is explained in the 'annex' which is attached to the tribunal's decision when it is sent to the parties.

18.3 RECOUPMENT PROCEDURE

The payment of the prescribed element is stayed until the Secretary of State either serves a recoupment notice on the employer or notifies the employer that he does not intend to serve a notice (reg. 7(2) and (3)). The notice must be served on the employer within 21-days of either the announcement or notification of a decision to make a monetary award or 'as soon as practicable thereafter'. Where judgment is reserved, the 21-day period will run from the date on which the decision is sent to the parties (reg. 8(6)(a) and (b)).

A copy of the notice must be sent to the employee and, if requested, to the Secretary of Tribunals (reg. 8(4)).

The notice operates as an instruction to the employer to deduct from the award the amount claimed by the Seretary of State. This is deemed to be a complete discharge of the employer's duty to pay the amount to the employee, though the employee may challenge the amount of benefit recouped by the Secretary of State (reg. 8(10)).

The maximum recoupable amount is the total benefit received in the period covered by the award for loss of pay. In cases where this is less than the prescribed element, the balance is paid to the employee (reg. 8(2) and (3)).

18.3.1 Challenging the determination

An employee who feels that the amount of benefit recouped is incorrect has a right of appeal to the Social Security Appeal Tribunal. In order to appeal, the employee must give notice in writing to the Secretary of State within 21 Days of receiving a copy of the recoupment notice. If the tribunal decides that the Secretary of State has recouped more benefit than the employee received, the excess must be repaid to the employee (reg. 10).

18.3.2 Balance of the monetary award

The amount awarded over and above the prescribed element is not affected by the regulations and is payable immediately. This covers compensation for future loss. In theory, those employees whose unfair dismissal compensation includes an award for future loss are ineligible for jobseeker's allowance during the period covered by the award, but how the relevant statutory regulation operates in practice is uncertain.

18.4 EFFECT OF REGULATIONS

The regulations apply only to awards of compensation made by the tribunal. This does not normally include settlements, though it has been suggested that they may apply where the terms of the settlement are recorded in full as an award of the tribunal (see Clayton, 'Practice and Procedure in Industrial Tribunals', *Legal Action*, March 1986). Normally, it will be impracticable to apply the regulations in such circumstances because, in general, the parties do not break down the settlement into its constituent parts, i.e., the settlement does not state the proportion of the payment relating to past loss of earnings, so in practice the regulations are not enforced. This gives employees a strong incentive to settle their claims and the effect of the regulations should always be borne in mind in settlement negotiations.

The regulations do not apply to compensation awarded under discrimination legislation (see Chapter 19).

18.5 TAX

The maximum award of unfair dismissal compensation falls below the tax threshold for lump sum payments (currently £30,000) and any award will therefore be free of tax (Income and Corporation Taxes Act 1988, ss. 148(2) and 188; Finance Act 1988, s. 74(1)).

18.6 INTEREST

The payment of interest on industrial tribunal awards is governed by the Industrial Tribunals (Interest) Order 1990 (SI 1990 No. 479), which came into force on 1 April

1990. This provides that interest is payable on any industrial tribunal award which is unpaid 42 days after the decision is sent to the parties, i.e., after the time for appealing against the decision has expired.

Tribunals are required to notify the parties of the relevant rate of interest (i.e., the rate specified by s. 17 of the Judgments Act 1838, currently 15 per cent) and the date from which it accrues.

Interest is not payable on:

(a) sums representing costs and expenses; or
(b) any sum which is payable to the Secretary of State under the Recoupment Regulations (see 18.1 above); or
(c) any sum which is payable to the Inland Revenue or Department of Social Security.

An important point to bear in mind is that interest will accrue after the 42 day period even if there is a review or appeal. So, where an employer's appeal is partly successful, interest will still be payable on the original award. However, where the 'relevant decision' is made by the Employment Appeal Tribunal, i.e., where it substitutes a finding of unfair dismissal and makes an award of compensation itself, interest will not accrue until its order is promulgated.

Note: A power to vary the award of interest is now to be found in the Industrial Tribunals Act 1996, s. 14.

PART III COMPENSATION FOR REDUNDANCY

19 Compensation for Redundancy

19.1 INTRODUCTION

Broadly speaking, the rules governing the calculation of a redundancy payment are the same as those used to calculate the basic award (see Chapter 5).

19.2 PRE-CONDITIONS FOR PAYMENT

Entitlement to a redundancy payment depends on the following basic qualifying conditions being met:

(a) the applicant must be an employee;
(b) the applicant must have been continuously employed for two years or more at the time he or she is made redundant;
(c) the applicant must have been dismissed by reason of redundancy.

A detailed consideration of the law on redundancy including all the relevant qualifications and exclusions is outside the scope of this book.

19.3 CALCULATING A REDUNDANCY PAYMENT

The amount of a redundancy payment depends on the length of the employee's period of continuous employment, the amount of a week's pay at the calculation date and the employee's age at the relevant date. The payment itself is then worked out by counting backwards from the relevant date to calculate the number of years of employment and allowing (ERA 1996, s. 162(1) and (2)):

(a) one and a half week's pay for each year of employment in which the employee was not below the age of 41;

(b) one week's pay for each year of employment in which the employee was not below the age of 22;

(c) half a week's pay for each year of employment in which the employee was between 18 and 21.

The maximum number of 'reckonable years' of employment is 20 (s. 162(3)).

The table at the end of the chapter is a ready reckoner for the calculation of a redundancy payment. It shows the number of weeks' pay to which an employee is entitled in view of his age and number of complete years' service.

19.3.1 Statutory extension of relevant date

The 'relevant date' for the purpose of calculating a redundancy payment may be extended in certain circumstances. Thus if the employee is dismissed without being given the required period of statutory notice, the 'relevant date' will be the date on which that notice would have expired (ERA 1996, s. 145(1)). Where the notice exceeds the employee's statutory entitlement, the 'relevant date' is the date on which the notice expires (ERA 1996, s. 145(2)(a)). Finally, where the contract is for a fixed term, the 'relevant date' is the date the term expires (s. 145(2)(c)).

19.3.2 Upper age limit

Entitlement to a redundancy payment is subject to an upper age limit of 65 for both men and women (ERA 1996, s. 156(1)).

Any redundancy payment is scaled down where it is payable in the final year before statutory retirement by one twelfth for each whole month between the relevant date and the employee's 64th birthday (ERA 1996, s. 162(4)).

The relevant date is not extended by the period of statutory notice where insufficient notice is given for the purpose of the scaling down provisions.

19.3.3 A week's pay

The rule governing the statutory calculation of a week's pay are considered in Chapter 7. There follows a synopsis of the main points.

(a) For most employees a week's pay is the amount they earn in the course of their normal working hours.

(b) Normal working hours are the minimum number of hours employees may be required to work under their contract of employment. Thus overtime hours are not included in an employee's normal working hours unless overtime is guaranteed by the employer (*Brownson* v *Hire Service Shops Ltd* [1978] IRLR 73).

(c) Not all payments received by employees in their pay packet count. Most 'contractual' payments are included in the calculation of a week's pay. Thus ordinary wages or salary, shift bonuses and productivity bonuses are all included. Other regular payments may also count (see *A & B Marcusfield Ltd* v *Melhuish* [1977] IRLR 484). However, tips and some other discretionary or ex gratia bonuses do not count.

(d) Benefits in kind such as the provision of a company car do not form part of a week's pay.

(e) A week's pay is based on an employee's gross earnings, i.e., earnings before tax.

(f) The amount of pay which qualifies as a week's pay is subject to a statutory ceiling fixed by the Secretary of State for Employment and reviewed annually. The current maximum stands at £210 (ERA 1996, s. 227(1)).

19.3.4 Statutory maximum

The statutory maximum award is fixed at 30 weeks' pay. The maximum amount of pay which qualifies as a week's pay is reviewed each year by the Secretary of State for Employment and varied by statutory instrument. Where the effective date of termination is on or after 1 April 1992, the maximum for a week's pay is £210. This means that the maximum total redundancy payment is £6,300 where the effective date of termination is on or after that date.

The maximum payment is available to any employee who is over 61 on the relevant date and earns £210 or more.

19.3.5 The calculation date

Under the Employment Rights Act 1996, s. 226(5) and (6), the calculation date for redundancy dismissals is either:

(a) the date x weeks before the date the employment ends, where x is the minimum period of notice required by s. 86(1) of the Employment Rights Act 1996; or

(b) the date the employment ended if the employee was dismissed with no notice, or with less notice than that required under s. 86(1).

Example

Dismissal with minimum period of notice required by statute. An employee with five years' service is dismissed with the statutory minimum period of notice, i.e., five weeks. The calculation date is five weeks before the last day of employment.

Summary dismissal. An employee with five years' service is summarily dismissed. The 'calculation date' is the last day of employment.

Dismissal with less than the statutory minimum period of notice. An employee with five years' service is dismissed and given three weeks' notice. The calculation date is the date on which notice expires.

19.4 REDUCING REDUNDANCY PAYMENTS

Apart from the 'scaling down' provisions (see 20.3.3 above), redundancy payments may be reduced where:

(a) an employee receives a pension payment either immediately after or within 90 weeks of dismissal;
(b) an employee commits an act of misconduct during the notice period;
(c) an employee leaves work before the redundancy notice period has expired without the employer's consent;
(d) an employee fails to comply with a notice of extension served by the employer after taking part in a strike in the obligatory notice period.

19.4.1 Pension payments

The Secretary of State has made a statutory instrument which affects the rights of those employees in receipt of a pension to a redundancy payment. This provides that a redundancy payment may be reduced if an employee receives a pension either immediately after, or within 90 weeks of the dismissal (ERA 1996, s. 158; Redundancy Payments Pensions Regulations 1965 (SI 1965 No. 1932)).

Before making such a reduction, the employer must serve a notice on the employee explaining how the reduction will be made. The notice should be served within a reasonable period of time after a redundancy payment claim is made (*Stowe-Woodward BTR Ltd* v *Beynon* [1978] ICR 609).

The amount of the reduction varies, depending on whether the pension is by way of a lump sum or periodic payment:

(a) If the payment is a lump sum, the percentage reduction is

$$\frac{30 \times \text{lump sum}}{52 \times \text{one week's pay}}$$

(b) If the pension is a periodic payment, the percentage reduction is

$$\frac{300 \times (\text{total pension over first 12 months of payment})}{52 \times \text{one week's pay}}$$

Special provisions apply if the payment does not start immediately after the dismissal. In such circumstances, redundancy pay is reduced by either the weekly value of the pension, or by one third of a week's pay, whichever is the greater, for each week between the date of dismissal and the date of the first payment. The weekly value of the pension in the case of a periodic payment is the amount of the pension over the first 12 months of payment divided by 52. In the case of a lump sum, the weekly value is the lump sum divided by 520.

Cases involving reductions under these provisions are rather rare, but may arise where an employee takes early retirement (see *Royal Ordnance plc* v *Pilkington* [1989] IRLR 489). Moreover, it is possible that the application of either of the above formulae may result in the employee's entitlement to a redundancy payment being excluded altogether (*British Telecommunications plc* v *Burwell* IRLIB 293, November 1985).

19.4.2 Misconduct

The general rule is that employees who are dismissed for misconduct are not entitled to a redundancy payment at all (ERA 1996, s. 140(1)). However, in certain circumstances, the industrial tribunal is given a discretion to award a proportion of the redundancy payment if it considers this to be just and equitable (s. 140(3)). These provisions do not apply where the employee is dismissed for taking part in a strike.

19.4.2.1 Entitlement excluded

There will be no entitlement to a redundancy payment where an employer is entitled to dismiss the employee by reason of the employee's conduct and the employer terminates the contract either:

(a) without notice; or
(b) by giving shorter notice than that required either by the contract or by the statutory provisions; or
(c) by giving the full entitlement to notice accompanied by a statement in writing to the effect that by reason of the employee's conduct the employer would have been entitled to terminate the contract without notice.

This covers the normal situation where the employer dismisses for misconduct and/or redundancy. It would also apply to a case where an employee was found to have been guilty of misconduct before being given notice though this was unknown at the time notice was given, as the Employment Rights Act 1996 preserves the common law rules regulating the right to terminate without notice (s. 86(4)). See *Boston Deep Sea Fishing and Ice Co* v *Ansell* [1888] 39 Ch D 339. The test for determining whether the employee is guilty of the alleged misconduct is an objective one. It is not sufficient for the employer to show a reasonable belief in the employee's guilt (*Bonner* v *H Gilbert & Co* [1989] IRLR 475).

19.4.2.2 Entitlement reduced at tribunal's discretion

Special provisions apply where the employee, having been given notice of redundancy, commits an act of misconduct in the notice period which would entitle the employer to terminate the contract without notice. In such circumstances, if the employer does nothing, the employee's right to the full redundancy payment is preserved. However, if the employer either:

(a) dismisses the employee immediately; or
(b) shortens the notice period; or
(c) allows the employee to continue to work out the notice as before but serves a notice in writing to the effect that the employer would have been entitled to terminate without notice,

the industrial tribunal is given a discretion to reduce the redundancy payment in such a way as it considers just and equitable in the circumstances (ERA 1996, s. 140(3)).

19.4.2.3 Examples of operation of the statutory provisions

In *Simmons* v *Hoover Ltd* [1976] IRLR 266, the EAT gave the following examples of the operation of this provision. In each example it is assumed that the contract may be terminated by giving the employee three months' notice.

(a) An employee is given two months' redundancy notice, either when it was already known or when it is subsequently discovered that he had stolen from the employers. Redundancy pay is lost under s. 140(1) of the Employment Rights Act 1996 for the reasons given above and is not saved by s. 140(3) because there is only one dismissal.

(b) An employee is given three months' notice, but is dismissed without notice one month later after he is discovered to have been stealing from the employers. Redundancy pay is not lost but may be reduced in whole or in part as the tribunal thinks fit (s. 140(3)).

(c) An employee is given six months' notice. During the last three months the employee is caught stealing and is dismissed immediately. The dismissal is still covered by s. 140(3) and the tribunal may award such proportion of the redundancy payment as it considers just and equitable.

19.4.2.4 Guidelines on the exercise of statutory discretion

In cases where s. 140(3) of the Employment Rights Act 1996 applies, it is for the tribunal to determine the proportion of the payment due to the employee. Although there have not been many reported cases involving these provisions, it is likely that the following factors would influence industrial tribunals in their judgment:

(a) the gravity of the misconduct;
(b) the employee's length of service;
(c) other penalties imposed on the employee such as the loss of notice pay and holiday pay and other fringe benefits.

In common with other areas where the tribunal is given discretion of this nature, the EAT will not overrule the tribunal simply on the ground that it would have reached a different conclusion. For example, in *Lignacite Products Ltd* v *Krollman* [1979] IRLR 22, Mr Krollman was summarily dismissed for stealing shortly before the end of his redundancy notice period. The industrial tribunal awarded 60% of his redundancy pay. On appeal, the EAT said that they were surprised that the tribunal had not reduced the award still further but refused to interfere on the ground that it was a matter for the tribunal to decide.

19.4.3 Early leavers

The statutory provisions lay down a strict procedure which has to be followed by employees who wish to leave their job before their notice period has ended. Failure to follow this procedure may result in the employee's redundancy payment being reduced or lost altogether (ERA 1996, s. 142).

The statutory procedure is as follows. Once the employer has given the employee notice, the employee may give written notice of an intention to leave before the

Compensation for Redundancy

expiry of the employer's notice. However, the employee's notice of intention must be given within what the statutory provisions call 'the obligatory notice period', i.e., the minimum period of notice an employer is required to give the employee by law and must indicate when the employee intends to leave (s. 136(3)).

Faced with such a notice, the employer may either agree to the employee's request, in which case the employee is entitled to the full amount of the redundancy payment, or serve the employee with a counter-notice requiring him to withdraw the notice of termination and to continue in the employment until the employer's notice expires. In addition, the counter-notice must state that if the employee fails to comply with the request, the employer will contest liability to pay the redundancy payment (s. 142(2)).

If the employee still leaves, the matter will have to be referred to a tribunal which, having regard to the reasons why the employee wishes to leave early and the reasons why the employer wants the employee to stay, must decide whether it is just and equitable for the employee to receive a redundancy payment and if so, how much (s. 142(3)).

The statutory procedure is not available in cases where the employee's contractual notice entitlement is longer than the statutory minimum until the start of the period equivalent to the statutory notice period. Thus an employee who is given eight weeks' notice having worked for the employer for four years will only be entitled to serve his notice of intention at the start of the last four weeks of the eight-week period. In some cases, the EAT has overcome this technical difficulty by finding a mutually agreed variation of the date of expiry of the employer's notice (see *Tunnel Holdings Ltd* v *Woolf* [1976] ICR 387), but the provisions still pose a potential trap for the unwary employee.

19.5 STRIKE DISMISSALS GENERALLY

The provisions in s. 140(1) of the Employment Rights Act 1996 do not apply where the employee takes part in a strike during the notice period. In such circumstances, the right to redundancy pay is preserved by s. 140(2), provided the dismissal occurs during the obligatory notice period. It would appear that where the dismissal occurs during the contractual notice period, the right to a redundancy payment is lost, though the point remains open to further argument.

These provisions apply only if employees take part in a strike after they have been given their redundancy notice. In cases where the workers are on strike before the redundancy notice is issued, the employer will normally be entitled to terminate their employment summarily as a result of the strike itself with the result that they will be disqualified from redundancy pay (see *Simmons* v *Hoover Ltd* [1976] IRLR 266).

19.5.1 Notice of extension after strike

Where after being given redundancy notice, an employee takes part in a strike during the notice period, the redundancy payment may be reduced in whole or in part if the employee fails to comply with a notice of extension served by the employer in the form prescribed by statute (ERA 1996, s. 143).

In broad terms, this provision allows the employer to request an employee who is taking part in a strike to extend his notice period by an additional period up to the number of days lost by the strike. An employee complies with the provision by either agreeing to the request or being available for work within the proposed period of extension. If the employee fails to comply, the tribunal is empowered to reduce the redundancy payment as it thinks fit.

19.6 TAX LIABILITY

A statutory redundancy payment is exempt from income tax under the normal Schedule E provisions (Income and Corporation Taxes Act 1988, s. 579(1)). Similarly in *Mairs (HM Inspector of Taxes)* v *Haughey* [1993] IRLR 551, the House of Lords confirmed that a non-statutory redundancy payment is not an emolument and therefore is not taxable as such. However, tax liability may arise if the redundancy payment either by itself, or when aggregated with other payments received on the termination of employment, exceeds £30,000, since s. 580(3) of the Income and Corporation Taxes Act 1988 brings such payments within the scope of s. 148 of that Act.

The position is therefore as follows:

(a) redundancy payments under £30,000 are tax free; and
(b) redundancy payments over £30,000 are subject to higher rate tax, currently 40%, on the excess.

For taxation generally see Chapter 2.

19.7 READY RECKONER FOR CALCULATING THE NUMBER OF WEEKS' PAY DUE

Age (years)	Service (years) 2	3	4	5	6	7	8	9	10	11	12	13	14	15	16	17	18	19	20
20	1	1	1	1	—														
21	1	1½	1½	1½	1½	—													
22	1	1½	2	2	2	2	—												
23	1½	2	2½	3	3	3	3	—											
24	2	2½	3	3½	4	4	4	4	—										
25	2	3	3½	4	4½	5	5	5	5	—									
26	2	3	4	4½	5	5½	6	6	6	6	—								
27	2	3	4	5	5½	6	6½	7	7	7	7	—							
28	2	3	4	5	6	6½	7	7½	8	8	8	8	—						
29	2	3	4	5	6	7	7½	8	8½	9	9	9	9	—					
30	2	3	4	5	6	7	8	8½	9	9½	10	10	10	10	—				
31	2	3	4	5	6	7	8	9	9½	10	10½	11	11	11	11	—			
32	2	3	4	5	6	7	8	9	10	10½	11	11½	12	12	12	12	—		
33	2	3	4	5	6	7	8	9	10	11	11½	12	12½	13	13	13	13	—	
34	2	3	4	5	6	7	8	9	10	11	12	12½	13	13½	14	14	14	14	—
35	2	3	4	5	6	7	8	9	10	11	12	13	13½	14	14½	15	15	15	15
36	2	3	4	5	6	7	8	9	10	11	12	13	14	14½	15	15½	16	16	16
37	2	3	4	5	6	7	8	9	10	11	12	13	14	15	15½	16	16½	17	17
38	2	3	4	5	6	7	8	9	10	11	12	13	14	15	16	16½	17	17½	18
39	2	3	4	5	6	7	8	9	10	11	12	13	14	15	16	17	17½	18	18½
40	2	3	4	5	6	7	8	9	10	11	12	13	14	15	16	17	18	18½	19
41	2	3	4	5	6	7	8	9	10	11	12	13	14	15	16	17	18	19	19½
42	2½	3½	4½	5½	6½	7½	8½	9½	10½	11½	12½	13½	14½	15½	16½	17½	18½	19½	20½
43	3	4	5	6	7	8	9	10	11	12	13	14	15	16	17	18	19	20	21
44	3	4½	5½	6½	7½	8½	9½	10½	11½	12½	13½	14½	15½	16½	17½	18½	19½	20½	21½
45	3	4½	6	7	8	9	10	11	12	13	14	15	16	17	18	19	20	21	22
46	3	4½	6	7½	8½	9½	10½	11½	12½	13½	14½	15½	16½	17½	18½	19½	20½	21½	22½
47	3	4½	6	7½	9	10	11	12	13	14	15	16	17	18	19	20	21	22	23
48	3	4½	6	7½	9	10½	11½	12½	13½	14½	15½	16½	17½	18½	19½	20½	21½	22½	23½
49	3	4½	6	7½	9	10½	12	13	14	15	16	17	18	19	20	21	22	23	24
50	3	4½	6	7½	9	10½	12	13½	14½	15½	16½	17½	18½	19½	20½	21½	22½	23½	24½
51	3	4½	6	7½	9	10½	12	13½	15	16	17	18	19	20	21	22	23	24	25
52	3	4½	6	7½	9	10½	12	13½	15	16½	17½	18½	19½	20½	21½	22½	23½	24½	25½
53	3	4½	6	7½	9	10½	12	13½	15	16½	18	19	20	21	22	23	24	25	26
54	3	4½	6	7½	9	10½	12	13½	15	16½	18	19½	20½	21½	22½	23½	24½	25½	26½
55	3	4½	6	7½	9	10½	12	13½	15	16½	18	19½	21	22	23	24	25	26	27
56	3	4½	6	7½	9	10½	12	13½	15	16½	18	19½	21	22½	23½	24½	25½	26½	27½
57	3	4½	6	7½	9	10½	12	13½	15	16½	18	19½	21	22½	24	25	26	27	28
58	3	4½	6	7½	9	10½	12	13½	15	16½	18	19½	21	22½	24	25½	26½	27½	28½
59	3	4½	6	7½	9	10½	12	13½	15	16½	18	19½	21	22½	24	25½	27	28	29
60 (men only)	3	4½	6	7½	9	10½	12	13½	15	16½	18	19½	21	22½	24	25½	27	28½	29½
61 (men only)	3	4½	6	7½	9	10½	12	13½	15	16½	18	19½	21	22½	24	25½	27	28½	30
62 (men only)	3	4½	6	7½	9	10½	12	13½	15	16½	18	19½	21	22½	24	25½	27	28½	30
63 (men only)	3	4½	6	7½	9	10½	12	13½	15	16½	18	19½	21	22½	24	25½	27	28½	30
64 (men only)	3	4½	6	7½	9	10½	12	13½	15	16½	18	19½	21	22½	24	25½	27	28½	30

Crown copyright reproduced by permission of the Controller of Her Majesty's Stationery Office from 'Department of Employment' booklet 16, 'Redundancy payments'.

PART IV   COMPENSATION IN DISCRIMINATION CASES

Introduction

Financial compensation is one of the remedies open to an employee who is the victim of unlawful discrimination contrary to the Sex Discrimination Act 1975 and/or the Race Relations Act 1976, i.e., is dismissed on the grounds of race, sex or marital status, or is the victim of religious discrimination in Northern Ireland contrary to the Fair Employment (Northern Ireland) Act 1989, and is one of the remedies open to an employee who is discriminated against on grounds of disability contrary to the Disability Discrimination Act 1995. The award is normally assessed in the same way as the compensatory award for unfair dismissal, but there are some differences. For example, compensation may be awarded for injured feelings in race, sex, disability and religious discrimination cases. There are also some important differences in the assessment of compensation in pregnancy dismissals. Lastly, it should be remembered that it is not necessary for a claimant to satisfy a service requirement before alleging that his or her dismissal is discriminatory.

This Part examines the rules and principles governing compensation in discrimination cases and their relationship with the tribunal's general power to award unfair dismissal compensation.

20 Compensation in Discrimination Cases

20.1 REMEDIES IN DISCRIMINATION DISMISSALS

Where an industrial tribunal finds a complaint of unlawful discrimination well-founded, it may, if it considers it just and equitable to do so, grant one or more of the following remedies (SDA 1975, s. 65; RRA 1976, s. 56(1)(a); DDA 1996, s. 8):

(a) an order declaring the rights of the employer and employee in relation to the act to which the complaint relates;
(b) an order requiring the employer to pay compensation to the employee;
(c) a recommendation that the employer take certain appropriate action within a specified period to obviate or reduce the adverse effects of the discriminatory act to which the complaint relates.

The power to make a recommendation under (c) does not include a power to recommend that the employee should be promoted to the next suitable vacancy (*British Gas plc* v *Sharma* [1991] IRLR 101). But a tribunal has recommended that a supervisor who was found to have sexually harrassed the applicant should be transferred to another post elsewhere within the employer's organisation and, in the meantime, suspended on full pay (*Whittington* v *P Morris and Greenwich Health Authority* (Case No. 17846/89) and *Wagstaff* v *Elida Gibbs Ltd and another* (1991) 141 NLJ 1514). It should be noted that awards of compensation may be made against named individuals as well as employers though tribunals are not bound to do so (*Armitage, Marsden and HM Prison Service* v *Johnson* [1997] IRLR 162).

20.1.1 Compensation — the statutory provisions

It is provided that compensation shall be assessed 'in like manner as any other claim in tort; i.e., on the same basis as if the employee had brought an action in damages for tort in the county court or an action in reparation for breach of statutory duty in the sheriff court (in Scotland) (SDA 1975, s. 66(1)(2); RRA 1976, s. 57(1); DDA 1995, s. 8(3)). This means that once the tribunal has decided that it is 'just and equitable' to order compensation, it has no discretion to adjust the compensation to what it thinks is just and equitable in the particular circumstances of the case, but must follow the principles established at common law for assessing damages in tort

(*Hurley* v *Mustoe (No. 2)* [1983] ICR 422). To this extent, compensation in discrimination cases differs from compensation for unfair dismissal (see Chapter 8).

Compensation is recoverable for foreseeable damage arising from the act of discrimination (*Skyrail Oceanic Ltd* v *Coleman* [1981] ICR 864). This includes compensation for loss of earnings, benefits and other compensatable items. It may also include compensation for being placed at a disadvantage in the labour market (*Moeliker* v *A Reyrolle & Co Ltd* [1976] ICR 253). However, there is no separate head of damage for loss of career prospects (*MOD* v *Cannock* [1994] ICR 918).

Compensation for loss of earnings is assessed on a tortious basis. The aim is to put the complainant into the position in which he or she would have been had he or she not been dismissed and is therefore not limited to loss suffered during the notice period (*MOD* v *Cannock*). However, the multiplier must take account of the personal characteristics of the complainant (see 9.5.4) and other contingencies (see 9.5.5) (see *MOD* v *Cannock*).

The normal rules on mitigation apply and credit must be given for jobseeker's allowance and other social security benefits received in the relevant period because the regulations relating to recoupment do not apply (see *Stones* v *Hills of London* EAT 12/83, where the applicant had been turned down for a job on racial grounds and the unemployment benefit he received was deducted from the award). The deduction made as a result of the duty to mitigate should be applied before allowance is made for the application of the multiplier or the percentage chance figure (*MOD* v *Hunt* [1996] IRLR 139). So, for example, if an employee earns £500 a week and finds a new job in which the earnings are £250 a week, the net loss is £250 and the percentage chance is applied to that figure. For public policy reasons, the same principle is likely to apply in race and disability discrimination cases.

20.1.2 Pregnancy dismissals

A claim for sex discrimination will arise where an employee is dismissed because she is pregnant, or for reasons connected with pregnancy.

Particular problems have arisen in relation to the assessment of compensation in sex discrimination cases brought either in anticipation of or after the ECJ's ruling in *Webb* v *EMO Cargo (UK) Ltd* [1994] IRLR 482. In *Webb*, the European Court ruled that a dismissal on grounds of pregnancy (or for pregnancy related reasons) was in breach of the Equal Treatment Directive (76/207/EEC). Such a dismissal could not be justified on the basis that an employer would have dismissed a man in comparable circumstances since pregnancy is a unique characteristic of the female sex and therefore a dismissal on grounds of pregnancy amounted to unlawful discrimination contrary to Article 5 of the Directive. Subsequently the House of Lords ruled that the Sex Discrimination Act both could and should be interpreted in a manner which gave effect to the ECJ's ruling ([1995] IRLR 645).

This led to a series of much-publicised cases against the Ministry of Defence which, until 1990, had a rule of automatically dismissing servicewomen who became pregnant. The high level of awards made in many of these cases largely reflected the fact that many of the complainants were commissioned officers with excellent career prospects. Nonetheless, the high awards led to concern in some quarters, and in *Ministry of Defence* v *Cannock* [1994] ICR 918, the EAT took the opportunity to review the principles applicable in such cases. Although the guidance was technically *obiter*, the EAT has since stated that the guidelines should normally be followed (see *Ministry of Defence* v *Bristow* (ante) and *Ministry of Defence* v *Hunt* [1996] IRLR 139).

20.1.2.1 Loss of earnings

As regards the assessment of loss of earnings, the EAT in *Cannock* stated that a tribunal should start by asking itself what are the chances that the complainant would have returned to work from maternity leave had she been given that opportunity. This was to be assessed on a 'chance' basis taking into account any relevant statistical evidence as well as the evidence given by the complainant. It would then be necessary to consider whether the woman, having regard to her domestic circumstances, would have been in a position to return. In this context, it would be relevant to take account of the 'obvious disruption to family life' caused by a posting overseas. However, in *Hunt*, the EAT ruled that it was open to a tribunal to conclude that there was a 100% chance of the complainant returning to work. The EAT said that whilst such a finding was 'unusual' and 'exceptional', it could not be regarded as 'perverse'.

Next, the tribunal should assess the length of service which the complainant has hypothetically lost and should take account of the contingencies and other factors, including the chances of the complainant having and returning to work after the birth of a second or third child (see 20.1 above). In *Hunt*, the EAT noted that where the tribunal finds that the chance of return diminished after the birth of a second or third child, this should be reflected in a cumulative percentage rather than by applying a different percentage at each stage of the calculation. So, for example, if a tribunal finds that there was an 80% chance of the woman returning after the birth of her first child and a 40% chance of her returning after the birth of her second child, the appropriate calculation for the second period would be 40% of the 80% and not 40% of the original 100%.

Allowance should also be made for the possibility of promotion, although in *Cannock* the EAT observed that 'tribunals should be wary of assessing the chances of promotion on the high side' since again this was a question of 'chance' not of 'fact'. Lastly, the tribunal should calculate the loss up to the date of the hearing (past loss) and calculate future loss 'by using the usual multiplicand and multiplier method'.

20.1.2.2 Child care costs

In assessing loss of earnings, a deduction should be made for the full child care costs which would have been incurred by the complainant had she returned to work. The argument that there should only be a set-off of half such costs as such costs would be shared between both partners, was rejected by the EAT in *Cannock*.

20.1.2.3 Mitigation

As stated above, the ordinary rules on mitigation of loss apply in discrimination cases. However, in *MOD* v *Sullivan* [1994] ICR 118, the EAT ruled that the duty would not arise until such time as a woman's physiology and state of mind had returned to normal after the birth. Allowance should also be made to protect the 'special relationship between a woman and her child' from being disturbed as a result of the simultaneous pursuit of employment. The duty to mitigate therefore would not normally arise until six months after the birth of the first child (also see *Cannock*).

The burden of proving a failure to mitigate is on the employer (see 15.1.1), and it is for that party to produce evidence of a failure to mitigate either by way of cross-examination or of its own, but, as the EAT noted in *Cannock*, after the six-month period the complainant is 'expected to be in the job market actively looking for work and applying for jobs'. Nonetheless, tribunals are entitled to take account of the fact that women with young children and child care responsibilities are at a disadvantage in the labour market (*MOD* v *Hunt*).

Mitigation of loss may involve complainants applying for work with their former employer, though this will not normally be considered reasonable where the complainant has found a new job (*Cannock*).

The deduction for mitigation should be applied before the deduction for the percentage chance of the complainant returning to work under 20.1.2.1 above (see *MOD* v *Hunt*).

20.1.3 Compensation for injured feelings

It is provided that 'damages in respect of an unlawful act of discrimination may include compensation for injury to feelings whether or not they include compensation under any other head' (SDA 1975, s. 66(4); RRA 1976, s. 57(4); DDA 1995, s. 8(4)). Compensation for injury to feelings should include compensation for the loss of congenial employment and damage to career prospects (*MOD* v *Cannock and Ors* [1994] IRLR 509). This contrasts with the position in unfair dismissal cases (see 12.2 above).

20.1.3.1 Size of awards — general principles
Awards for injury to feelings have increased substantially since the Court of Appeal's rulings in *Alexander* v *The Home Office* [1988] IRLR 190 and *Noone* v *North West Thames Regional Health Authority* [1988] IRLR 530. In the former case May LJ reviewed the policy considerations which should influence the level of such awards. He pointed out that, unlike cases of pure financial loss, it is often impossible to quantify the loss suffered as a result of the humiliation and insult caused by racial discrimination. He added that:

> awards should not be minimal because this would tend to trivialise and diminish respect for the public policy to which the Act give effect. On the other hand, just because it is impossible to assess the monetary value of injury to feelings, awards should be restrained. To award sums which are generally excessive does almost as much harm to the policy and the results which it seeks to achieve as do nominal awards.

In *Noone* the Court of Appeal suggested that awards for injury to feelings should normally be no more than £3,000. This was justified on the basis that, at that time, the maximum award of compensation in discrimination cases was £8,500. The

Noone decision preceded the abolition of the statutory limit on compensation and in *Orlando* v *Didcot Power Station Sports & Social Club* [1996] IRLR 262, it was argued that tribunals should no longer be bound by the guidance given by the Court of Appeal in *Noone*. However, in rejecting this argument, the EAT stated that, in its view, the Court of Appeal was not so 'linking the amount of an award for injury to feelings to the compensation limit that it could be legitimately argued that without the limit which then applied, the award would thereby have been higher'. Nonetheless, even prior to the removal of the statutory limit, it was clear that tribunals might award more than the normal maximum in 'exceptional' circumstances (see, for example, *Wagstaff* v *Elida Gibbs Ltd* (1991) 141 NLJ 1514, where an industrial tribunal awarded £8,925 for injury to feelings in a sexual harassment case, and *Duffy* v *Eastern Health & Social Services Board* [1992] IRLR 251, where £15,000 was awarded as compensation for injured feelings in a religious discrimination case under the Fair Employment (Northern Ireland) Act 1989). Moreover, in *Armitage, Marsden and HM Prison Service* v *Johnson* [1997] IRLR 162, the EAT, in upholding an award of £21,000 for injury to feelings in a racial discrimination case, no longer felt inhibited by the ceiling imposed by the Court of Appeal in *Noone*, although the EAT's in *Johnson* does not appear to have been referred to its earlier ruling in Orlando. At the time of writing, the highest reported award for injury to feelings is £25,000 in *Chan* v *London Borough of Hackney* (COIT 400002/92), again a race discrimination case.

At the other end of the spectrum, in *Ministry of Defence* v *Sullivan* [1994] ICR 193, the EAT acknowledged that an award of some kind should be made where injury to feelings is proved, and recent cases tend to suggest that an award of between £500 and £750 is at or near the minimum (see *Sharifi* v *Strathclyde Regional Council* [1992] IRLR 259 and *Ministry of Defence* v *Hunt* [1996] IRLR 139).

The EAT in *Johnson* identified five guiding principles which should be taken into account in assessing such awards:

(a) awards for injury to feelings are compensatory. Such awards should be just to both parties and should compensate fully without punishing the tortfeasor. Feelings of indignation at the tortfeasor's conduct should not be allowed to inflate the award;

(b) awards should not be so low as that would diminish respect for the policy of the anti-discrimination legislation. Society has condemned discrimination and awards must ensure that it is seen to be wrong. On the other hand, awards should be restrained, as excessive awards could be seen as a way to untaxed riches;

(c) awards should bear some general similarity to the range of awards in personal injury cases, though this should be done by reference to the 'whole range of such awards' rather than to particular cases;

(d) tribunals should take into account the 'value in everyday life' of the sum they are awarding; and

(e) tribunals should bear in mind the need for 'public respect' for the level of awards made.

The latest survey in *Equal Opportunities Review* (EOR 67) confirms that removal of the statutory limit has led to an increase in the average and median awards of compensation for injured feelings in both sex and race discrimination cases. The median award for both types of discrimination case in 1994/1995 stood at £1,500.

However, on average, sucessful race discrimination complainants received 60% more compensation for injury to feelings than sex discrimination complainants.

20.1.3.2 Proving injury to feelings

An award for injury to feelings should not be made automatically whenever unlawful discrimination is proved or admitted (*Cannock*). The complainant must satisfy the tribunal that:

(a) he or she actually suffered injury; and
(b) this was caused by the employer's discriminatory conduct.

There may be a further requirement that the employee knows that the employer's conduct is discriminatory.

Furthermore, it is also for the complainant to show the nature and extent of the injury to feelings which has been caused by the employer's discriminatory conduct (including any injury to career prospects). However, in both *Cannock* and *Sullivan*, the EAT acknowledged that the burden on the complainant is not that great since it will normally be easy to satisfy a tribunal that at least some injury has been caused by the act of discrimination (see *Murray* v *Powertech (Scotland) Ltd* [1992] IRLR 254).

20.1.3.3 Assessing compensation for injured feelings

In most cases the size of the award will reflect the seriousness of the employer's conduct and the effect this had on the particular complainant since the employer must take the 'victim as he or she is' (*Orlando* v *Didcot Power Station Sports and Social Club* [1996] IRLR 262). Relevant factors will include the distress and shock caused by the discrimination, the age of the victim, the impact the discrimination had on the victim's health (see, for example, *Wagstaff* v *Elida Gibbs Ltd* (1991) 141 NLJ 1514, where the harassment was particularly severe and resulted in the complainant needing psychiatric help, and *Longmore* v *Dr Bernard Kei Kam Lee* (Case No. 021743/88), where the victim, who became very ill and required counselling, was awarded £3,000), the duration of the discriminatory treatment, the impact of that treatment on the victim's career, and the resilience of the victim.

Past toleration of discriminatory conduct will not preclude an award of compensation for injury to feelings since 'the mere fact that one has lived in conditions of some adversity does not necessarily mean that one has no feelings' (*Hurley* v *Mustoe* [1981] IRLR 208). But in *Orlando*, the EAT accepted that a tribunal is entitled to take into account the nature of the lost employment and, in appropriate cases, a lower award may be justified where the job is part-time since a 'person who unlawfully loses an evening job may be expected to be less hurt and humiliated by the discriminatory treatment than a person who loses their entire professional career', but this will not always be so.

Another relevant factor is the behaviour of the employer. There is some evidence to suggest that awards will be higher where the employer contests liability than where the employer admits liability and takes steps to remedy the discrimination (see

Duffy v *Eastern Health & Social Services Board* [1992] IRLR 251; *Armitage, Marsden and HM Prison* v *Johnson* [1997] IRLR 162). On the other hand, evidence of the complainant's general attitude to matters of sexual behaviour is admissible to show the degree of injury suffered by the complainant (*Snowball* v *Gardner Merchant Ltd* [1987] IRLR 397).

Awards for injury to feelings are highest in sexual and racial harassment cases. For example, in one case, two young waitresses who were subjected to questions of an intimate sexual nature and to assaults of a sexual nature by the manager received £10,000 each (*A and B* v *R1 and R2*, reported in EOR 67). Similarly in *Armitage, Marsden and HM Prisons Service* v *Johnson* [1997] IRLR 162 the EAT upheld an industrial tribunal award of £21,000 (including two awards of £500 each against the named individuals) for injury to feelings where a campaign of victimisation, humiliation, ostracism, ridicule and contempt had lasted for over 18 months. The latest survey in EOR 67 shows that all but one of the cases where the award for injury to feelings exceeded the pre-1994 statutory maximum involved instances of sexual harassment. The EOR survey also confirms the previous trend of significant awards being made in cases of race discrimination, particularly where someone is denied promotion or subjected to racial abuse for a prolonged period. The average award in race discrimination cases in 1995 was £3,129 compared to £1,873 in sex discrimination cases.

20.1.3.4 Causation
Compensation for injured feelings may be reduced or even eliminated if it is shown that the injury complained of is unrelated to the act of discrimination.

This is illustrated by the Court of Appeal's ruling in *Skyrail Oceanic Ltd* v *Coleman* [1981] ICR 864. Mrs Coleman was dismissed after she became engaged to a man who worked for a rival company. Both companies feared that there would be a real risk of confidential information being disclosed once the couple were married, but Mrs Coleman was chosen for dismissal on the 'discriminatory' assumption that she was not the 'breadwinner'. For this reason, the dismissal was found to be contrary to the Sex Discrimination Act 1975, and the industrial tribunal award Mrs Coleman the sum of £1,000 to compensate her for the damage to her reputation caused by the dismissal. The Court of Appeal reduced the award to £100, saying that damage to reputation was not 'properly attributable to an unlawful act of sex discrimination' and therefore should have been disregarded.

20.1.3.5 Knowledge
It has been suggested that there is a further requirement that the employee must know that the act which caused the dismissal was contrary to discrimination law. Thus in *Skyrail Oceanic Ltd* v *Coleman* it was said *obiter* that 'any injury to feelings must result from the knowledge that it was an act of sex discrimination'. However, the court's *obiter* remarks are open to doubt, since the requirement of 'knowledge' is not found elsewhere in the law of tort and there would seem to be no good reason in logic or principle why it should apply in discrimination cases. To take an example, it should not matter whether the victim of a discriminatory selection procedure knows whether the selection was contrary to discrimination law, though the award may be increased if the discrimination is shown to be intentional.

20.1.4 Aggravated damages

In *Alexander* v *The Home Office* [1988] IRLR 190, the Court of Appeal accepted that an award for injury to feelings could include aggravated damages where there is evidence that the employer behaved in a 'high-handed, malicious, insulting or oppressive manner' though it is not entirely clear whether or not this forms part of the overall award of compensation for injury to feelings (see *Armitage, Marsden and HM Prison Service* v *Johnson* [1997] IRLR 162). On the other hand, in determining the amount of the award, tribunals should take account of the mitigating circumstances, i.e., whether or not the employer has apologised for the discriminatory behaviour. For such an award to be made there must be a causal connection between the exceptional or insulting conduct or motive in committing the wrong and the injury suffered by the complainant, and this will normally require some knowledge on the part of the complainant that the discriminatory treatment was unlawful at the time it took place. So, for example, in *Ministry of Defence* v *Meredith* [1995] IRLR 539, the EAT ruled that such an award could not be made where a complainant was not aware that her employer's conduct was unlawful at the time of her dismissal.

The latest EOR survey (EOR 67) suggests that aggravated damages are awarded in fewer than 3% of successful cases. The awards in the period 1994–5 averaged £1,857, the median award being £1,000. The highest award of £7,500 was made in a race case involving a campaign of victimisation against a black prison officer (*Johnson* v *(1) Armitage (2) Marsden and (3) HM Prison Service* [1997] IRLR 162). An award of £1,500 was made to a young woman who was sexually harassed by one of her managing directors on the basis that this amounted to 'high handed and oppressive conduct' (*A* v *Solitaire Ltd* case no: 16862/95) and an award of £1,000.00 was made to an employee who was dismissed for pursuing an equal pay claim (*Evans* v *Crown Eye Glass plc* case no: 47660/92). In less serious cases awards may be as low as £500.

20.1.5 Punitive or exemplary damages

In *Deane* v *London Borough of Ealing* [1993] IRLR 209, the EAT ruled that exemplary or punitive damages could not be awarded under the Race Relations Act 1976. The EAT reached this conclusion as a result of the Court of Appeal's ruling in *AB* v *South West Water Services* [1993] 1 All ER 609, to the effect that exemplary damages could only be awarded on statutory or other torts recognised before the ruling of the House of Lords in *Rookes* v *Barnard* in 1964 and therefore could not be made under the Race Relations Act 1976.

The EAT's ruling is also likely to apply in cases of discrimination on grounds of sex and disability. Similarly, in *Ministry of Defence* v *Cannock* [1994] ICR 918, the EAT stressed that awards for injury to feelings should not include a deterrent element.

Exemplary damages are also not available under the Equal Treatment Directive (*Ministry of Defence* v *Meredith* [1995] IRLR 539).

20.1.6 Overall size of awards

There has been a marked increase in the overall level of awards since the abolition of the statutory limit. The latest EOR survey reports that race discrimination awards are up by 63% and sex discrimination awards are up by 31% (excluding MOD cases). However, in *MOD* v *Cannock* the EAT stressed that tribunals should not make excessive awards, particularly in pregnancy dismissals. Nonetheless, there is nothing wrong in principle with tribunals simply adding up the awards made under each head and awarding the total (incuding interest) in full (*MOD* v *Hunt and Ors* [1996] IRLR 139).

20.1.7 Compensation for indirect discrimination

Since 25 March 1996, tribunals have had the power to award compensation for indirect discrimination in cases of sex discrimination and equal pay (Sex Discrimination and Equal Pay (Miscellaneous Amendment) Regulations SI 1996 No. 438) where it would not be just and equitable merely to make a declaration and/or a recommendation.

In cases of indirect race discrimination, s. 57(3) of the Race Relations Act 1976 provides that compensation may not be awarded in cases of indirect race discrimination unless it is shown that a discriminatory requirement or conduct was applied with the intention of treating the complainant less favourably on the grounds of race. In *J H Walker Ltd* v *Hussain* [1996] IRLR 11 and *London Underground* v *Edwards* [1995] IRLR 355, the EAT ruled that such an intent may be shown if, at the time the relevant act took place, the employer:

(a) wants to bring about the state of affairs which constitutes the unlawful act of discrimination; and
(b) knows that the prohibited result will follow from those actions.

A tribunal may infer that a person wanted to produce certain consequences from the fact that the employer acted knowing what those consequences would be.

The result is that compensation for indirect race discrimination may be awarded where the employer knows that the requirement or condition has an indirectly discriminatory effect but still seeks to enforce it by dismissing an employee who refuses to accept that condition etc. So, for example, in the *Hussain* case, the EAT held that the tribunal was entitled to make an award of compensation for indirect discrimination where the company knew that the requirement to work on a holy day would indirectly discriminate against its Indian Moslem workforce. An award of compensation for injury in such circumstances may include compensation for injury to feelings (*J H Walker Ltd* v *Hussain* [1996] IRLR 11).

Note: There is no statutory liability for indirect discrimination in cases of disability, although some forms of indirect discrimination may amount to discrimination for a 'reason which relates to the disabled person's disability' within the meaning of DDA 1995, s. 5(1).

20.1.8 Compensation for failure to observe a recommendation

If, without reasonable justification, an employer fails to comply with a recommendation made by an industrial tribunal pursuant to the powers conferred on it by s. 65(1)(c) of the Sex Discrimination Act 1975, s. 56(1)(c) of the Race Relations Act 1976 or s. 8(5) of the Disability Discriminatin Act 1995, it may either:

(a) increase the amount of compensation awarded; or
(b) if no award has been made, make an award of compensation,

if it considers it just and equitable to do so (SDA 1975, s. 65(3), RRA 1976, s. 56(4), DDA 1995, s. 8(5)).

20.1.9 No statutory limit to compensation

There is no statutory limit to the amount of compensation which can be made in cases of unlawful sex discrimination, the previous limit in sex discrimination cases having been removed by the Sex Discrimination and Equal Pay Regulations 1993 (SI 1993 No. 2798) following the ECJ's ruling in *Southampton and South West Hampshire AHA* v *Marshall (No. 2)* [1993] IRLR 445. These Regulations had retrospective effect (*Harvey* v *The Institute of the Motor Industry (No. 2)* [1995] IRLR 416).

The statutory limit on compensation in cases of race discrimination was removed by the Race Relations (Remedies) Act 1994, and in cases of religious discrimination the previous £35,000 maximum was removed by the Fair Employment (Amendment) (Northern Ireland) Order 1995 (SI 1995 No. 758(NI4)).

There is no statutory limit on compensation which can be awarded in cases of unlawful discrimination under the Disability Discrimination Act 1995 (DDA 1995, s. 8).

20.1.10 Interest

At the same time as removing the statutory limit to compensation in cases of unlawful discrimination, provision was also made for the award of interest in discrimination cases. These provisions, which are now to be found in the Industrial Tribunals (Interest on Awards in Discrimination Cases) Regulations (SI 1996 No. 2803), are more complex than those in unfair dismissal cases (18.6).

20.1.10.1 Interest on loss of earnings
Interest on loss of earnings normally runs from the mid-point date between the unlawful act and the calculation date (that is the date of the remedies hearing).

20.1.10.2 Injury to feelings
Interest on injury to feelings runs from the date on which the unlawful act took place to the date of the hearing.

20.1.10.3 *Exceptional circumstances*

In 'exceptional circumstances' (whether relating to the case as a whole or the particular sum in the award), where the award of interest on the above bases would cause 'serious injustice' to either party, the industrial tribunal may order that interest runs from some other period (Industrial Tribunals (Interest on Awards in Discrimination Cases) Regulations 1996, reg. 6(3)).

What is 'exceptional' is a matter for an industrial tribunal to determine, but in *Ministry of Defence* v *Cannock* [1994] ICR 918, the EAT indicated that a tribunal would be entitled to award interest over a longer period where the loss has continued over an exceptionally long period.

20.1.10.4 *Interest after award*

Interest on the tribunal award itself runs from the day immediately following the tribunal's award (Industrial Tribunals (Interest on Awards in Discrimination Cases) Regulations 1996, reg. 8).

20.1.10.5 *Rate of interest*

The rate of interest is a simple rate of interest which accrues from day to day as prescribed by r. 27(1) of the Court Funds Rules 1987 or, in Scotland, by the Act of Sederant (Interest in Sheriff Court Decrees or Extracts) 1975.

The industrial tribunal's decision must include a statement of the total amount of interest awarded.

20.2 RELATIONSHIP WITH UNFAIR DISMISSAL

Where a dismissal is both unlawful under the Sex Discrimination Act 1975 or the Race Relations Act 1976 and unfair under the Employment Rights Act 1996, the tribunal may make a basic award and an additional award as well as awarding compensation for the financial loss suffered as a result of the dismissal.

To avoid the possibility of an employee being compensated twice for the same loss, it is provided that where compensation falls to be awarded under both the Employment Rights Act 1996 and under one or both of the Sex Discrimination Act 1975 and the Race Relations Act 1976:

> An industrial tribunal shall not award compensation under any one of those two or three Acts in respect of any loss or other matter which is or has been taken into account under the other, or any of the others, by the tribunal (or another industrial tribunal) in awarding compensation on the same or another complaint in respect of that act (ERA 1996, s. 126(2)).

20.2.1 Additional award

Where a dismissal is unfair as well as unlawful under the Sex Discrimination Act 1975 or the Race Relations Act 1976, the tribunal has the power to order re-employment. Such an order may be made even in cases of indirect discrimination

(*Dick* v *University of Dundee* 1982 SCOIT 3814/81). A additional award is made if the employer fails to comply with an order for reinstatement or re-engagement unless the employer satisfies the tribunal that it was not practicable to comply (ERA 1996, s. 117(3)(b) and (4)). The additional award is dealt with more fully in Chapter 4.

In sex and race discrimination cases, the additional award is between 26 and 52 weeks' pay. The award is therefore higher than in non-discrimination cases (ERA 1996, s. 117(5)(b) and (6)).

Appendix   Tribunal Form*

1 346/485 (2)

UNFAIR DISMISSAL — ASSESSMENT
OF COMPENSATION   *Sheet I*
BASIC AWARD (s. 119) (max £210 p.w.)   £

Less
(a)   Unreasonable refusal of reinstatement
        (s. 122(1))   £
(b)   Conduct before dismissal (s. 122(2) and
        (3)) %   £
(c)   Redundancy award/payment (s. 122(4))   £ _____   _____
                                           NET BASIC AWARD   A

COMPENSATORY AWARD (s. 123) (max £11,300)
Loss of wages to date of hearing/
promulgation (after allowing for failure to mitigate)
Net average wages £   p.w.
From   to   (weeks)
Less
(a)   Post dismissal earnings/money in lieu of notice £   £
(b)   Any balance of (i) and (ii) not deducted
        from C below   £   £ _____

Less   Contributory fault (s. 123(6)) and/or
           Conduct before dismissal (s. 123(1))   %   £ _____
                                          PRESCRIBED ELEMENT   B   £
(1)   Estimated future loss of wages (after
        allowing for failure to mitigate)
        Net average wages £   p.w. for   weeks   £
(2)   Loss of other benefits (before and after
        hearing)   £
(3)   Loss of statutory industrial rights   £

(4)   Loss of redundancy rights in excess of
            statutory entitlement: (s. 123(3))   £
(5)   Loss of pension rights   £
(6)   Expenses incurred   £ _____
                                          TOTAL (1) to (6)   £ _____

Less (i) Any other payment by respondent   £
        (ii) Excess of redundancy payment over
             Basic Award (s. 123(7))   £ _____   £ _____
Less Contributory fault (s. 123(6)) and/or
        Conduct before dismissal (s. 123(1))   %
                                          NET TOTAL   C £ _____

*See Author's note at end of Form
ADDITIONAL AWARD s. 117(5)(a), (b)
Applicant not reinstated/re-engaged under
  Order
Award 26 to 52 or 13 to 26 weeks'
  pay   TOTAL   D £ _____

(a)	MONETARY AWARD		TOTAL	A £
	Grand Total	£		B £
(b)	PRESCRIBED ELEMENT	£		C £
(c)	PERIOD OF PRESCRIBED			D £ _____
	ELEMENT		GRAND	
	to		TOTAL	£ _____
(d)	EXCESS OF (a) over (b)	£		

UNFAIR DISMISSAL — ASSESSMENT
OF COMPENSATION (trade union related cases)

                                                                  Sheet II

I   *Reinstatement/Re-engagement not requested
        by applicant* — Calculate on Sheet I save that
        the Basic Award is not less than £2,770 before
        reductions (s. 120(1))
II   *Reinstatement/Re-engagement requested but
        no order made*
        Basic Award — Calculate on Sheet I subject to
        £2,770 minimum before reductions (s. 120(1))   A £ _____
        Compensatory Award — Calculate on Sheet I
        (i) To date of hearing/promulgation
                              PRESCRIBED ELEMENT   B £ _____
        (ii) Future loss etc   C £ _____
        Special Award (s. 125(1))
        £   (1 week's pay) × 104
        (minimum £13,775: maximum £27,500 see I
        above)   £

Less
(i)	reduction for age (over 64 (s. 125(3)))	£			
(ii)	Conduct before dismissal (s. 125(4)) %	£		£ _____	
(iii)	Prevented Order being complied with or refused offer (s. 125(5)) %	£	E	£ _____	

III *Reinstatement/Re-engagement ordered but not complied with (unless not practicable s. 125(2))*

Basic Award — Calculate on Sheet I subject to £2,770 minimum before reductions (s. 120(1)) A £

Compensatory Award — Calculate on Sheet I
  (i) To date of hearing/promulgation
                                 PRESCRIBED ELEMENT B £ _____
  (ii) Future loss etc C £ _____

Special Award (s. 125(2))
£   (156 weeks' pay)
(minimum £21,000: no maximum)

Less
(i)	Deductions for age (over 64) (s. 125(3))	£			
(ii)	Conduct before dismissal (s. 125(4)) %	£			
(iii)	Prevented order being complied with or refused offer (s. 125(5)) %	£ _____	E	£ _____ £ _____	

(a)	MONETARY AWARD Grand Total	£	TOTAL	A	£
(b)	PRESCRIBED ELEMENT	£		B	£
(c)	PERIOD OF PRESCRIBED ELEMENT to		GRAND TOTAL	C D	£ £ _____
(d)	EXCESS OF (a) over (b)	£			£ _____

IT 58A(2)

Author's note:
This form assumes that a full award of compensation is made. Where a *'Polkey'* reduction is made pursuant to ERA s. 123(1) (see Chapter 17), it should be made after the loss is calculated but before the reduction for contributory fault in accordance with the EAT's ruling in *Digital Equipment Ltd* v *Clements (No. 2)* (see 17.1.2). Similarly, where an employer makes an ex gratia payment or an enhanced redundancy payment, this is brought into account in the calculation of loss prior to a *'Polkey'* reduction being made and prior to any reduction for contributory fault (see 17.3.2). It should also be noted that where the award is reduced for contributory fault, the prescribed element should be reduced in proportion to the reduction for contributory fault (see Chapter 18).

Index

'A week's pay'
  calculation 56, 62, 80–3
    calculation date 78–80
    recent recruits 83
  defining 66
  normal working hours
    time rates 80–1
    variable hours 81–2
  redundancy pay and 188–9
  statutory maximum 83
Additional award 39, 49–50, 51
  calculation date 78, 79
  discrimination and unfair dismissal 207
  union-related dismissal 51
Age
  basic award and 54, 56
    scaling down 56
  loss of future earnings and 105
  redundancy payments and 188
  special award and 62, 63–4
    scaling down 62

Back-dated payments 79
Back-pay 10, 46, 48, 50, 177
Basic award
  calculation 54–6
    age at dismissal 54, 56
      scaling down 56
    calculation date 78–9
    effective date of termination 55
    length of service and 54
    straddling years of employment 55
  deductions from 60
  maximum 57
  minimum 56–7
    redundancy dismissals 57
      union dismissals 57

Basic award — *continued*
    'unreasonable' employee 57
    union-related dismissals 56
  reducing 140
    automatically unfair dismissal 59
    contributory fault 58, 163–4
    redundancy 59, 175
    restrictions in union membership
      dismissals 59
    matters to be disregarded 59
    minimum award 59
    unreasonable refusal of reinstatement
      offer 58–9
  redundancy pay and 57, 59, 96, 175
  see also Additional award
Bonuses 10–11
  pay in lieu and 19
  remuneration and 73

Career prospects, damage to 16
Commission 10–11
  remuneration and 73
Company car 111–13
  damages for loss 13
  pay in lieu 19
  private use 111
  remuneration, as 76
  valuing use 111–13
    cars provided on HP 113
    Inland Revenue scales 112
    purchase and resale 112–13
    running costs 111–12
Compensatory award
  calculation
    date of assessment 85–6
    decision in *Gilham* 86
    hearing on quantum 85–6

Compensatory award — *continued*
  exception 86
  expenses and *see* Expenses
  fringe benefits *see* Fringe benefits
  loss of earnings *see* Earnings loss
  pensions *see* Pensions
  deductions
    ex gratia payments 176–7
    deduction from total loss or final award 179–80
    payments which count 177–9
    statutory maximum 180–2
    redundancy payments 175–6
      enhanced 176
      statutory 175
    state benefits 183
  discrimination dismissals *see* Race discrimination; Sex discrimination
  fair dismissal and 141, 142
  heads of compensation 90–1
    loss arising from manner of dismissal *see* Dismissal, manner of
    loss of earnings *see* Earnings loss
    loss of pension *see* Pensions
    loss of statutory rights *see* Statutory rights
    proof of loss 91
  industrial pressure 91
  interest on 185–7
  misconduct 141–2
  not punishment 85–6
    exceptions 85
  notice pay, loss 85
  prescribed element 183–4
  recoupment of benefits from *see* Recoupment
  reducing 140, 141
    alternative reasons for dismissal 148–9
    capability 146–7
    contributory fault 149–50, 163
    degrees of injustice 143–4
    disciplinary procedure breach 148
    failure to appeal 150
    health grounds for dismissal 147–8
    inevitability of dismissal 143
    insufficient evidence of employee's guilt 142
    mitigation of loss *see* Mitigation of loss
    no injustice, no award 141–2
    notice period, dismissal during 149

Compensatory award — *continued*
    onus on employees 150
    post-dismissal conduct 150
    procedure and substance 142–3
    redundancy
      dismissals 144–6
      future risk 146
    secondary employment loss 149
  remoteness 86–90
    attributable to employer's action 89–90
    consequential loss 89
    period of training 88–9
    permanent new employment 87–8
  statutory maximum 92
  wrongful dismissal *see* Wrongful dismissal
  see also Additional award; Basic award; Damages; Special award
Conduct
  post-dismissal 150
  see also Contributory fault, reduction of award; Misconduct
Constructive dismissal, contributory fault and 169–70
Contract
  breach
    anticipatory 5
    damages 4
    fundamental 4, 5–6
    pay in lieu and 20
  damages
    for breach 4
    for distress and 15–16
  employment *see* Contract of employment
  fixed term 4, 6
  frustration 6, 7
  fundamental breach 4, 5–6
  intention not to be bound 2, 5
  notice *see* Notice
  performance 3
  repudiation 5, 7
  restricted grounds for dismissal 4
  specific task, for 4
  termination
    agreement 6
    dismissal for cause 6
    expiry 6
    frustration 6
    giving proper notice 6
    lawful 6–7
    summary dismissal 6–7

Index

Contract — *continued*
  wrongful dismissal 5
  'elective theory' and 5–6
Contract of employment
  agreed damages clause 19
  breach
    by employee 18
    fundamental 5
  disciplinary procedures 3–4
  frustration 7
  fundamental breach 5
  pay in lieu 18–19
  pay rate 94–5
  redundancy pay 96–7
  working hours 67, 68–9, 70
  variation 70–1
Contributory fault
  additional award 163
  compensatory award 163
  conduct
    agents 168
    constructive dismissal 169–70
    culpable or blameworthy, meaning 164–6
    employee's alone relevant 168
    ill-health dismissal 167
    industrial action 165–6
    internal appeals 169
    judged objectively 167
    linked to the dismissal 168–9
    in notice period 169
    power to limit compensation and 170
  industrial action 165–6
  industrial pressure 172–3
  pension loss 128
  reduction of award 27, 149–50
    amount 171–3
      100% reduction 172
      industrial pressure 172–3
      no reduction 171–2
      not proportional to employer's loss 173
    basic award 58, 163–4
    consistent 173–4
    dismissal for incapacity 166–7
    new evidence after the hearing 174
    special award 163–4
  see also conduct

Damages
  breach of contract 4
  damages period 8–9, 10, 22
    pay increase during 10
  distress 15–16
  employee should not profit 21
  injured feelings 135–6, 200–3
  interest 30
  mitigation of loss *see* Mitigation of loss
  reduction 21–7
    contingencies and accelerated receipt of payments 26–7
    annuity method 27
    multiplier 27
    contributory fault 27
    deducting tax from 27, 28–9
  wrongful dismissal *see* Wrongful dismissal
  see also Compensatory award
Directors, payments to 29–30
Disciplinary procedures 3–4, 9, 148
Discrimination, dismissal on grounds of *see* Race discrimination; Sex discrimination
Dismissal
  alternative reason for 148–9
  automatically unfair *see* Unfair dismissal
  for cause 6
  constructive, contributory fault and 169–70
  discrimination *see* Race discrimination; Sex discrimination
  during notice period 149
  incapacity, contributory fault and 166–7
  manner of, compensation for 90
    disadvantage in the labour market 136
    injured feelings 135–6
  pregnancy ground 39
  reasons for 7, 38
    procedural fairness 39
    reasonableness 38–9
    written 7
  restricted grounds 4
  summary *see* Summary dismissal
  unfair *see* Unfair dismissal
  wrongful *see* Wrongful dismissal
Distress
  damages for 15–16
  see also Injured feelings

Earnings loss
  assessment 103
  credits for payments received

Earnings loss — *continued*
  from new employer 99–101
    during notice period 100–1
    pay rises in new job 102
    permanent new employment
      99–100
    payments in lieu 99
    state benefits 102
  expenses, out-of-pocket 97–8
  future 90, 103–8
    age and 105
    assessment
      contingencies 106
        deducting 106
      multiplier 106
      no set amount 107
      personal characteristics of employee
        105
      power to review 107–8
      state of the labour market 105–6
    less well paid 104
    new job, equivalent or better 104
  holiday pay 95–6
  immediate 90, 103
  interest 99
  notice pay 95
  pay 93–4
    calculation 94–5
      contract of employment 94–5
      piece workers 94
      shift workers 94
      tips, bonuses, commission 94
    redundancy 96–7
    rises in 95
  redundancy pay 96–7
  remoteness 102–3
  social security credit loss 98
  tax implications 98
Ex gratia payments 46, 48, 60, 176–7
  claims for damages and 25
  deductions from compensatory award
    176–82
    payments which count 177–9
    statutory maximum 180–2
    total loss of final award 179–80
Expenses 14–15, 76
  assessing loss of
    costs of finding new job 116
    legal expenses 117
    starting up business 116–17
  'bogus' 98

Expenses — *continued*
  out-of-pocket 97–8

Fixed-term contract 4, 6
  damages period and 8–9
Fringe benefits 13, 109–16
  accommodation 13, 76, 113–14
  company car *see* Company car
  company loans 114–15
  food 115
  loans 13
  medical insurance 13, 115
  mortgage subsidy 13, 19
  pay in lieu and 19
  remuneration, as 76
  share ownership 115–16
  telephone 115
  travel allowances 13, 115
  valuing 110

Golden handshakes 20

Hadley v *Baxendale* rule 15
Health, grounds for dismissal 7, 147–8,
  155, 167, 170
Holiday pay 10, 18, 46, 75, 95–6
  stamp system 75
Hours of work *see* Working hours

Industrial action *see* Strikes
Industrial relations 85, 101
  re-employment and 43–4
Industrial tribunals
  awards, interest on 185–6
  jurisdiction 30
  recoupment regulations 183–5
  reemployment orders 41–6
    duty to give reasons 46
Injunctions 33–4
Injured feelings
  discrimination cases 200–3
  no compensation for 135
    exceptions 135–6
  see also Distress
Insolvency of employer 25
Interest
  compensation for discrimination
    206–7
  compensatory award 185–7
  damages 30
  earnings loss 99

Index

Loss of earnings *see* Earnings loss
Lump sum payments   19, 20, 29
   tax and   185

Maternity leave, loss of right   137, 138
Misconduct
   compensatory award and   141, 142
   redundancy payments   191–3
Mitigation of loss
   alternative employment
      offers   154
      re-training   157
   damages reduction   21–7
      assessing deduction   23, 161–2
      credit for benefits accrued   22
      onus of proof   23
      seeking alternative employment   21–2
   discovery   161
   duty to find employment   155–8
      personal characteristics of the applicant   155–6
      pregnancy dismissals   158, 199–200
      reasonable offers   156–7
         flexibility   156–7
      retraining   157–8
      setting up business   157
      'signing on' for sickness benefit   158
      state of the labour market   155
   duty to mitigate
      disability insurance   26
      earnings from new job   23–4
      employment benefits, collateral   26
      ex gratia payments   25
      in fact   22, 23–5, 152, 162
      in law   22–3, 152
      limits   159–60
         compensation negotiations   160
         duty arises after dismissal   159
         failure to use grievance procedure   159
         internal appeals   159–60
      onus of proof   160–1
      payments in lieu   25
      private pensions   26
      redundancy pay   26
      remoteness   25–6
      social security benefits   24–5
      state benefits   24–5
      statutory notice and   23
      statutory notice pay   24–5
      unfair dismissal   25, 151–2

Mitigation of loss — *continued*
   early retirement offers   155
   failure, loss of damages and   18
   onus of proof   160–1
   pensions and   123
   re-employment
      non-compliance by employee   52
      offers   152–5
         reasonableness test   153–4
      orders   50, 152
      starting up a business   116–17
      statutory provisions   151
Multiplier
   compensatory award   110
   damages reduction   27
   earnings loss   106
   pension loss calculation   125–6

Notice
   agreement to reduce   3
   calculation date   79
   contractual, statutory compared   18
   dismissal without   2–3
   duty to specify length   3
   'garden leave'   19
   pay   95
   pay in lieu   18–21
   performance contracts   3
   period
      dismissal during   149
      reasonable *see* reasonable period
   proper   6
      dismissal without   2–3
   reasonable period
      employee's status   2
      established custom or practice   2
      period by which pay is calculated   2
      type of job   2
   seamen and dockers   3
   statutory
      calculating entitlement   16–18
      contractual and   18
      duty to mitigate   23
      failure to give   3
         effective date of termination   55
      formula   17–18
      pay   10, 24–5
         calculation   18
      periods   3
         employees outside Great Britain   3
         exceptions   3

Notice — *continued*
  written statement of entitlement 3

Overseas employees 28
  statutory notice 3
Overtime 19, 67–8, 74–5

Pay
  calculation 94–5
  in lieu *see* Pay in lieu
  loss of earnings and 93–4
  notice 95
  rises 95
  see also 'A week's pay'; Holiday pay; Remuneration
Pay in lieu 18–21, 46, 48
  claims for damages and 20, 25
  contract of employment and 19
  ex gratia payments and 177
  payment gross or net 21
  summary dismissal and 19
  taxation of 20, 28
  what the payment should cover 19–20
Pension
  additional voluntary contributions (AVCs) 120
  Blue Book 118–19, 128–34
  loss
    actuarial evidence 128
    calculation
      benefits method 126–7
      contribution rate and interest 125
      contributions method 125–6
      cost of annuity 126–7
      multiplier 125–6
      new employment 127
      partial discontinuance method 127
    contributory fault 128
    proof 127–8
    type of loss
      future 124–5, 130–1
        allowance for accelerated payment 124–5
        credit for future employee contributions 124
        period of unemployment 124
        withdrawal 124
      non-compensatable 120–1
      past 121–3
        deferred pensions 123
        mitigation of loss 123

Pension — *continued*
    return of contributions 123
    transferability 122
    withdrawal 122–3
    relationship with other heads of compensation 128
  remuneration, as 76–7
  types
    additional voluntary contributions (AVCs) 120
    defined benefits 13–14, 119, 121
    defined contribution 13, 119, 121
    final salary 119, 121, 130, 132–4
    money purchase 119, 129, 132
    State 120
    State Earnings Related Pension Scheme (SERPS) 120
  types of pension loss 129–34
    final salary schemes 130
    loss of enhancement of accrued rights 132–4
      final salary schemes 132–4
      money purchase schemes 132
    loss of future rights 130–1
Perks *see* Fringe benefits
Piece work 67, 74, 94
Post-dismissal conduct 150
Pregnancy
  child care costs 199
  dismissals 198–200
    ground 39
    mitigation 158, 199–200
  duty to find employment and 156
  loss of earnings 199
  mitigation of loss 158, 199–200
Profit-related pay schemes 11
Profit-sharing schemes 11, 74, 115–16

Race discrimination 39, 50
  compensation
    aggravated damages 204
    failure to observe recommendation 206
    interest 206–7
    punitive or exemplary damages 204
    statutory limit 206
    statutory provisions 197–8
    see also injured feelings
  indirect 205
  injured feelings 136, 200–3
    aggravated damages 204

Index

Race discrimination — *continued*
  assessment 202–3
  causation 203
  knowledge 203
  relevant factors 202–3
  size of awards 200–2
  unfair dismissal and 207–8
    additional award 207–8
Recoupment
  monetary award and 183–4
  procedure 184–5
  regulations 183–5
    effect 185
Redundancy
  breach of agreed procedure 39
  early retirement offers and 155
  enhanced notice entitlement 26
  payments *see* Redundancy payments
  selection procedure 9
Redundancy payments 96–7
  basic award and 57, 59, 96, 175
  calculation 187–9
    age limits, upper 188
    date 79, 188, 189
    statutory extension of relevant date 188
    statutory maximum 189
    week's pay 188–9
  claims for damages and 25, 26
  compensatory award 176
  enhanced 96, 176
  loss of chance 15, 137
  pre-conditions 187
  ready reckoner 195
  reducing 144–6, 189–93
    early leavers 192–3
    misconduct 191–3
    notice of extension after strike 193–4
    pension payments 190
    strikes 193–4
  tax liability 194
Re-employment
  contributory fault 44–5
  enforcement of orders 48–52
    additional award 49–50, 51
    defence of impracticability 50–1
    failure to reinstate or re-engage 49
    fixing the penalty 50
      tariff approach 50
    non-compliance by employee 52
      failure to mitigate 52

Re-employment — *continued*
  partial compliance 48–9
    failure to comply distinguished 49
    union-related dismissal 51
  fundamental loss of trust 44
  'inexpediency' 44
  interim relief 52–3
    continuation order 53
  orders for 41–6
    compliance 43–4, 50–1, 62–3
    duty to give reasons 46
    industrial relations and 43–4
    see also enforcement of orders
  permanent replacements 45, 63
  practicability of compliance 43–4, 50–1, 63
  special award and 62–3
  re-engagement 39, 42
    terms 47–8
  reinstatement 34, 39, 42
    terms 46–7
    unreasonable refusal 58–9
  size of employer organisation 44
  statutory procedure 42–3
    re-engagement 42
    reinstatement 42
  terms 46–8
    tribunal's duty to state 48
  wishes of the complainant 43
Remuneration
  allowances 75
    abnormal conditions 75
    anti-social hours 75
    attendance 75
    London weighting 75
    travelling time 75
  bonuses 73
  commissions 73
  discretionary payments 74
  employment with no normal working hours 77–8
  expenses 76
  fringe benefits 76
  guarantee payments 77
  holiday pay 75
    stamp system 75
  meaning 72–3
  overtime pay 74–5
  pensions 76–7
  productivity schemes 73
  profit sharing schemes 74

Remuneration — *continued*
  rate of pay 73
  state benefits 77
  tips 74
  wages council orders 73
Rota workers 67, 74

Sex discrimination 39, 50
  compensation
    aggravated damages 204
    failure to observe recommendation 206
    injured feelings *see* injured feelings compensation
    interest 206–7
    punitive or exemplary damages 204
    statutory limit 206
    statutory provisions 197–8
  indirect 205
  injured feelings compensation 136, 200–3
    aggravated damages 204
    assessment 202–3
    causation 203
    knowledge 203
    relevant factors 202–3
    sexual harassment 203
    size of awards 200–2
  pregnancy
    child care costs 199
    dismissals 198–200
    loss of earnings 199
  unfair dismissal 207–8
    additional award 207–8
  see also Women
Sexual harassment compensation 203
Share option schemes 11–12
Shift work 19, 74, 94
Sick pay 18
Special award
  calculation 62–4
    date 78, 79
    re-employment and 62–3
    review of statutory payments 63
    scaling down 63–4
    week's pay 63
  entitlement 61–2
    age and 62
      scaling down 62
    redundancy 61
    reemployment order 39, 61

Special award — *continued*
  reduction 63–5, 140–1
    complaint well-founded 65
    contributory fault 163–4
    general grounds 64
    joinder provisions 65
    matters to be disregarded 64–5
    special grounds 64
    union-related dismissal 39, 51, 61, 62, 64–5
Specific performance, order for 33, 34
  rule against 34–5
State benefits 24–5
  attendance allowance 24
  compensatory award and 102
  income support 24, 183
  mobility allowance 24
  recoupment from final award 183–5
  remuneration, as 77
  unemployment benefits 24, 25, 183
Statutory rights, compensation for loss 90, 137–9
  maternity leave 138
  no award 138–9
    remoteness 138
  reduced award 139
  redundancy and unfair dismissal 137
  statutory notice 138
Strikes 65
  dismissal and 193–4
  mass dismissals 39
Summary dismissal 6–7
  calculation date 78
  effective date of termination 55
  pay in lieu 19

Tax
  damages and 27, 28
  final award 28–9
  'Gourley principle' 28, 29
  lump sum payments 185
  overseas employees 28
  pay in lieu 20, 28
  redundancy payments 194
Tips 74, 94
  'troncs' 74
Trade unions, dismissal related to 39, 49, 64–5
  additional award 52
  basic award, minimum 56, 59
  closed shop 65

Index

Trade unions, dismissal related to
— *continued*
  interim relief 52–3
  redundancy 57
  short-time working 71–2
  special award 39, 51, 61, 62
    joinder provisions 65
    reducing 64–5
Transfer of business dismissals 39

Unfair dismissal
  automatically unfair 39, 59
  basic award *see* Basic award
  breach of agreed redundancy procedure 39
  closed shop dismissal 65
  compensation *see* Compensatory award
  financial settlement *see* Settlement
  industrial pressure 172–3
  loss of right to bring claim 15, 137
  pregnancy 39
  procedural fairness 39
  qualifying conditions 38
  special award *see* Special award
  transfer of business 39
  see also Race discrimination; Sex discrimination

Women
  child care 156, 199
  duty to find employment 156
  maternity leave 137, 138
  pensions 77
  pregnancy
    child care costs 199
    dismissals 198–200
      ground 39
      mitigation 158, 199–200
    duty to find employment and 156
    loss of earnings 199
    mitigation of loss 158, 199–200
  sexual harassment compensation 203
  unfair dismissal, scaling down basic award 56
  see also Sex discrimination
Working hours 66
  agricultural workers 68
  coach drivers 68
  contract of employment and 67
  employment contract 70
  employment without 68–9, 77–8

Working hours — *continued*
  hours counting as 69–70
  normal 67–72
  overtime 19, 67–8, 69–70, 74–5
  piece workers 67
  regular overtime 67–8
  rota workers 67
  short-time working 71–2
  variation
    agreed 71
    implied 71
Wrongful dismissal
  actions
    court proceedings 30
    time limits 30
    tribunal proceedings 30–1
  damages
    assessment 7–16, 31–2
      damages period 8–9
        breach of contractual procedure 9
        fixed term contract 8–9
        notice period 8
        pay increase taking effect during 10
      payments which count 9–16
        commission and bonus 10–11
        company car 13
        damage to career prospects 16
        damages for distress 15–16
        discretionary payments 9
        expenses 14–15
        Hadley v *Baxendale* rule 15
        loss of chance of redundancy 15
        loss of right to bring unfair dismissal claim 15
        medical insurance 13
        pay 10
        pensions 13–14
          calculation of loss 14
          'contributions method' 14
          defined contributions 13
        perks 13
        profit sharing schemes 11
        profit-related pay schemes 11
        rent-free accommodation 13
        share option schemes 11–12
        subsidised loans or mortgages 13
        travel 13
    interest on 30
  definition 2

Wrongful dismissal — *continued*
  disciplinary procedures breach
    3–4
  employment contract and breach of
    disciplinary procedures   3–4
    fixed term   4
    frustration   7
    fundamental breach   4, 5–6
    repudiation   5
    restricted grounds of dismissal   4
    specific task   4
  notice

Wrongful dismissal — *continued*
    dismissal without   2–3
    failure to give   3
    statutory entitlement calculation
      16–18
  remedies
    declarations   36–7
    equitable   33–5
    injunctions   33–4
    public law   35–6
    specific performance   33, 34
      rule against   34–5